Drawn to Sound

Genre, Music and Sound

Series editor: Mark Evans, Macquarie University, Sydney

Over the last decade screen soundtrack studies has emerged as a lively area of research and analysis mediating between the fields of cinema studies, musicology and cultural studies. It has deployed a variety of cross-disciplinary approaches to illuminate an area of film's audio-visual operation that was neglected for much of the late twentieth century. This new series extends the field by addressing the development of various popular international film genres in the post-war era (1945–present), analysing the variety and shared patterns of music and sound use that characterize each genre.

Published titles

Terror Tracks: Music, Sound and Horror Cinema
Edited by Philip Hayward

Forthcoming titles

Earogenous Zones: Sound, Sexuality and Cinema
Edited by Bruce Johnson

Fantasy, Cinema, Sound and Music
Edited by Janet K. Halfyard

Sounding Funny: Sound and Comedy Cinema
Edited by Mark Evans

Drawn to Sound
Animation Film Music and Sonicity

Edited by
Rebecca Coyle

LONDON   OAKVILLE

First published in 2010 by

UK: Equinox Publishing Ltd, 1 Chelsea Manor Studios, Flood Street, London, SW3 5SR
USA: DBBC, 28 Main Street, Oakville, CT 06779

www.equinoxpub.com

British Library Cataloguing-in-Publication Data

A catalogue record for this book is available from the British Library.
ISBN 978 1 84553 352 6 (paperback)

Library of Congress Cataloging-in-Publication Data
Drawn to sound: animation film music and sonicity / edited by Rebecca Coyle.
    p. cm. — (Genre, music and sound)
 Includes bibliographical references (p.   ) and index.
 ISBN 978-1-84553-352-6 (pb)
1. Motion picture music—History and criticism. 2. Animated films. I. Coyle, Rebecca. ML2075.D73 2010
781.5'42—dc22
                                    2009021280

Typeset by S.J.I. Services, New Delhi
Printed and bound in Great Britain by Latimer Trend & Company Ltd, Plymouth, Devon

Contents

Part III: Music and Sonicity

Part IV: Music and Industrial Contexts

Acknowledgements

Thanks are due to the following individuals and institutions:

All the authors who allowed themselves to be persuaded into the project, submitted inspiring essays, and stuck with it through to the end. Series editor Mark Evans, and Equinox editor Sandra Margolies, editorial assistant Suzie Khamis and various Equinox staff, plus anonymous chapter readers and referees. Kerry Drumm, Events and Exhibitions at Aardman Animations Ltd for provision of research materials. Macquarie University PhD student Christoforo Garigliano for translation assistance. Library assistance at AFI, AFTRS and SCU, and particularly the document supply staff, SCU library. My colleagues in the Media program and technical officers (especially Rodney Douglass) in the School of Arts and Social Sciences for various assistances. Additional individuals are named in relation to various chapters.

Thanks to my daughters Rosa and Amelia for those constant updates on the latest cool anime and animation images and sounds. This book would not have been possible without the loving guidance, knowledgeable input and patient tolerance of my husband, Phil. Thanks for letting it take up so much space in your life.

About the Authors

Rebecca Coyle teaches in the Media Program at Southern Cross University, Australia, and has edited two anthologies on Australian cinema soundtracks, *Screen Scores* (1998) and *Reel Tracks* (2005). She is currently researching film music production within an Australian Research Council funded project, is Research Director for the School of Arts and Social Sciences, and has recently edited a special issue of *Animation Journal* (published 2009).

Jon Fitzgerald teaches in the contemporary music programme at Southern Cross University, Australia. He has previously written on a variety of musical and screen sound topics and he is the author of *Popular Music Theory and Musicianship* (1999/2003). He is also an experienced performer and composer.

Daniel Goldmark is Associate Professor of music at Case Western Reserve University in Cleveland, Ohio. He is the series editor of the Oxford Music/Media Series, and is the author and/or editor of several books on animation, film, and music, including *Tunes for 'Toons: Music and the Hollywood Cartoon* (2005).

Janet K. Halfyard is Director of Undergraduate Studies at Birmingham City University Conservatoire. Her publications include *Danny Elfman's Batman: A Film Score Guide* (2004), an edited volume on Luciano Berio's *Sequenzas* (2007), and a wide range of essays on music in film and cult televison.

Philip Hayward is Director of Research Training at Southern Cross University, Australia and an adjunct professor in the Department of Media, Music and Cultural Studies at Macquarie University, Sydney. His previous screen sound books include *Off the Planet: Music, Sound and Science Fiction Cinema* (2005) and *Terror Tracks: Music, Sound and Horror Cinema* (2009).

Kentaro Imada is a research fellow in the Kyoto City University of Arts Research Centre for Japanese Traditional Music. He completed his doctorate at Osaka University, with a study of incidental music for silent film. His entry on film and animation music in Japan appears in the *Garland Encyclopedia of World Music: East Asia – China, Japan and Korea* (2001).

Ian Inglis is Reader in Popular Music Studies at Northumbria University, Newcastle upon Tyne. His books include *The Beatles, Popular Music and Society* (2000), *Popular*

Music and Film (2003), *Performance and Popular Music* (2006), *The Words and Music of George Harrison* (2010), and *Popular Music and Television in Britain* (2010).

Kyoko Koizumi is an associate professor in the School of Social Information Studies at Otsuma Women's University, Tokyo, Japan. Her chapter 'Creative Soundtrack Expression: Tôru Takemitsu's Score for *Kwaidan*' appeared in *Terror Tracks: Music, Sound and Horror Cinema* (2009), edited by Philip Hayward, and she is on the editorial board of *Screen Sound*.

Neil Lerner, Associate Professor of Music at Davidson College, USA, regularly teaches courses on music history and on film and media studies. After a dissertation on music in selected US documentaries, he has written essays on music in a variety of films and television shows. He serves on the editorial boards of *American Music* and *Music, Sound, and the Moving Image*.

Peter Morris is Director of Undergraduate Studies in Music and Sound Recording at the University of Surrey. He is a specialist in music for film, particularly animated cartoons, technology in the creative process and the works of Stephen Sondheim. After training in piano and conducting at the Royal Academy of Music, he spent many years as a jobbing keyboard player and musical director in Europe and the United States, primarily for theatre works but also as a jazz performer and solo pianist.

Janice Esther Tulk is a SSHRC Postdoctoral Fellow in the Mi'kmaq College Institute at Cape Breton University, Canada. Her current research revolves around the relationship between expressive culture, Mi'kmaw soundscapes, and colonial encounter. She is the producer of *Welta'Q – "It Sounds Good": Historic Recordings of the Mi'kmaq* (2009).

Paul Wells is Director of the Animation Academy in the School of the Arts, Loughborough University, UK. He has published widely in the field of animation studies, including *Understanding Animation* (2nd edn 2009), *Re-Imagining Animation: The Changing Face of the Moving Image* (2008, with Johnny Hardstaff), and *The Animated Bestiary: Animals, Cartoons and Culture* (2009). He is also an established writer and director for radio, television and theatre, and conducts workshops worldwide based on his book, *Scriptwriting* (2007).

Aki Yamasaki is a part-time lecturer in Sociology at Kansai University, Japan. Her papers include 'Selling Sound Track', published in *Annals of Human Sciences* (in Japanese, 2007).

To the Coyle (gar)goyles – Jacqueline, Alice, Jinny and Gabrielle – and to Stephen, for those shared times wishing upon a star

Introduction
Audio Motion: Animating (Film) Sound

Rebecca Coyle

Animation has become the design element and medium of choice in a multitude of contemporary cultural practices, from installations to online media. As a film form, animation increasingly engages with expressive tools and techniques, whether as drawn components or three-dimensional modelled or computer-generated imagery (CGI). Popular appreciation for animation is manifest in audience and critical response to animation feature films. As importantly, animation feature films today offer a major challenge to live action in terms of box-office performance and profits, especially in the powerful US entertainment industry. This book spotlights animation as an audio-visual film form but positions the focus on its audio elements.

The discipline of film studies has recently begun to acknowledge the importance of animation and there has been a corresponding increase in animation publications. Film-music research has also flourished, with numerous books and journals, study programmes, conferences, network forums, and research outcomes evolving in the last decade. Yet relatively little attention has been given to a link between these two fields, that is, the deployment of sound and music in animation film. This book bridges these worlds and explores the shared terrain of animation-film sound as one that constitutes a unique and distinctive field of film and film-music studies.

Drawn to Sound's sustained attention to music and sound does not attempt to displace the visual but rather to highlight the equally crucial role that sound plays in our experience of (animation) films. The book emphasizes how sound is a central component of animation that initiates, assists and extends its critical expressive tools. Sound – including music – operates with motion, storytelling and space. Even at its most functional, sound enables animation film to leap out of the screen and engage the viewer's imagination. Cumulatively, the chapters demonstrate the rich sonic resources to be gathered from a study of animation films. This introduction defines the research territory and contextualizes the films discussed by outlining the project's framework, background literature, and significant precursors.

Project brief

Drawn to Sound specifically concentrates on feature films released in the post-World War II period. Each chapter offers a detailed critical analysis of a single film or group of films, as well as contributing to a thematic subgroup (outlined below) and the volume as a whole. The collection adds to the few animation-film sound studies that exist by offering a series of 'field studies' that cumulatively suggest a procedural approach for further development. As such, *Drawn to Sound* generates groundwork for the construction of broader theories and provides an overarching, inclusive and interdisciplinary direction for future investigations. The chapters explore their sonic subjects from a variety of research angles and employ different analytical tools derived from media and art history, music, and cultural studies.

Insofar as animation techniques and visual outcomes are markedly different between individual studios and producers, analysis of the sound cannot be restricted to a single approach, and the chapters in this book propose a range of perspectives, showing how music and sound in animation film cannot be overly generalized (and thereby challenging the notion of animation as a 'genre'). Animation music methods range from those that use old-style heavily synchronized music, to animated dramas using music somewhat like live-action film, to comedies in which the music contributes to the gag, and musicals in which songs and musical themes are woven into the score as an overall music track. Music also operates as sonic affect, and sounds for animation include 'atmospheres' and sound FX, dialogue and vocal performance, and the overall sound design.

The specific focus on feature films in this series restricts the studies to music and sound in extended forms. *Drawn to Sound* has adopted Edera and Halas's definition of 'feature' as commencing at a minimum of 50 minutes duration (1977: 12), although most films discussed run to the more usual feature length of 80 to 90 minutes. As several chapters show, sonically adventurous feature films by studios, specific writers/ directors, or auteurs often developed from a portfolio of short film forms that initiated a significant emphasis on sound and music (see, for example, Janet Halfyard's reference to Tim Burton's innovative shorts produced prior to his features). A consideration of feature-film soundtracks positions the studies in the context of the growing field of screen-sound scholarship (rather than being marginalized by formats such as experimental, music video, documentary or other short forms; see Elsey and Kelly, 2002).

The analyses in this anthology refer to films released in the 1940s (e.g., Halas and Batchelor's *Handling Ships*, 1944–45) through to the first decade of the new millennium (e.g., George Miller's *Happy Feet*, 2006), by which time animation feature production had greatly expanded. This fifty-year timeframe links the studies to newer technologies available for sound and music and reflects a significant period of transition as animation production moved into the digital era. Alongside computer-generated animation image techniques, sound has increasingly been recorded, mixed and mastered in digital forms, occasioning changes in the production process for animation film as an audio-visual product. In addition, sound fidelity and spatiality for both cinema and home consumption has increased audience awareness and expectations of sonicity, a move that was exploited as early as 1940 by the Disney studio with the stereo sound system developed for *Fantasia*. Film animation has become a fundamental locus of research into digital film and media theory (see especially Manovich, 2001, 2002).

While the majority of chapters in this volume predominantly focus on music, several also explore the aural architecture of the overall soundtrack. Daniel Goldmark's discussion of *Les Triplettes de Belleville* (Sylvain Chomet, 2003; released as *The Triplets of Belleville* in the USA, and *Belleville Rendez-Vous* in the UK), for example, shows how sound not only communicates wihout dialogue but also powerfully conveys place and period. Jon Fitzgerald and Philip Hayward's analysis of the performed 'voices' of the appliances in *The Brave Little Toaster* (Jerry Lees, 1987) identifies that these songs are tightly integrated into the narrative and dialogue. Sonic components such as sound design and dialogue for animation are, in this regard, worthy subjects for publications in their own right (extending the work of, for example, Lawson and Persons, 2004).

In *Drawn to Sound*, the term 'sound' is used to denote both music and non-musical sound (and all aspects of this) and 'soundtrack' refers to the overall sonic elements accompanying the image track (rather than merely a recorded soundtrack CD released in conjunction with the film that has a more or less direct relation to the film release soundtrack). A discussion of such terms highlights a problem for analysis of sound and music in animation (as for film, and other screen forms, per se), that is, the semantic tools available for this task. However, as Beauchamp notes, just as "the audience will notice poor sound design even though most cannot articulate what was lacking" (2005: 17), unfamiliarity with terms and terminology should not detract from animation-sound studies. Indeed, this offers a significant challenge to the field.

Analysing animation (film)

It is appropriate to introduce this book with a few points about its title. 'Drawn to sound' refers to the animation process of an image track constructed in relation to a soundtrack as well as to the perceptual and analytical emphasis on sound in this volume. 'Animation film music and sonicity' acknowledges both the identification of cinema forms as well as the interrelation between music and sound. I have borrowed the term 'sonicity' from science, where it refers to the transmission of power by periodical forces and movements. This sense has been mobilized by researchers and artists aligned with the World Soundscape Project (see Stanza and Kandola, online[1]). As the project's ultimate aim is "to find solutions for an ecologically balanced soundscape where the relationship between the human community and its sonic environment is in harmony",[2] it is apposite for the discussion of sound in animation, in which the idealized creation of a world, its inhabitants and their activities is a *shared* project of sound and image.

In its most inclusive definition, animation is a way of representing motion. Scholarly studies of animation have concerned themselves with this notion in terms of whether animation is "drawings-that-move" or "movements-that-are-drawn" (Cholodenko,

1991: 18). These discussions centre on the image track, and adding sound to this debate contributes a further dimension of movement in space and time. Like the light waves that realize images, sound reaches our ears as waves that are inherently 'in motion'. Sound fills space through time and is difficult to contain. Furthermore, sound arrives in our ears as packages of elements. Indeed, for the 'sonic universe' of animation, Leslie observes:

> All noises take their place on the soundtrack and get their turn. A violin phrase is no better than a cracking walnut or a squelching kitten body. The art lies in the arrangement of materials, from wherever they stem. (2002: 28)

Added to this, for the viewer/listener the contoured and mastered sound on an animation film is heard in conjunction with the other sounds in a space – mobile phones and popcorn-crunching noises in the cinema, the sounds of domesticity as we view a DVD at home. Sound cannot be freeze-framed in the same way that images can be presented on the page, despite the best efforts of musicologists to capture dynamic elements by notating melodies and arrangements. Sound is constant movement. The inspirational Canadian animator and researcher Norman McLaren observed the animator's role in creating action that is "outside the vocabulary offered by its mainstream counterpart" (paraphrased by Wells, 2002: 6) and dependent on what occurs *between* the frames. Sound also moves around stereo space and transitions across scenes, frames and juxtapositions. It provides its own segues, foreshadowings and momentum for narrative, 'gag points' to highlight the animator's hand, and 'personality'. The title of this introduction – 'Audio Motion' – acknowledges these traits. As the notion of 'animating' suggests, this book is an attempt both to breathe life into analyses about sound in animation studies, as well as to reflect those debates within sound studies (and film studies) that can be employed, exploited and extended for and by animation film research.

Animation *film* is an audio-visual form of creating and staging motion that is linked to specific distribution and exhibition contexts. As such, animation film bridges many genres and appears in different forms, from the scratched, calligraphic and paper cut-out experiments from many different countries over a hundred years, to 'clay' animation and stop-motion figures, drawn cel animation and anime,[3] recent computer-generated imagery (CGI) from major studios, and hybrid forms incorporating live-action characters and/or backgrounds. The variety of film styles included under 'animation film' is represented in this volume, which features studies of films made using different techniques. Increasingly, live-action film incorporates aspects of animation, a recognition of which is central to *Who Framed Roger Rabbit* (Robert Zemeckis, 1988), as discussed in Neil Lerner's chapter. Indeed, the blurring of boundaries between live action and animation has led to Mark Langer's discussion of the "end of animation history", meaning the end of "a historical period where theorists and practitioners commonly conceived of animation as a distinct form of image generation defined by its opposition to live-action cinema".[4]

A re-examination of animation in this regard can shed light on its ability to order the world depicted in film in a different way – one that both references (and simulates) 'reality' and yet surpasses it, presenting scenarios that we recognize as simultaneously other and the same. Animation scholarship has focused on how writers and film-makers as diverse as Sergei Eisenstein (see Leyda, 1988), Walter Benjamin,[5] and Taihei Imamura (1992) have been fascinated by animation's potential to radically refigure the human (and animal) body and its activities.[6] Indeed, as Alan Cholodenko (1991) explores, film per se can be defined as a form of animation. It is this level of abstraction that offers a particularly malleable and potent form for *sonic* exploration, given the way sound exploits motion, time and space. Leslie notes how Robert Field's early analysis of Disney's output appreciated "the cerebral nature of animation" (Leslie, 2002: 30).

Recently, scholars such as Lev Manovich (2001), Joanna Bouldin (2001), Esther Leslie (2002) and others have used animation to reframe arguments in classical film theory regarding cinematic representation, as well as to provide a counter-history of the cinema that is not based in photographic indexicality. As Cholodenko discusses, "animation as film and animation as idea" (1991: 24) enable an engagement with both the significance of animation forms and its contribution to theories of authorship, genre and other analytical forms. Nevertheless, animation has been relatively marginalized in film scholarship, as well as relatively under-examined in film-sound research (with some notable exceptions, as discussed below).

Animation's marginalization in film scholarship may be due to the history of short animation film formats that in part reflect the cost and effort required for construction of each frame. Despite CGI innovations, animation is still costly and induces wariness in film investors.[7] However, Cohen *et al.* (2009) guesstimate[8] that "animation may now represent up to 25 per cent of the world's audio-visual market … in both commercial and independent film contexts" (337). It is therefore timely to examine animation, given the box-office successes of animation features (from US blockbusters such as *Shrek*, 2001, and *Shrek II*, 2004, to the transnational work of Studio Ghibli), the number of productions, and their recognition in terms of Academy and other awards.[9]

In his 2007 volume of essays, Cholodenko notes that there has been a remarkable increase in scholarly attention coinciding with "a quantum increase, expansion and diversification in animation production, distribution, exhibition and consumption around the world" (2007: 15). According to US box-office statistics,[10] sixteen of the all-time highest US box-office performers produced between 1992 and 2008 were animation features, and the same number of animation features are also in the Top 50 films in worldwide box-office performance statistics (although these are less reliable data). Notably, these figures do not take into account the lucrative DVD sales and rental incomes that accrue to animation feature films, nor the number of feature films that make significant use of digital and/or animation effects. So far from animation film being an outmoded format, it has achieved new prominence. In addition, the interest in soundtrack releases is relevant to this book. Alongside marketing strategies for live-action films, animation films have assisted their promotion and profits through CD soundtracks. As early as ten years ago, Essex (1998) noted that in 1990 fewer than twenty soundtracks appeared on the *Billboard* album chart but this figure had jumped to more than 50 by 1998. Interestingly, in that year, a month before DreamWorks launched their animated feature *The Prince of Egypt* (Brenda Chapman, Steve Hickner, Simon Wells), three separate soundtracks for the film were released in pop, country and inspirational formats.[11] Beyond the US market, Aki Yamasaki's chapter in this book provides an analysis of the way soundtracks relate to the film products released by the Japanese animation industry.

Animation film's connection with less culturally valued genres and formats has contributed to its critical marginalization. Such formats include children's and family-oriented films, slapstick comedy (especially TV cartoons), educational and propaganda films. These associations with (often) low-resolution forms have impacted on the scholarly attention to *sound*, given that, particularly in the last thirty years, industry demands for fast turnaround have resulted in somewhat formulaic sound and music – soundtracks that are frequently deemed unworthy of sustained study. Industrial formats like television cartoons are generally little researched in terms of their sonic components due to the dismissive attitude to computer-generated music (rather than original, live recorded or orchestral scores) and to soundtracks that include pre-recorded and/or library music. Nevertheless, deeper analysis of cartoons and animation films suggests they continue to be sites for musical and sonic experimentation and innovation. Roy Prendergast (1977), paraphrasing composer Ingolf Dahl's observations, notes that cartoon music in the 1940s and 1950s differed from the common use of popular music and folk tunes in the 1930s in its "sustained use of twentieth-century musical language" (in contrast to the use of these musical idioms in live-action dramatic feature films). Prendergast argues that this arises from the "incessant and lively motion" in animation, representing "a kind of dance" (*ibid.*: 190) that complemented the often balletic neoclassic works of composers such as Stravinsky and Milhaud. Prendergast argues that "music can give definition to screen action and it can invest the drawn characters with personality" (*ibid.*). This tentative argument is reinforced and enhanced in studies of more recent cartoons (as discussed below) and films. In his chapter, Philip Hayward's discussion of the action-charged dancing and singing penguins in *Happy Feet* shows various ways that this is performed in the contemporary animation film industry.

Animation film's audio

Critical literature addressing sound and music in animation film is surprisingly scarce despite the fact that, as audio-visual texts, the audio is often notably crucial to the narrative and the film's emotional impact. Sound can enhance the perceptual elements of the animation. As Beauchamp claims, "sound facilitates and accelerates the audience's ability to develop meaning and commit the scene to visual memory" (2005: 18). For these reasons alone, it is relevant to explore animation-film sound in the context of music and sound studies as well as in media, film and cultural studies. As audio-visual text that is entirely constructed (that is, in addition to animation's constructed *visual* locations, there are no existing on-location recorded *sounds* as in live action), animation is demanding of music and the films are often musically saturated. Linked to this, the sound is often overtly synchronized to the on-screen action. While at Disney, Carl Stalling composed from bar sheets, a notated blueprint of the music, dialogue and animation timing that enabled precise synchronization of soundtrack and action. This systematized approach to scoring was a significant industry innovation. The songs for on-screen performance were composed first so that mouth movements could be timed to them, a practice (known as mickey-mousing) that is still employed in both animation and film musicals (including music videos) today.[12]

Early animators, especially in the USA in the synchronized-sound era, understood the connection between image and sound. As Leslie (and others) note, for example, Walt Disney and the Fleischer brothers depicted noise-making events, objects and activities not just as part of the narrative, but as the storyline itself. Following in the footsteps of experimental film-makers such as Walter Ruttmann,[13] Norman McLaren also experimented with a form of "animated sound" (see McLaren, 1995; and Russett, 2004). Wells contends that McLaren's work was particularly significant for the nexus of sound and image in animation because he explored "sound itself, the imagery of movement and dance" (2002: 12). Such sound experiments with animation show how it can meld from one entity to another and that image and sound can synthesize. As Halas and Manvell argued (1959: 81):

> The animator is responsible for the vision, the control of the total medium, including sound as well as sight. He [sic] must think sound as well as picture. He is only half an animator if his skill is limited to drawing. (emphasis in original)

Paul Wells, in his chapter, describes how John Halas applied these ideas about sound and music in features produced by the British Halas & Batchelor studio. More recently, Beauchamp (perhaps too emphatically) claimed that "many experienced animators credit sound with contributing as much as 70% of the success of a project" (2005: 17). While experimental approaches were explored as part of the avant-garde (notably by Len Lye, Oscar Fischinger, and others), Beauchamp focuses largely on animators who engaged in experimentation and innovation in commercial industrial settings. Yet sound scholarship in the main has not caught up with these initiatives.

The lack of emphasis on sound in animation literature is due to several factors relating to animation production and aesthetics. A considerable proportion of animation output and, therefore, research and writing has derived from design and graphics centres rather than film schools.[14] As a result, the connection with sound as part of an audio-visual screen product has been peripheral. Also, much animation output has been produced by auteur directors or high-profile studios and little credit has been given to production personnel, including composers and sound designers. In many cases, sound and music have been designated as a post-production activity that is out-sourced and underfunded (a problem shared with live-action films). In addition, the contribution by sound personnel is deemed marginal to the director's 'vision' for the film and, as Hanna notes, "the medium remains occulocentric" (2008: 33). In his chapter on the music track for *Yellow Submarine* (George Dunning, 1968), Ian Inglis discusses how the film exemplifies this by being primarily devised by the musical director George Martin, who drew on existing songs by the Beatles, with little creative input on the part of the group. Animation literature tends to concentrate on visual aesthetics and style while marginalizing the form's reliance on dialogue and/or sound effects and sound design, much of which is closely aligned with the image track (sometimes to the point of being overly literal or functional, for example, in creating or highlighting gags at comic moments).[15] Where location sound is absent, music can be particularly impor-tant for functional reasons, such as continuity and flow, narrative purposes or aesthetic contribution. Warner Bros. directors like Chuck Jones (and even Tex Avery, as Steve Allen, 2009, argues) created cartoons that were highly musically oriented and featured characters with little dialogue, such as Road Runner and Coyote, thereby enabling music to effectively 'speak for' the central protagonists and highlight the action. Exactly how this occurs is worthy of exploration in terms of animation-film-sound research. Some analytical tools can be found in the modest literature currently available.

Selected scholarly literature on animation sound

Literature on animation music and sound is dispersed across a range of scholarly texts, industry guides, and 'craft and technique' information. One important work that recog-nizes the role of sound in animation and the value of its analysis is a volume (not yet translated into English) edited by Italian animation scholar, Giannalberto Bendazzi, together with Manuele Cecconello and Guido Michelone, titled *Coloriture: Voci, rumori, musiche nel cinema d'animazione* (Colourings: Voices, Noises, Music in Ani-mation Cinema), which was published in 1995. It includes theoretical overviews, generic approaches to music (e.g., uses of popular, 'classical', jazz and dance music), profiles of specific animators and composers, as well as case studies of specific films or cartoon animation forms. In addition, appendices offer insights into other sonic components and processes such as dialogue dubbing, effects and synaesthesia.[16] The broad brief of this book – covering short- and long-form films and various musical genres – is globally far-reaching, and its mix of research paradigms demonstrates the wealth of opportunities available for exploration in the field.

A major contribution to bringing sound 'up in the mix' was the 2002 anthology, *The Cartoon Music Book*, edited by Daniel Goldmark and Yuval Taylor. This attempts to identify various approaches to animation-music analysis, and therefore offers a useful model for more extended analyses. The volume demonstrates the rich history of 'cartoon music' with excerpts of writing by seminal early cartoon and film composers alongside interviews with contemporary composers, analyses of particular US programmes, a discussion of the role of soundtrack merchandise and, significantly, an informative bibliography of books, articles and 'mentions' of animation music and composers.

Several animation books include chapters on sound and music, although these are often functional and descriptive of the process, adopting a 'craft'-based approach along the lines of many animation production volumes and online resources such as Animation World Network. Often more descriptive accounts are available in general film-music guides for composers; for example, Richard Davis (1999) includes a chapter on animation in which he emphasizes the different approaches to music in television animation series, feature-length animation musicals and dramas.[17] A more relevant volume covering sound design as a broad field is Robin Beauchamp's informative production book, *Designing Sound for Animation* (2005), which effectively signposts conceptual topics and details technical and production aspects of animation music and sound. Teaching sound design at the Savannah College of Art and Design, Beauchamp also works as a music editor and sound designer for independent animators, and as a freelance composer and arranger on commercial projects, and this background informs his book.

Published in the same year (2005), Daniel Goldmark's PhD thesis-based book, *Tunes for 'Toons: Music and the Hollywood Cartoon*, analyses the relation and operation of music to cartoons in the early synch-sound period, often characterized as the Golden Age of US studio animation prior to the arrival of television. This book reflects Goldmark's experience as an archivist and librarian at Spümcø International animation company and in the music industry with Rhino Entertainment in Los Angeles. Cartoons, argues Goldmark, have a unique approach to screen scores in their use of Tin Pan Alley, folk and popular US parlour songs, excerpts of film musicals, and themes from classical, jazz and operatic works. Directing his study to those composers who helped establish the "paradigmatic sound" (2005: 7) of Hollywood cartoons, Goldmark details how during his time at Warner Brothers (1936–58) Carl Stalling employed a building-block approach to his cartoon scores, working with individual segments towards the whole, a technique that contrasted with the slow crescendos employed by Scott Bradley. In contrast to Stalling's use of published and library music, Bradley expressed disdain for popular music (especially songs with regular rhythmic pulses) and, in almost twenty-five years of composition for MGM (1934–57), prided himself on original "illustrative" (*ibid.*: 44) scoring. Bradley's music, Goldmark argues, conveys both action and emotion, that is, feelings or effects associated with a situation on screen, through the register of instruments (conveying weight), complexity and speed of melodic line (for violence) and stinger chords (suggesting pain). Stinger (or 'shock' chords) were used – often in anticipation of the action – in place of the traditional sound effects that Bradley believed had become a cartoon cliché.

While Stalling treated his cartoon compositions as merely a form of work, Bradley wanted to extend and develop cartoon music and improve the perception of it. Bradley's 1941 essay 'Cartoon Music of the Future'[18] reflected an idealized concept of the cartoon in which the storyline and music would have equal narrative significance. Towards this aim, he envisaged discarding dialogue from future cartoons, using the orchestra for tone colour and sound effects, and ultimately pre-composing scores that would direct the animation (rather than the reverse, as then currently practised).

The bricolage approach of contemporary television series like *South Park* evokes those predecessors analysed by Goldmark. While shows like *The Powerpuff Girls* may be scored to driving electronic dance beats rather than jazz combos or orchestras, modern cartoons have "a century's worth of cartoon music to draw upon" (*ibid.*: 163). The legacy of Stalling, Bradley and early cartoon composers,[19] Goldmark concludes, is that "music does more nowadays than tell stories or provide an emotional barometer" (*ibid.*: 162). *Drawn to Sound* provides analyses that support this claim.

The Australian film-maker and researcher Philip Brophy has contributed to both animation and film-sound analysis. In his paper at 'Quick Draws', the 1988 Australian/ International Animation Festival (subsequently published as a chapter in Cholodenko's 1991 collection *The Illusions of Life*), Brophy offered a way to "pass over the visuality of film" (1991: 71) and acknowledge the audio-visual nature of animation. Focusing on rhythm as movement in time, he characterizes animation as "*separate* images ... combined with *continuous* sound" (*ibid.*: 74), thereby highlighting how animation operates through the practical application of sound to the impression of movement (suspension of disbelief) in the image track. His flow chart of relationships between "real time and music time" (*ibid.*: 76) is applicable for animation designed for cinema or for the small screen, whether television, music video,[20] online or computer games. Brophy also emphasized the value of analysis of non-Anglophone forms, particularly anime. In his chapter for Cholodenko's follow-up book, *The Illusion of Life II: More Essays on Animation*, published in 2007, he claims that it is in anime that "radical sound-image configurations" are "liquefied as a vast reservoir of metaphysical possibilities" (2007: 206). Such a characterization informs the present book's inclusion of chapters on products stemming from the anime industry in Japan, notably Aki Yamasaki's study of music products and marketing for *Cowboy Bebop* films, and Kentaro Imada's analysis of musical elements informed by both western and Japanese musical histories evident in the Lupin III films.

Although early studies of animation attended to its global outcomes, there was a period when scholarly research tended to be nationally – or continentally – based and Anglophone-centric. Other production centres (featuring, for example, Japanese animators like Osamu Tezuka, Laiming Wan in China, etc.) were generally dissociated from those of North America and Europe. The success of *Spirited Away* (*Sen to Chihiro no kamikakushi*; Hayao Miyazaki/Kirk Wise, 2001) as a transnational product reinforced the limitation of this critical perspective. (See Kyoko Koizumi's chapter in this volume for an analysis of the compositional approaches employed by Joe Hisaishi in his film collaborations with Hayao Miyazaki.) While the work of John Lent was important in increasing information on animation in other regional centres (see, for example, his 2001 volume *Animation in Asia and the Pacific*), as with many animation studies, sound and music barely rate a mention. One modest contribution to this international agenda is the book chapter by animation academic Michael Hill (1998). This essay discussed the musicality of feature films by European/Australian Yoram Gross, whose Australian-based animations ranged from *Dot and the Kangaroo* (1977) to the internationally successful *Blinky Bill* products (including the feature-film release in 1992). Hill's study not only attempts to show how the filmed Australian bush settings for the animated characters are brought to life by their idiosyncratic sounds but also how Guy Gross's character songs add value to narrative impact in the films.

A major contribution to animation film-music research is associated with the products of the US corporation Disney, although much of this work is uncritically euphoric and suggests corporate input to research.[21] As Wells observes, the term 'Disney' can be redefined "as a metonym for an authorially complex, hierarchical industrial process, which organizes and executes selective practices with the vocabularies of animated film" (cited from Davies and Wells, 2001, in Wells, 2002: 85). David Tietyen's *The Musical World of Walt Disney* (1990) shows how Walt's musicality inspired not only a musical orientation in the animation films up to his death in 1966 but also informed the animation style and lucrative merchandising strategies. This last aspect was explored in Michael Murray's study of fifty years of Walt Disney records (1997) and more recently in Tim Hollis and Greg Ehrbar's 2006 study. Disney's musical animation productions have evolved through several technological and compositional periods, and composer and critic Ross Care's work overviews the 'Golden Age' of studio animation (see his chapter in Goldmark and Taylor, 2002) and includes an oft-cited study (Care, 1985) of the music for *Bambi* (1942) and other composer profiles (Care, 1977). Adding to this, a considerable number of studies have concentrated on *Fantasia* (1940), thanks to its music-informed concept and address to known musical 'classics' (see, for example, published work by Taylor, 1940; Culhane, 1983, and also his examination of *Fantasia 2000*, 1999; Granata, 2002; Clague, 2004). Ultimately, the Disney corporation feature films demonstrate the central place music can inhabit in a work's emotion, narrative engagement and sonic signature. These elements are analysed in the *Drawn to Sound* chapters by Janice Esther Tulk, Jon Fitzgerald and myself.

The dispersed literature for animation-film music and sound has arisen from various scholarly and industry sources that reflect a range of disciplinary foci. However, this is reflective of animation studies more generally as well as film-music/sound studies.

Animating film sound analyses

Scholarly texts on animation film are increasing in number and range, from the seminal works published in the 1990s (see Bendazzi, 1994; Furniss, 1998; Wells, 1998; Pilling, 1999) to more recent volumes (Buchan, 2006a; Cholodenko, 2007; and others). The commitment to animation studies on the part of publishers like John Libbey has assisted this development of the field. In addition, there are now various animation research periodicals, from the *Animation Journal*, edited by leading scholar Maureen Furniss in the USA and running since 1991,[22] and the *International Journal of Comic Art*, edited, since 1999, by John Lent, through to three new journals launched in 2006: the Society for Animation Studies's online *Animation Studies*, John Libbey's *Cartoons: The International Journal of Animation*, edited by Chris Robinson (in Ottawa), and Sage's *Animation: An Interdisciplinary Journal*, edited by Suzanne Buchan (in the UK).[23] Curiously, despite their relatively recent introduction and claims to a fresh, inclusive approach (see Buchan's editorial, 2006b), these newer journals also display a 'deafness' to sound and music and largely emphasize visual and narrative aspects of the form as separate from sound and music. If not ignored, in these publications the audio analyses are mostly either confined to a passing reference under post-production or marginalized to brief mentions located through the index or endnotes.[24] Some reasons for such a paucity of address to sound and music have already been outlined. Perhaps more importantly, the neglect emanates from a dearth of analytical models from which to develop workable methods. Approaches applicable to animation film music/sound may be adopted or adapted from literature on film music.

Screen sound – especially music – research has rapidly expanded in the last few years, with several publishers' catalogues featuring books, three mid-2000s journals (*The Soundtrack*; *Music, Sound and the Moving Image*; and, online, *Music and the Moving Image*) adding to established periodicals such as *The Film Music Journal*, *Film Score Monthly* and *Soundtrack*, and several conferences hosted by institutions in the USA and UK.[25] Some music journals[26] offer useful profiles of composers and add to industry contributions – such as interviews with sound designers – in publications like *Mix* or *Audio Technology*. There is now a significant body of work available around film music and several 'schools' offering analytical models. Music-in-film scholarship located in music faculties is often based on a largely musicological approach that treats film music as somewhat removed from the film image track and mostly focuses on original music composed specifically for the film text under examination. Interdisciplinary film-music scholarship enables analysis of all (or more) of the components of the music track, including pre-recorded songs, which increasingly feature in film soundtracks (and CD releases). Popular music studies have contributed to this perspective, although often by hearing the songs without the soundtrack (and without address to animation film – see, for example, Powrie and Stilwell, 2006). Another analytical school that significantly arose from popular-music studies considers the broader industrial context of the music track in relation to the marketing and distribution of the film (see Smith, 1998), and this is acknowledged and extended in the studies by Yamasaki, Fitzgerald, Peter Morris and Rebecca Coyle in this volume. A further analytical model considers the production process for the music and soundtrack in relation to the personnel involved and their operational method. This approach demonstrates that, certainly in the major studio productions, there is rarely ownership of the music by a single named composer but instead the music track (including all of its components) is the product of several (often many) creators working as composer, orchestrator, sound designer, music editor, music supervisor, mixers and others. This is a useful model for animation film, given the variable production processes employed for each film project.[27]

Overall, along the same lines as the marginalization of animated film in film studies programmes, film-music/sound research has rarely attended to animation soundtracks. While it is notoriously difficult to generalize about animation film, the form has different requirements of sound and music from live-action film. Indeed, it is important that the analytical approach is applicable to the film music usage. For example, an issue that has particularly intrigued animation-sound scholars is that of 'funny music', that is, the ways that music and sound are used for humour (see Mera, 2002) and this is outlined in the chapter by Morris and Coyle in this volume. Goldmark's *Tunes for 'Toons* (2005) shows an awareness of the analytical approaches of film-music scholars, drawing on neologisms and concepts originated by Claudia Gorbman (1987), Michel Chion (1994), Krin Gabbard (1996) and Jeff Smith (1998), and he attempts to differentiate the unique properties of animation music. Many film-music terms, Goldmark argues, are inapplicable to cartoon music given that music is "far more integral to the construction of cartoons" (2005: 4). As Paul Wells notes in his chapter in this volume, current debates occurring within film-music studies cannot necessarily be applied to animation film (for example, concerning diegetic/nondiegetic, source/underscore, etc.). In addition, there is often a high proportion of music included in an animation film, whether original or adapted. The Aardman DreamWorks feature *Wallace & Gromit: The Curse of the Were-Rabbit*, for instance, included 72 minutes of music for the 80-minute film.

It is inappropriate, however, to argue that everything about sound and music in animation film is different from live action. Indeed, Stephen Deutsch argues that recent US-made CGI feature films "so thoroughly emulate the structural and narrative worlds of live-action films, that the scores owe far less to the gestures of cartoon music and sound than they do to feature film soundtrack production practices" (2008: 98). In addition, while animators may be "responsible for ... a highly detailed process of *creating* a world rather than merely *inhabiting* one" (Wells, 2002: 26), this may not be a new situation for music personnel who have devised a sound location to convey a science-fiction or otherwise 'other-worldly' location. Furthermore, all voices are generated as recordings of actors, regardless of how those voice recordings may be manipulated later, and synched to animated drawings rather than to live-action performances (in ADR or real time). Animation excels in enabling creatures and objects to gain a 'voice' or sound signature released from 'realism', whether they be the spiders and maggots in Tim Burton's films or the mutating houses and creatures in Hayao Miyazaki's films. The chapters in this book therefore contribute to these debates within film-sound studies as well as to the dispersed and wide-ranging volume of animation studies.

Themes and framework of this book

The structure of *Drawn to Sound* relates to ways of dealing with music – as composed, adapted, used as/with sounds, and in relation to the industry. As a result, the chapters are grouped under section headings comprising scoring approaches, intertextual music tracks, sound design and sonicity, and industrial contexts. While highlighting the variety of approaches available for analysing animation-film music and sound, these broad categories are, of course, porous and accommodate overlapping issues and interweaving lines of argument.

Moving beyond a phenomenological approach, *Drawn to Sound* also extends debates about socio-political dimensions in animation films. Animation has a long history of engaging with social and political issues in abstracted ways not commonly exploited in conventional film-making (and not without controversy – see Cohen, 1997). In this sense, animation film has often both challenged and reinforced institutional structures: discourses surrounding race, ethnicity and sexuality, among others, have often found a space in animation that would have been silenced or censored in mainstream film-making. These concepts can be significantly carried in soundtracks, as the chapters by Tulk, Lerner, and Fitzgerald and Hayward demonstrate. Tulk, for instance, draws on focus-group discussions of the musical themes in *Brother Bear* (Aaron Blaise and Robert Walker, 2003) to analyse the plundering of indigenous and other 'world' musical motifs.

While providing input to animation-sound studies, *Drawn to Sound* does not aspire to being a definitive text, but rather offers both studies of specific films and analytical models. The films discussed are not the only – or even necessarily the most significant – films that might be analysed. Neither are the models the only ones available for use in analysis of animation-film music and sound. The films examined and methods employed have been determined by the availability of authors engaged in scholarly research and writing within the brief of this book (that is, post-World War II animated feature-film music and sound), and those scholars come from complementary research backgrounds, including sociology, music, cultural studies, media and film disciplines. This highlights how music and sound in animation does not need to be hived off from other areas of analysis but can be core to film, animation and music explorations, as well as a significant domain, trigger or medium for interdisciplinary studies.

The films studied in *Drawn to Sound* were produced in the USA, Europe, Japan and Australia. While this indicates the global fascination with animation, it does not reflect the centres of production proportionately (especially if we take into account major centres of short-film production, particularly since the 1930s). Several films studied in this volume derive from the Disney corporation's animation studio (e.g., *The Little Mermaid*) or through a Disney-schooled director (auteur Tim Burton) or even creative personnel in a company production from the Disney talent pool (*The Brave Little Toaster*). As previously noted, it is difficult for a book that focuses on feature-length film, with a concentration on music, to avoid a major emphasis on a corporation with such a considerable track record in this production form and audio orientation. Similarly, the Japanese industry is so influential in the contemporary period that it warrants several chapters illustrating various approaches and showing that 'the industry' does not necessarily operate monolithically. Several chapters suggest that the transnational nature of animation film and music products is as much to do with economic imperatives as with cultural globalization (or glocalisation – see Quigley, 2002). However, not all the films spotlighted in these studies were commercially successful and some chapters investigate films produced on relatively modest budgets.

Drawn to Sound is structured around four sections. In the first section, 'Scoring Animation Film', three chapters provide overviews of different musical approaches. Film and television music theorist Janet Halfyard examines Tim Burton's stop-motion animation films, *The Nightmare Before Christmas* (directed by Henry Selick, 1993) and *Corpse Bride* (2005), and argues that music and songs help to structure these films and allow horror and humour to be juxtaposed so distinctively. Animation authority Paul Wells discusses long-form films (including the now-famous *Animal Farm* [1954]) from the prolific Halas and Batchelor studio by providing a national industrial context and showing how the studio's approach to animated musical forms offered a distinct form arising from the UK in the postwar period. Kyoko Koizumi's overview of Joe Hisaishi's music for feature films produced as part of his longtime collaboration with Hayao Miyazaki identifies four broad approaches to composition. These are influenced by Miyazaki's and Hisaishi's blending of Japanese and western-themed cultural influences and contribute to the construction of narratives in a selection of the films.

The second section of *Drawn to Sound* offers four studies of 'Musical Intertextuality'. British popular-music sociologist Ian Inglis examines the music track for George Dunning's *Yellow Submarine* (1968) and shows how producer George Martin deployed three categories of music – familiar and new Beatles songs together with an original score – to create an integrated aural and visual production. Cinema and popular-music scholar Philip Hayward analyses John Powell's music and its operation with popular songs and tap-dance music in George Miller's digital animation blockbuster *Happy Feet* (2006). Music and cinema historian Neil Lerner discusses *Who Framed Roger Rabbit* (Robert Zemenckis, 1988) in terms of musical framing and its vestiges of US minstrelsy, and argues that the film's repression of race as an issue is evident in its music. Canadian ethnomusicologist Janice Esther Tulk scrutinizes the 'world musics' rendered for Disney's *Brother Bear* (Aaron Blaise and Robert Walker, 2003) and describes the manner in which the music is ambiguous in its time and cultural setting rather than being representative of specific indigenous peoples.

The third section of *Drawn to Sound* offers three studies of 'Music and Sonicity'. US cartoon music specialist Daniel Goldmark analyses how Sylvain Chomet's musicscapes and soundscapes of two eras and two continents operate without dialogue in *Les Triplettes de Belleville*, a film that now has cult status. Sound organizes historical eras, plotlines and characterizations to effectively create spaces for nostalgia. This use of sonic affect to explore the past is also discussed in the chapter by musicologist Jon Fitzgerald and Philip Hayward on *The Brave Little Toaster* (Jerry Rees, 1987), a drawn cel animation film in which the narrative is largely carried by songs presented anthropomorphically by old-fashioned and defunct household appliances. Contemporary music theorist Kentaro Imada analyses the western-styled music in three feature films from the highly successful *Lupin III* (*Rupan sansei*) Japanese anime series. Imada draws on a socio-historical discussion of musical derivation to contextualize the case study and shows how the music in these features operates at a point of confluence between traditional Japanese stage and media sound and music and western musical accompaniment.

The last section of the volume, 'Music and Industrial Contexts', explores music in terms of animation and music industries, demonstrating how an understanding of film texts can be enriched by analysis of their production backgrounds. UK music and comedy researcher Peter Morris and I analyse the feature film that arose from a collaboration between the successful British claymation studio Aardman Animation and a Hollywood partner, namely, *Wallace & Gromit: The Curse of the Were-Rabbit* (Nick Park and Steve Box, 2005). We found that the music created by Julian Nott was informed by the studio's transition from a relatively small company to a collaboration with a major US animation producer, DreamWorks Animation SKG, and their deployment of Hans Zimmer's musical approach. In her analysis of *Cowboy Bebop* feature-film music production, Aki Yamasaki brings a media studies perspective to the music products – including soundtrack, theme song and character song releases – associated with the television series and films. Her characterization of corporate strategies for animation music in Japan shows how industry changes in the 1980s initiated new approaches to music genres and the marketing of animation CDs. In the final chapter, as a media studies researcher, I collaborated with musicologist Jon Fitzgerald to examine the extraordinary success of two Disney Corporation films in the post-Walt era: *The Little Mermaid* (1991) and *The Lion King* (1994). We argue that the overt deployment of Broadway musical-theatre approaches in the films enabled Disney to launch a new generation of animation feature-film production. These provided a fertile ground for seeding future CGI successes, such as John Lasseter's *Toy Story* (1995), that radically changed animation production.

Each section of *Drawn to Sound* offers a different perspective on animation as film, and together the chapters show not just a way of experiencing film but a textual analysis that Michael Bull and Les Back call "thinking with our ears" (2003: 2). This approach, they argue, "offers an opportunity to augment our critical imaginations, to comprehend our world and our encounters with it according to multiple registers of feeling" (*ibid.*).

As a collection of essays, *Drawn to Sound*'s contribution to animation and film-sound studies is multifarious and aims to extend discussions about sound and music, not just in film or even in animation.

Conclusion

The studies in *Drawn to Sound* show how animation is a malleable, mutable form that requires a flexible and innovative approach to its audio component. The book's historical time period and focus on the feature-film format also indicate the areas requiring detailed and sustained scholarly research, such as short-form sound/images experiments (especially in Europe), animation film precursors such as vaudeville, star voices employed in animation, the flourishing children's television industry,[28] and the frame-by-frame operation of sound in the audio-visual text. Unlike the differentiation of approaches and splintering of methods from psychoanalysis, semiotics, production study, industry, etc. present in film studies, this book offers a convergent way of experiencing animation films (hearing *and* seeing them) as audio-visual texts, industries, corporate and auteurial cultures, and conceptual explorations.

Drawn to Sound's international perspective shows how globally pervasive animation is but also how the film industry – particularly in relation to features – is increasingly a transnational one, which is now devised via digital and online media without necessarily strong geographical connections. In analysing animation and placing sound centre stage, *Drawn to Sound* offers a counter-history of screen media, and a fresh perspective on moving-image cultural experience. Ultimately, then, engaging the ear with the eye allows appreciation of animation film as an integrated and dynamic audio-visual media form.

Notes

1. Stanza's 'Sonicity' can be found online at http://www.soundcities.com/info.html (undated). Ajmir Kandola's discussion of 'Sonic/Sonicity' work can be found on the Silent Aether site at http:www.silentaether.com/content/view/17/72/ (accessed 7 June 2007).
2. H. Kallmann, A. P. Woog and H. Westerkamp (2008), 'World Soundscape Project', in *The Canadian Encyclopedia*, Historical Foundation of Canada, http://www.thecanadianencyclopedia.com (accessed 4 July 2008).
3. The abbreviated term anime arose in the 1970s and is thought to derive from the French phrase *dessin animé*. Most often, 'anime' describes animation from Japan that has a specific colourful art style (and often adult themes). Often evolving from comic-book (manga) series, anime can appear in television series, film, games, internet sites and commercials. Once hand-drawn and rendered as 2-D, now most anime is computer-generated and can be 3-D in style
4. M. Langer (2002), 'The End of Animation History', *Society for Animation Studies*; http://asifa.net/SAS/articles/langer1.htm.

5. In the first version of 'The Work of Art in the Age of Its Technical Reproducibility', published in 1935, as discussed in Leslie, 2002: 104–7.
6. See also Siegfried Kracauer (1960) and René Clair's work.
7. See, for example, http://www.your3dsource.com/most-expensive-3d-animated-films.html for figures on the ten highest-cost animation features.
8. Unsourced estimation.
9. The category of Best Animated Feature was introduced to the US Academy Awards in 2001 and is only awarded if eight or more animated feature films (of at least 70 minutes duration) have been theatrically released in Los Angeles in the year of the awards. Animated features have won Best Picture in the past, for example, *Beauty and the Beast* in 1991. Of course, there are specific awards for animation films, such as the Annie Awards presented by the Los Angeles branch of the International Animated Film Association. Significantly, an animation feature, John Lasseter's *Up!* opened the 2009 Cannes Film Festival.
10. http://www.boxofficemojo.com/alltime/adjusted.htm. Accessed 15 July 2008.
11. *The Prince of Egypt: Nashville* CD; *The Prince of Egypt: Inspirational* CD; and *The Prince of Egypt: Music from the Original Motion Picture Soundtrack* CD.
12. Although the term is often employed derogatively to imply lack of imagination or ingenuity on the part of the composer.
13. See discussions of his work in Kahn, 1999, and Leslie, 2002.
14. Also, more recently, IT and computer-generated imaging schools focus on animation. See the proposal by Eric Farrar at Ohio State University, 'A Method for Mapping Expressive Qualities of Music to Expressive Qualities of Animation', http://accad.osu.edu/~efarrar/thesis/proposal120602.pdf.
15. See Jeff Smith's discussion of comic allusion employed in film songs (Smith, 2001).
16. Thanks to Cristoforo Garigliano, PhD student at Macquarie University, Sydney, for his translations summarizing this volume.
17. See also various informative sections in Furniss, 2008.
18. Reproduced in an appendix in Goldmark (2005), pp. 167–8.
19. See also Goldmark's 2007 chapter that discusses cartoons from the 1920s.
20. See, for example, the work of Bill Plympton at http://www.plymptoons.com.
21. See, for example, the discussion of the title and cover image for Bell, Haas and Sells (1995).
22. See also Furniss's useful literature review (1999).
23. Other journals provide more technical discussions, for example, the *Journal of Visualisation and Computer Animation* that has been published since the late 1980s.
24. With this in mind, I guest-edited a special issue of *Animation Journal* featuring articles on sound and music, published in October 2009. The issue includes articles on television, short-form animation and feature-film productions released at various time periods.
25. Brophy coordinated three Cinesonic conferences on film sound and music, held in Melbourne in the late 1990s/early 2000s.

26. See, for example, the *Sounds Australian* periodical from the Australian Music Centre, and the *Popular Music* journal.
27. See, as a useful, industry-informed study, Jack Curtis Dubowsky's paper delivered at the Music and the Moving Image conference in New York, 2008, titled 'The Evolving Temp Score in Animation'.
28. See, for example, the overwhelming success of the British-originated series *Bob the Builder*, with its chart-hitting theme song 'Can We Fix It?' See Chieko Tsuneoka, 'Arts Abroad: A Little Puppet's Popularity Has No Strings Attached', *New York Times*, 7 August, 2001; http://query.nytimes.com/gst/fullpage.html?res= 9B04E7D6113CF934A3575BC0A9679C8B63

References

Allen, S. (2009), 'Audio Avery: Sound in Tex Avery's MGM Cartoons', *Animation Journal*, 17, 7–22.

Beauchamp, R. (2005), *Designing Sound for Animation*, Amsterdam: Elsevier/Focal.

Bell, E., Haas, L., and Sells, L. (1995), *From Mouse to Mermaid: The Politics of Film, Gender, and Culture*, Bloomington and Indianapolis: Indiana University Press.

Bendazzi, G. (1994), *Cartoons: One Hundred Years of Cinema Animation*, Eastleigh, Hampshire: John Libbey.

Bendazzi, G., *et al.* (1995), *Coloriture: Voci, rumori, musiche nel cinema d'animazione*, Bologna: Pendragon.

Bouldin, J. (2001), 'The Body, Animation and the Real: Race, Reality and the Rotoscope in Betty Boop', in A. Koivunen and S. Paasonen (eds), *Conference Proceedings for Affective Encounters: Rethinking Embodiment in Feminist Media Studies*, University of Turku, Finland, School of Art, Literature and Music, *Media Studies*, Series A, no. 49 (available at http://www.uut.fi/hum/mediatutkimus/affective/proceedings.pdf).

Brophy, P. (1991), 'The Animation of Sound', in A. Cholodenko (ed.), *The Illusion of Life: Essays on Animation*, Sydney: Power Publications/Australian Film Commission, pp. 67–112.

Brophy, P. (2007), 'Sonic-Atomic-Neumonic: Apocalyptic Echoes in *Anime*', in A. Cholodenko (ed.), *The Illusion of Life II: More Essays on Animation*, Sydney: Power Publications, pp. 191–208.

Buchan, S. (ed.) (2006a), *Animated 'Worlds'*, Eastleigh, Hampshire: John Libbey Publishing.

Buchan, S. (2006b), 'Editorial', *Animation: An Interdisciplinary Journal*, 1(1), 5–8.

Bull, M., and Back, L. (2003), 'Introduction: Into Sound', in M. Bull and L. Back (eds), *The Auditory Culture Reader*, Oxford/New York: Berg, pp. 1–18.

Care, R. (1977), 'The Film Music of Leigh Harline', *Film Music Notebook*, 3(2), 32–48.

Care, R. (1985), 'Threads of Melody: The Evolution of a Major Film Score – Walt Disney's *Bambi*', in I. Newsom (ed.), *Wonderful Inventions: Motion Pictures, Broadcasting, and Recorded Sound at the Library of Congress*, Washington, DC: Library of Congress, pp. 81–115.

Care, R. (2002), 'Make Walt's Music: Music for Disney Animation, 1928–1967', in D. Goldmark and Y. Taylor, *The Cartoon Music Book*, Chicago: A Capella Books, pp. 21–36.

Chion, M. (1994), *Audio-Vision: Sound on Screen*, trans. C. Gorbman, New York: Columbia University Press.

Cholodenko, A. (ed.) (1991), *The Illusion of Life: Essays on Animation*, Sydney: Power Publications/Australian Film Commission.

Cholodenko, A. (ed.) (2007), *The Illusion of Life II: More Essays on Animation*, Sydney: Power Publications.

Clague, M. (2004), 'Playing in 'Toon: Walt Disney's "Fantasia" (1940) and the Imagineering of Classical Music', *American Music*, 22(1), Spring, 91–109 (special issue on Cinema Music, edited by Gillian B. Anderson, Thomas L. Riis, and Ronald H. Sadoff).

Cohen, H., Salazar, J. F. and Barkat, I. (2009), *Screen Media Arts: An Introduction to Concepts and Practices*, South Melbourne: Oxford University Press.

Cohen, K. F. (1997), *Forbidden Animation: Censored Cartoons and Blacklisted Animators in America*, Jefferson, NC: McFarland & Co.

Culhane, J. (1983), *Walt Disney's "Fantasia"*, New York: H. N. Abrams.

Culhane, J. (1999), *Fantasia 2000: Visions of Hope*, New York: Disney Editions.

Curtis, S. (1992), 'The Sound of the Early Warner Bros. Cartoons', in R. Altman (ed.), *Sound Theory Sound Practice*, New York/London: Routledge, pp. 191–203.

Davis, R. (1999), *Complete Guide to Film Scoring: The Art and Business of Writing Music for Movies and TV*, Boston: Berklee Press.

Deutsch, S. (2008), 'Aspects of Synchrony in Animation', *The Soundtrack*, 1(2), 95–105.

Edera, B., with J. Halas (eds) (1977), *Full Length Animated Feature Films*, London/New York: Focal.

Elsey, E., and Kelly, A. (2002), *In Short: A Guide to Short Film-making in the Digital Age*, London: BFI Publishing.

Essex, A. (1998), 'Music; Forget the Movie. Listen to the CD.' *New York Times*, 27 December; http://query.nytime.com/gst/fullpage.html.

Furniss, M. (1998), *Art in Motion: Animation Aesthetics*, Sydney: John Libbey.

Furniss, M. (1999), 'Animation Literature Review', *Animation Journal*, http://www.animationjournal.com/books/reviews/litrev.html.

Furniss, M. (2008), *The Animation Bible: A Guide to Everything – from Flipbooks to Flash*, London: Laurence King.

Gabbard, K. (1996), *Jammin' at the Margins: Jazz and the American Cinema*, Chicago: University of Chicago Press.

Goldmark, D. (2005), *Tunes for 'Toons: Music and the Hollywood Cartoon*, Berkeley/Los Angeles/London: University of California Press.

Goldmark, D. (2007), 'Before Willie: Reconsidering Music and the Animated Cartoon of the 1920s', in D. Goldmark, L. Kramer, and R. Leppert (eds), *Beyond the Soundtrack: Representing Music in Cinema*, Berkeley/Los Angeles/London: University of California Press, pp. 225–45.

Goldmark, D., and Taylor, Y. (eds) (2002), *The Cartoon Music Book*, Chicago: A Capella Books.

Gorbman, C. (1987), *Unheard Melodies: Narrative Film Music*, London/Bloomington: BFI Publishing/Indiana University Press.

Granata, C. L. (2002), 'Disney, Stokowski, and the Genius of *Fantasia*', in D. Goldmark and Y. Taylor (eds), *The Cartoon Music Book*, Chicago: A Capella Books, pp. 73–92.

Halas, J., and Manvell, R. (1959), *The Technique of Film Animation*, London: Focal.

Hanna, S. (2008), 'Composers and Animators – the Creation of Interpretative and Collaborative Vocabularies', *Journal of Media Practice*, 9(1), 29–41.

Hill, M. (1998), 'Life in the Bush: The Orchestration of Nature in Australian Animated Feature Films', in R. Coyle (ed.), *Screen Scores: Studies in Contemporary Australian Film Music*, Sydney: AFTRS/Allen & Unwin.

Hollis, T. and Ehrbar, G. (2006), *Mouse Tracks: The Story of Walt Disney Records*, Jackson: University Press of Mississippi.

Imamura, T. (1992), *Manga Eiga Ron [Comic Animation Film Theory]*, rev. ed., Tokyo: Iwanami Shoten.

Jones, C. (1989), *Chuck Amuck*, New York: Farrar, Straus and Giroux.

Kahn, D. (1999), *Noise, Water, Meat: A History of Sound in the Arts*, Cambridge, MA/London: MIT Press.

Kracauer, S. (1960), *Theory of Film: The Redemption of Physical Reality*, Oxford: Oxford University Press.

Lack, R. (1997), *Twenty-four Frames Under: A Buried History of Film Music*, London: Quartet.

Lawson, T., and Persons, A. (2004), *The Magic Behind the Voices*, Jackson: University Press of Mississippi.

Lent, J. A. (2001), *Animation in Asia and the Pacific*, Eastleigh, Hampshire: John Libbey Publishing.

Leslie, E. (2002), *Hollywood Flatlands: Animation, Critical Theory and the Avant Garde*, London: Verso.

Leyda, J. (ed.) (1988), *Eisenstein on Disney*, London: Methuen.

Manovich, L. (2001), *The Language of New Media*, Cambridge, MA: MIT Press.

Manovich, L. (2002), 'What Is Digital Cinema?', in N. Mirzoeff (ed.), *Visual Culture Reader*, New York: Routledge, pp. 405–16.

McLaren, N. (1995), 'The Definition of Animation: A Letter from Norman McLaren', *Animation Journal*, Spring, 62–6.

Mera, M. (2002), 'Is Funny Music Funny? Contexts and Case Studies of Film Music Humor', *Journal of Popular Music Studies*, 14, 91–113.

Murray, M. R. (1997), *The Golden Age of Walt Disney Records 1933–1988*, Antique Trader Books.

Pilling, J. (1999), *A Reader in Animation Studies*, Bloomington: Indiana University Press.

Powrie, P., and Stilwell, R. (2006), *Changing Tunes: The Use of Pre-existing Music in Film*, Aldershot: Ashgate.

Prendergast, R. (1977), *Film Music: A Neglected Art. A Critical Study of Music in Films*, New York: W. W. Norton.

Quigley, M. (2002), 'Glocalisation versus Globalization: The Work of Nick Park and Peter Lord', *Animation Journal*, 10, 85–94.

Russett, R. (2004), 'Animated Sound and Beyond', *American Music*, 22(1) (Spring), 110–21.

Smith, J. (1998), *The Sounds of Commerce: Marketing Popular Film Music*, New York: Columbia University Press.

Smith, J. (2001), 'Popular Songs and Comic Allusion in Contemporary Cinema', in W. P. Robertson and A. Knight (eds), *Soundtrack Available: Essays on Film and Popular Music*, Durham, NC: Duke University Press, pp. 407–30.

Taylor, D. (1940), *Walt Disney's* Fantasia, New York: Simon and Schuster.

Tietyen, D. (1990), *The Musical World of Walt Disney*, New York: Harry N. Abrams.

Wells, P. (1998), *Understanding Animation*, London: Routledge.

Wells, P. (2002), *Animation: Genre and Authorship*, London: Wallflower.

Part I
Scoring Animation Film

1 "Everybody Scream!"
Tim Burton's Animated Gothic-Horror Musical Comedies

Janet K. Halfyard

Animation, thanks in large part to the Disney corporation, has a long and illustrious history in the genre of musicals, the first full-length animated musical being *Snow White and the Seven Dwarfs* (1937), followed by a host of titles through the following decades. The Disney animations of the 1970s and 1980s were generally less high-profile than those of the previous decades and it was only in 1989, with *The Little Mermaid*, and 1991, with the astonishingly successful *Beauty and the Beast* – the only animated film ever to be nominated for an Academy award in the Best Picture category – that the animated musical became a truly mainstream genre again. It was, perhaps ironically, the success of these films that led to Disney's willingness to go ahead with a production as unorthodox and therefore potentially risky as *Tim Burton's The Nightmare Before Christmas* (Henry Selick, 1993).

Disney's animated musicals have tended to be romanticized fairy-tales: their essential character is that of life-affirming, often humorous, stories of conventional hopes and loves overcoming grim and treacherous adversity; the songs are a major factor in communicating the uplifting elements of narratives that otherwise have the potential to be quite disturbing. Meanwhile, Tim Burton's version of the animated musical might best be described as Disney seen through a glass darkly. Whilst Burton's *The Nightmare Before Christmas* and *Corpse Bride* (2005) are still fairy-tale-like stories of love and redemption, they are certainly not conventionally life-affirming: the principal characters tend to be dead, and the songs include jauntily sung lines such as "Everybody scream" (*Nightmare*) and "Die, die, we all pass away" (*Corpse Bride*). Burton creates a blackly comic version of the musical, informed not only by the visual tropes and clichés of the horror genre, but also by Danny Elfman's music. Regularly described as combining elements of both the 'dark' and the 'quirky', Elfman's music is a significant element of Burton's overall filmic style, and he was a major contributor to both of these films in terms of music, songs (including lyrics) and his own performances.[1] The songs in these two films – *Tim Burton's The Nightmare Before Christmas* (henceforth *Nightmare*) and *Tim Burton's Corpse Bride* (henceforth *Corpse Bride*) – comprise one of the more atypical aspects of Elfman and Burton's work together. Until *Big Fish* (2003), for which he wrote the Siamese twins' song, 'Twice The Love', Elfman did not write songs for any more of Burton's films after the two animations. This is a more curious fact than might at first appear, as it was on the basis of his work as a singer–songwriter for his band, Oingo Boingo, that Elfman originally came to be writing film scores with Burton in 1985, and he regularly wrote songs for films by other directors until the early 1990s.[2]

The combination of horror and comedy – the dark and the quirky – in both Burton's work and Elfman's music reflects their shared love of all things macabre and an attitude towards these things which goes against the grain of convention. This is shown in Elfman's Oingo Boingo album titles – *Dead Man's Party* (1985), *Skeletons In The Closet* (1989), *Dark At The End Of The Tunnel* (1990) – and in his extensive collection of occult objects, such as an Ecuadorian shrunken head known as Uncle Billy that received a credit as 'mascot' in *Edward Scissorhands* (Tim Burton, 1990) and on the CD recording of *Batman Returns* (Tim Burton, 1992). In Burton's life and work, the same shrunken-head motif is visible in the final waiting-room scene of *Beetlejuice* (1988) and in Burton's general outlook:

> It goes back to childhood: I just remember that feeling that what people call 'normal' is not normal and what people call 'abnormal' isn't abnormal. And that's why I always responded to characters and monsters, and cultures like Mexico and its Day of the Dead, because I always felt there was more life there … I came from a sort of puritanical suburban existence where death was looked upon as dark and negative. But it happens to everybody, and I always responded to cultures that made death feel more a part of life.
> (Salisbury and Burton, 2006: 252–3)

The fact that *Nightmare* and *Corpse Bride* are musicals brings Elfman himself more prominently into the foreground in terms of the creative contribution of music. This chapter discusses that contribution, the working practices involved in realizing the films and the way in which both Burton and Elfman place their individually distinctive imprint on the outcomes in truly collaborative works. I examine the ways in which music and songs help to structure the films themselves and allow humour and horror to be juxtaposed so distinctively.

Burton's animations

Since the late 1980s, Tim Burton has occupied a unique position in Hollywood as a film-maker who is as comfortable with animation as he is with live action and who has at times combined animation with his live-action work. Thanks to computer-generated imagery (CGI), animation has become a regular but often invisible element of live-action film, a near-seamless blending of the realism of living actors in physically authentic locations with animated elements that allow actors to achieve the impossible in entirely imaginary locations. Burton's directorial style, however, prefers to make his animations completely visible, a stylistic element that intentionally disrupts the surface realism of his films rather than a technique used to preserve it (see McMahan, 2005: 80–120). We see this in the pointedly brief and stylistically intrusive stop-motion sequences of *Pee-Wee's Big Adventure* (1985), in the sandworms and transformations of *Beetlejuice* (1989) and in the overtly cartoonish CGI aliens of *Mars Attacks!* (1996), as well as in brief intrusions of stop-motion into live action in *Sleepy Hollow* (1999), and the CG Oompa-Loompa clones of *Charlie and the Chocolate Factory* (2005).

The visibility of his animations is just as important stylistically in his animated films as it is in his live-action work. Many animated films seek to create and maintain an alternative and equally convincing sense of realism through the consistency and coherence of their animated visual language. Burton's use of stop-motion, the combination of 2-D and 3-D elements in his animated work, and his creation of grotesque fantasy worlds inhabited by the dead disrupts the surface realism in a way comparable to the introduction of overt animation into live-action film. We are invited not to suspend our disbelief but to embrace the surreal and anti-realistic nature of the worlds he creates. Disney animations – including more recent Pixar CGI films – promote a smoothness in the visual image, a lack of visual texture; and it is arguably this lack of visual information that makes such characters and landscapes more credible. While they do not contain all the information they need to be instantly read as real rather than animated, they do not contain significant additional visual information that could not possibly be real, so allowing the viewer's imagination to fill in the gaps. Burton's work, on the other hand, is often heavily textured and anti-realistic: the landscape of *Nightmare*, for example, transforms Burton's line drawings into three dimensions, so that the ground and sky appear furrowed, a 3-D version of Munch's painting *The Scream* (1893). Sally, the leading lady, is quite literally sewn together from scraps, her seams showing and her stuffing occasionally falling out; and Jack, whose head has to be removed and swapped by the animators in order for his mouth to move when he speaks or sings, demonstrates the fact that his head can be taken off in 'Jack's Lament'. Disney's Belle and Aurora (from *Beauty and the Beast* and *Sleeping Beauty* (1959) respectively) are just as much animated constructs as Sally and Jack, but only Burton's characters are willing to advertise the fact so unashamedly to their audience.

Vincent and *Frankenweenie*

Burton's first job in film was as an animator for Disney in 1979, straight out of the California Institute of the Arts. He joined Disney, therefore, at one of its lowest points as an organization, when the animation department had shrunk to less than a third of its former size and many of the films being produced – *Pete's Dragon* (Don Chaffey, 1977), *The Fox and the Hound* (Ted Berman, Richard Rich, Art Stevens, 1981) and *The Black Cauldron* (Ted Berman and Richard Rich, 1985) – never truly joined the canon of 'famous' Disney works.

After several unhappy years during which he found he "couldn't even fake the Disney style" (Salisbury and Burton, 2006: 9), Burton was given the go-ahead to produce two short films of his own, the animated *Vincent* (1982) and the live-action *Frankenweenie* (1984). *Vincent* captures the essence of Burton's mature visual style: the morbid little tale of a thin, pale child with a shock of black hair, triangular face and mournful eyes (a credible puppet-double for Burton himself), who is obsessed with death and madness. The visual images construct various binary oppositions: the animation is entirely in black and white, and combines both 2-D drawings and 3-D stop-animation work. Other elements support such binaries: the text, narrated by Vincent Price, is a bizarre combination of the rhyming couplets of Dr Seuss with the macabre stories of Edgar Allan Poe; and the central character, Vincent Malloy, over-identifies with his narrator and namesake, Vincent Price. Central to the narrative is the juxtaposition of the normality of Vincent's domestic situation with the gothic horror of his fantasies, often signalled by the visual switch from his well-lit, white-painted bedroom to the dark, shadow-infested version of the same room when the door is shut or the lights switched out.

The music, by Ken Hilton, mirrors this series of juxtapositions in yet another binary pairing, this time the sound of a recorder against that of organ and harpsichord. The recorder corresponds to the daylight/childhood side of the equation – it is the archetypal instrument of childhood music lessons – while the organ and harpsichord music clearly references the world of the gothic horror films with which Price is associated. The film begins with the recorder, slightly out of tune, playing unaccompanied the melody of a song entitled 'The Streets Of Cairo', written by James Thornton in 1895, although it is better known as used by generations of American children for the playground rhyme 'Oh, they don't wear pants in the southern part of France'. The combination of its status as a children's rhyme with the recorder rendition – which turns out, in the opening shots of the film, to be played by Vincent himself – is then used to articulate his transformation from Vincent Malloy into his Vincent Price alter ego: from a seven-year-old boy to a grizzled and care-worn Vincent in a smoking jacket, as the recorder itself transforms into a long cigarette-holder. At the same time, the melody transforms, performed on the harpsichord instead of the recorder.

This short film establishes a very specific visual, narrative and musical world for Burton's animations that is carried over into his live-action films. Like *Vincent*, *Frankenweenie* is a film about death; in fact, both Vincent and Victor Frankenstein (the child at the centre of *Frankenweenie*) have pet dogs that they transform into zombies, Vincent in his imagination and Victor for real. In both films, the central character is a slightly built boy with dark hair, large eyes and a triangular face. Divorced from a human actor, Vincent comes across as a far more macabre and morbid character than Victor (played by Barret Oliver), who is a real child with a normal human physique. Vincent is constructed as an emaciated stick figure – he is too thin to pass for a real human being, his eyes too large, his limbs too attenuated, his mouth too small, pinched and down-turned. However, the major difference between them is that the live-action film has a genuinely happy ending, with all the previously hostile neighbours rallying round with jump-leads to shock Sparky the dog back into zombie life after he saves Victor's life; *Vincent*, on the other hand, ends with Vincent's apparent death.

Musically, the score of *Frankenweenie* is fairly generic, reflecting perhaps the relative inexperience of the two composers working on the project. David Newman and Michael Convertino were both scoring film for the first time. Their music successfully references the conventions of classic horror and plays with ironic grandness against the comic-horror of Burton's brief narrative, alluding to the gothic style that Elfman later provided so effectively for Burton in the *Batman* (1989) score, but it lacks the contrasts of *Vincent* that were to become a feature of Burton's later films. With its series of binary pairings, *Vincent* demonstrates in embryonic form a characteristic of Burton's live-action films: the juxtaposition of two different types of music, normally a more conventionally orchestral score against a pre-existing and/or immediately recognizable music. This is heard in several of the early films in particular, with the combination of Elfman's score and songs from Harry Belafonte (*Beetlejuice*), Prince (*Batman*) and Tom Jones (*Edward Scissorhands*).

Tim Burton's *The Nightmare Before Christmas*

One of the most curious aspects of both *Nightmare* and *Corpse Bride* is that, alone among Burton's films, he directed neither of them. In fact, he had a very hands-off approach to both of them: he did not write them and was not practically involved with the animation process. He *was* responsible for the plot outline and the drawings on which both characters and sets were based – the pet cemetery of *Frankenweenie* is reproduced very faithfully in the cemetery that lies on the border of Halloween Town in *Nightmare* – but his involvement was largely one of inspiring and giving approval to the work of others based on his ideas.

The starting point for *Nightmare* was a poem that Burton wrote after completing *Vincent* in 1982, and he originally thought Vincent Price might be the narrator. As with *Vincent*, the project was again a response to Burton's childhood fascinations and obsessions, this time not with Vincent Price movies but with Christmas holiday movies, particularly *How the Grinch Stole Christmas* (Chuck Jones, 1966) and *Rudolph the Red-nosed Reindeer* (Kizo Nagashima and Larry Roemer, 1964). However, having first conceived *Nightmare* at Disney in 1982, Burton had to wait until 1991 to begin working on the production, when Disney handed the project over to its more adult-oriented division, Touchstone Pictures.

The first problem that ensued was creating a script: Burton scripted *Vincent* using his own poem but, from *Frankenweenie* onwards, he has handed over to others the scriptwriting from his original ideas. Elements of the original *Nightmare* poem are found in the film, and are more extensively incorporated into the film's soundtrack release (1993), where Patrick Stewart acts as a narrator, using the original poem to link together the film's songs, creating a second, parallel version of the work. However, as the film was gearing up to go into production in 1991, there was still no script, merely Burton's three-page poem.

In the event, it was music that came to stand in place of a script as the backbone of the film, and this is one of the reasons why *Nightmare* has so many songs —ten complete songs were written before the film was shot, as well as underscore music written after the event. Both Burton and Elfman have variously recounted the process: over a relatively short period of time, they got together every few days and worked through the film chronologically.[3] Burton described what he wanted to happen in terms of action and how the characters concerned should react; Elfman took this information away and wrote a song around it. Once one song was complete, they moved on to the next section of the story, which resulted in a new song, and so on. Caroline Thompson, who had written the screenplay for *Edward Scissorhands*, was then brought in to write a script *around* the songs.

Elfman's music, used in all but one of Burton's feature-length films, has always played an integral role in how Burton's work is understood.[4] It is an axiom of Hollywood film-making practice that music "interprets the image, pinpoints and channels the 'correct' meaning of the narrative" (Gorbman, 1987: 58) and so gives control to the director (and, increasingly, to the producer) over interpretation. However, the level of Elfman's involvement with *Nightmare* is almost problematic on some levels. It is called *Tim Burton's The Nightmare Before Christmas*, but could just as easily be thought of as Danny Elfman's film, borne out by the fact that Burton himself describes it as less like a musical and more like an operetta. This label suggests how the important role played by the music and its composer goes well beyond that of normal film practices (Salisbury and Burton, 2006: 121.) The characters and the outline are Burton's, but the songs and their lyrics that drive the film's narrative are Elfman's creations. Elfman also sings several characters in the film, including the central character, Jack; is one of the five or six voices multi-tracked to provide the chorus for all the ensemble numbers; and wrote the underscore music which binds the film as a whole. Burton, meanwhile, was much less actively engaged in its making and was directing *Batman Returns* throughout a substantial part of *Nightmare*'s production.

The music largely belongs to Jack, sung by Elfman and played by Chris Sarandon, who was cast because his speaking voice was a credible match for Elfman's singing.[5] The exceptions to Jack's dominance of the music are 'Oogie Boogie Song', 'Sally's Song', both sung by their eponymous characters, and 'Kidnap The Santy Claws', sung by the trio of Lock, Shock and Barrel that again includes Elfman. Stylistically, the music comes across as old-fashioned, and this is a property that is relatively unique to Burton's animated musicals: both *Nightmare* and *Corpse Bride* allude to 1930s jazz on the one hand and to Kurt Weill and Gilbert and Sullivan on the other. This is in contrast to his live-action films, which tend to have 'classical' Hollywood scores, provided by Elfman, that only rarely identify the film's music with a particular style or era.

The old-fashionedness of the music is entirely intentional. As Elfman said in an interview, twelve years after completing *Nightmare*:

> the only concept [Tim and] I had was that ... we didn't want anything to sound like it could possibly have come from contemporary Broadway; and that all the references had to be archaic in some way. I wanted the songs to have a timeless feel – is this from the forties? is this from the twenties? is this from the sixties? when is this from? So I mixed up Kurt Weill and Gilbert and Sullivan ... and out came Nightmare ... It was kind of an anti-Broadway statement.[6]

This is primarily an articulation of Elfman's musical aesthetic and has a direct precedent in the work he did with his brother, Richard Elfman, on the latter's film *Forbidden Zone* (1980). Danny wrote music and songs for this, as well as being one of its principal performers, almost precisely the situation he found himself in when working on *Nightmare*. The music of *Forbidden Zone* likewise reflected a conscious avoidance of anything that was obviously related to contemporary pop, rock or musicals; instead, it made use of 1920s and 1930s jazz alongside distinctly avant-garde music.

Where Burton's aesthetic makes itself felt is in the way the film, visually and musically, articulates the sense of several different worlds existing alongside each other, and the differentiation of these worlds is evident in their musical soundscapes. There are four worlds in *Nightmare*: Halloween Town; Oogie Boogie's realm, which exists as an adjunct to Halloween Town itself; Christmas Town; and our own world. There is also a transitional space, the wood between the worlds, with doorways that evidently lead to holiday towns responsible for Thanksgiving, Easter and Valentine's Day.

All of the four worlds we encounter in *Nightmare* are both visually and musically distinct. Halloween Town is characterized by the colours black, white and orange (the colour of pumpkins) and by heavily textured surfaces. It is particularly associated with minor-key music that owes a great deal to Kurt Weill in terms of the melody and harmony of the songs, particularly the angular melody and slightly unpredictable harmonies of 'Sally's Song' and the wheezing, discordant band that persistently lurks on a street corner of the town. Their minor-key, rhythmically slowed and generally mournful version of 'Jingle Bells', played when Jack is attempting to explain Christmas to the Halloween folk epitomizes the macabre quirkiness that characterizes Halloween Town overall. Lyrically, there is more than a hint of Dr Seuss. This is perhaps the most obvious connection to *Vincent* and to Burton as a writer. In writing the lyrics for the songs, Elfman not only attempted to retain the rhythms and rhymes of Burton's Dr Seuss-inspired style, but also incorporated some of Burton's lines directly into his songs, such as "Perhaps it's the head that I found in the lake" in the 'Town Meeting Song' (Thompson, 1993: 177).

Christmas Town, by contrast, is full of bright reds, greens, yellows and blues. Where the base colour of Halloween Town is black, Christmas Town's is white, provided by its snow; and where Halloween Town has a two-dimensional sense created by the way many surfaces gain their sense of rough and uneven texture from (flat) line drawings, in Christmas Town everything is smoothly three-dimensional. The inhabitants of Halloween Town are ragged, vividly textured, physically distorted monsters and broken toys of infinite variety; those of Christmas Town are neat, smooth and identical childlike elves, with Santa Claus a very much larger and older version of them. Musically, Christmas Town causes Jack to sing the only major-key song in the film, 'What's This?' Its breathless lyrical rhythm, major key and the generally rising tendency of phrases identify the music as belonging to Christmas Town, despite being sung by Jack, since nothing that musically resembles this originates from Halloween Town itself.

   The 'real' world is musically identified by having no songs of its own; nor do any of the adults have heads, as these are consistently cut off by the top of the frame, leaving only children to be seen in their entirety; and the colours here tend towards slightly washed-out pastels. Oogie Boogie's realm goes to the other extreme: here, the colours are vibrant, psychedelic fluorescents in what are basically Christmas Town colours set against a black rather than white ground. Oogie's song is very evidently inspired by Cab Calloway, and there are distinct similarities with one of Calloway's best-known songs, 'Minnie The Moocher' (1930).[7] The location of Oogie's realm, underneath Halloween Town and in the dark, evokes the hidden-away speakeasies of the Prohibition era with which this style of music is often associated. With that comes the suggestion of danger and organized crime, with Oogie in charge and Lock, Shock and Barrel as his hoodlums.

Tim Burton's *Corpse Bride*

Thirteen years separate Burton's two feature-length stop-motion animation musicals. The technical process of making stop-animation – both the use of digital cameras and the mechanical process of manipulating puppets' facial expressions – improved so much between 1993 and 2006 that one might be forgiven for thinking that *Corpse Bride* is CGI in the style of stop-animation. However, there is an overall look to the two films that readily identifies them as works from the same stable, most notably the marvellous variety of grotesque characters. Burton's imprint remains clear in the creation of another set of opposing worlds, the land of the dead and the land of the living. The living inhabit a Victorian world largely devoid of colour – everything tends towards shades of grey and extremely muted pastels in the green/blue/purple range, a much more sombre version of the human world in *Nightmare*. The land of the dead has much in common with Oogie Boogie's realm, although not quite as garish. Nonetheless, this is another nighttime, subterranean realm that makes use of much brighter, more intense colours. Bone Jangles's big number, 'Remains Of The Day', uses the same idea of brightly fluorescent colours against a black background that was seen in Oogie Boogie's song, and, again, the location in the bar where new arrivals turn up suggests a speakeasy.

   The style of *Corpse Bride*'s songs acts as a musical metaphor and corollary for the visual characterization of each realm more overtly than in *Nightmare*. The main theme of the film – effectively Victor Van Dort's theme – is first heard in the main title sequence, played on the piano over images of Victor drawing and then releasing a butterfly, which connects to the end of the film when his actions release the Bride and she disintegrates into butterflies in the moonlight accompanied by the same theme.

As the camera follows the butterfly into the town, the sound of a clock ticking infiltrates the musical soundtrack, providing the pedestrian rhythm that continues throughout the camera's exploration of the town, and is then speeded up slightly to segue into the song. The fact that it is time itself that creates the plodding rhythm here acts as a revealing statement on the nature of life, indicating that time is responsible for the extreme differences between the lands of living and dead: the dead have no concern with time, and their lives are joyful and liberated as a result, reflecting Burton's general attitude toward death in his work.

The ticking motif is also specifically a mechanized one: we do not immediately see the source of the ticking but it starts as the camera pans across the town rooftops and is then diegetically linked to several clocks in the window of a shop. All their pendulums swing in time to the same ticking rhythm; the shopkeeper outside sweeps to this rhythm, the strokes of his brush becoming an additional pendulum. Everyone's actions in this sequence are apparently dictated by mechanical time, from the twitching of the cat's tail to the repetitive chopping of fish heads by two Van Dort employees. The orchestral sound is largely replaced at this point by a harpsichord, a much more mechanical-sounding instrument, which adds to the sense of things here being mechanized and ordered rather than lively and spontaneous.[8] Townsfolk walk and work to the rhythm of life, which in this case is the way that the seconds of their lives are inexorably measured out. The dead, freed from this constraint, are far more vigorous as a result.

The ensuing song, 'According To Plan', continues this characterization. Sung by the two sets of prospective parents-in-law, the Everglots and the Van Dorts, it is in many ways a very odd opening to the film, in that (like the world of the living in general) it is rather dour, the rhythm plodding and the melody lacking any kind of lyricism. The melodic line is quite repetitive and is so dull that when characters lapse into rhythmic speech, as they regularly do, there is little noticeable difference musically. This unexpectedly downbeat opening number is in keeping with the overall plot and the contrasting characterizations of the land of the living and the dead but, at this point in the film, the audience does not know this. The use of such an intentionally unappealing song is perhaps indicative of Burton's willingness to open with something which is not obviously crowd-pleasing. The interest in the song lies instead in the lyrics, which, like songs from *Nightmare*, take a very regular form and rely on slightly quirky images and rhymes for their humour, such as "our daughter with the face/Of an otter in disgrace", which is how Victoria is described by her parents.

The remaining songs all belong to the land of the dead, the first of these being 'Remains Of The Day', inspired by Sammy Davis Jr and sung by Elfman, in which Bone Jangles recounts the story of how the Bride was seduced and murdered by her treacherous lover. This is the first big production number of the film, twenty minutes in, and, just as 'According To Plan' was our introduction to the living, so this forms part of our introduction to the dead. The music contrasts on every level: where the first song is drab and plodding, this is an exuberant jazz number, with an overall improvisatory feel to sections between the verses, where Elfman scats and the skeletons dance. Like Oogie Boogie's song, this effectively affirms the exuberance of the non-living, although Oogie is a far more malevolent character than Bone Jangles.

The final song, sung by the full chorus of the dead, is a halfway point between these first two. 'The Wedding Song' is, like 'According To Plan', a song about weddings, and there is no influence of jazz in the music. Instead, this is an unambiguous pastiche of Gilbert and Sullivan, particularly *The Pirates of Penzance* (1879), which is alluded to visually as well, with a phantom major general atop a horse and a group of skeleton pirates led by their very own pirate-king dwarf. It has on the one hand, therefore, the exuberance and ironically life-affirming nature of the land of the dead but delivered in the more Edwardian/Victorian style of the land of the living; appropriately enough, as this is the moment that the dead make the decision to go 'upstairs' to the land of the living to perform the wedding ceremony for Victor and his Corpse Bride.

The other song in the film is 'Tears To Shed'. This is effectively two songs that alternate verses, the Bride's own lament and the duetting interjections from her friends, a maggot and a spider. It is again not obviously lyrical and the melodic range is quite limited, with stepwise sequences that generally end on the note they started on, perhaps indicating the Bride's dejection and the circular nature of her thoughts at this point. It does not clearly refer to any particular style or writer, although it perhaps owes more to Weill than any other number in the film. Musically, it has far more in common with 'According To Plan' than with either of the other two songs sung in the land of the dead, and this is arguably because the Bride's connection with Victor has made her depressingly aware of the fact that she is not alive – "I feel my heart is aching/ Though it doesn't beat, it's breaking". Time has caught up with her in that she is now connected to the living Victor, and this has infected her with the dourness of the living.

Nightmare is primarily about its music: the songs provide the overall structure of the film and are integral to the plot, defining the different worlds in consistent and coherent ways. *Corpse Bride* has far fewer songs and the use of musical style is therefore less thoroughgoing but music remains central to the narrative because two of the main characters are pianists. In technical terms, just as the songs for both films had to be written before the animation was created, the piano music that the characters play in *Corpse Bride* also had to be written before the film went into production, and the animated piano-playing, while not always lining up logically with the keyboard (low notes are sometimes played rather high on the keyboard during Victor and the Bride's duet) is nonetheless very credible. Mike Johnson, the co-director, attributes this to the animator for the piano-playing sequences, Phil Dale, who plays the piano himself (Johnson, 2005: online) but it is also an aspect of the meticulousness of Burton's own approach and the extent to which he demands as much detail in his animations as one might expect from a live-action sequence.

Although he himself never sings, Victor is therefore a musician and he initially bonds with both Victoria and the Bride over the piano. When he comes to the Everglots' house for the wedding rehearsal, he lingers by the piano and starts to play his theme, where he is overheard by Victoria, and their first conversation results from her praise of his playing. Later, in the land of the dead, he finds the Bride playing the theme from her song on the piano. Their reconciliation takes place without words, as he replies musically, first by imitating the phrases she plays from her theme, and then by encouraging her into a true duet when he plays his theme to her. The two themes are actually not that different – both are in a minor key and both are capable of switching between triple and duple time – and there is a strong indication given through this scene that, apart from the inconvenience of Victor being alive, the two are actually very well suited.

Gothic horror, musical comedy

The elements of horror and comedy are most successfully combined through allusion to other films, both visually and musically. Possibly the most humorously absurd moment occurs in *Corpse Bride* when, towards the end of the film, a moustachioed skeleton is repeatedly hit over the head by what turns out to be his still-living wife. As she realizes who he is, and protests that he has been dead for thirty years, he sweeps her into his bony embrace and declares, "Frankly, my dear, I don't give a damn" to the swelling sound of Max Steiner's recognizable theme from *Gone with the Wind* (Victor Fleming, 1939).

There are also some obvious sonic/visual references to horror films. The most overt of these is the timbral allusion to Peter Lorre's voice for the Bride's friendly maggot, who also manages to look a little like the co-star of *The Beast with Five Fingers* (Robert Florey, 1946) and suggests other horror classics. That film, in fact, haunts the edges of *Corpse Bride* because of the presence of pianos: the Everglots' entrance hall, a vast and shadowy space dominated by a piano and a staircase, refers to the main set of *The Beast with Five Fingers*, which of course also starred Burton's idol, Vincent Price; and the moment when the Bride's skeletal hand detaches itself from her wrist and continues to play the piano is another allusion to that film.

Mark Salisbury has noted the resemblance between the Bride and Elsa Lanchester in James Whale's *The Bride of Frankenstein* (1935), and there is also an obvious narrative correspondence in her name and the film's title (Salisbury and Burton, 2006: 252). The Bride has some textbook horror moments of her own. The most elaborate is when she rises from her grave after Victor has inadvertently slipped the ring onto her desiccated finger. The Bride's hand then comes to life and attempts to pull him down into the ground, referring to the scene at the end of Brian de Palma's *Carrie* (1976), in which Carrie's hand emerges from her grave to grasp the wrist of Amy Irving. When Victor pulls away and pulls the hand with him, we are back in the realms of *The Beast with Five Fingers* as the hand continues to creep towards him.

Musically, Elfman uses the full orchestra augmented by a choir and occasional organ for heightened effect, employing exactly the same techniques as those he used in other 'gothic' films for Burton from *Beetlejuice* to *Sleepy Hollow*, layering orchestral groups so that one (here, mainly the strings or the voices) has the melody whilst the other groups (brass, woodwind, percussion) create dense, busy textures around this. As her ethereal, hideously smiling, floating form pursues Victor through the woods, she herself appears to have no weight and the force of her assumed malevolence comes largely from her full-bodied musical sound.

The humour here and also in *Nightmare* often lies in the utter seriousness of the music, which would not be out of place in a live-action horror film but which takes on a slightly absurd feel in the context of an animation. There is a discontinuity between the depth and 'seriousness' of the full-scale Hollywood orchestral sound and the animated circumstances of these characters that automatically hints at this being a spoof. We are not supposed to be genuinely scared, as would be the intention in a 'true' horror film. In horror, we are supposed to believe that the Other could be real and threatening us via the proxy of the human characters in the narrative. In Burton's animation, the intentional artifice created by his physically non-realistic characters in a stop-motion genre places more distance between our credulousness and our identification with the characters. Likewise, in a more conventional horror film, as in real life, characters would not break into song; the moment they do, then – like Burton's stylistically distinctive animations themselves – the surface realism of the narrative is disrupted, particularly given the nature of the songs in both *Nightmare* and *Corpse Bride*, with their patter, Dr Seuss-style rhyming schemes and allusions to familiar musical styles.

Burton resists standard animation practice, perhaps seen most clearly in the way he continues to prefer stop-motion in the era of CGI. Although CGI has allowed computer modelling to produce much more detailed and realistic movement, one of the main conventions of non-CGI animation is that, just as visual appearances are 'smoothed' and simplified, actions are often condensed and stylized, using a visual shorthand that communicates effectively without necessarily connecting all the points between movements that would form part of a live-action sequence. However, in Burton's stop-motion, they are not condensed: actions are completed in minute and painstaking detail, and this has its corollary in sound. In animation, sounds are often metaphorical rather than realistic, and non-essential, ambient sound is frequently eliminated; in Burton's work, sounds are consistently and realistically detailed. Occasionally, for comic effect, and especially in moments of musical silence, sounds do become exaggerated, such as the classic cartoon convention of being able to hear someone moving very fast, which occurs with the Everglots' butler in the wedding rehearsal scene of *Corpse Bride*, accompanied by 'busy' musical notes. However, overall, *Corpse Bride* in particular produces footsteps and other incidental sounds with the kind of depth and realism that would be expected in live action, reflecting the persistent blending of an animation and live-action aesthetic in Burton's films overall.

This blending is also present in the music itself. As a film composer, Elfman generally resists the impulse to 'mickey-mouse' but, on occasion, the whole idea of non-diegetic sound being used to imitate a diegetic action is used quite playfully. The best example of this is when Victor and the Bride play the piano: at one point, her hand breaks off, continues playing an elaborately decorated passage as it fingers its way up the keyboard, and then continues up Victor's arm and across his shoulders, delicately trilling all the way – but, of course, the moment the hand leaves the keyboard the sound of the piano notes becomes diegetically impossible and the music, which only a moment before was clearly issuing from the piano, is now effectively mickey-mousing the hand's actions. This is one of those moments when the extent to which Burton's – and Elfman's – work blurs the usual boundaries of live action and animation, with the technically convincing piano duetting of the two characters belonging more closely to live-action narratives, and the visual joke of the independently moving skeleton hand and its impossible piano trills clearly belonging more to the realms of animation.

Musically, the one aspect of the animations that does not have obvious correspondence with Burton's live-action work is the songs. In terms of orchestration, harmony, texture and the insistence on minor-key melodies, the underscores of both *Nightmare* and *Corpse Bride* could as easily be sections of *Batman* or *Sleepy Hollow*, but both animations use 'non-diegetic' songs in a directly narrative manner,[9] something absent from the live-action films until *Charlie and the Chocolate Factory*.[10] Burton has consistently used songs in films in a way that is very different from the 'song from the movie' device of placing a song in the end credits and incorporating its theme into the underscore, as in *Robin Hood, Prince of Thieves* (Kevin Reynolds, 1991) and *Titanic* (James Cameron, 1997). In his early films, Burton tended to use small groups of songs by specific artists which were then associated with specific spaces and characters in the film: however, until *Charlie*, none of his live-action films crossed over into the territory of musicals in the way that the animations do, in which characters themselves start singing and making music as a means of progressing the narrative.

Conclusion

Burton and Elfman clearly love both the horror and the comedy genres, and, while some of Burton's live-action films have strayed away from one or other of these (perhaps most notably *Planet of the Apes* in 2001, which explores neither), the area in which they have been able to explore them together most consistently and successfully is the animations. Here, the joyful exuberance of the instruction "everybody scream" is able to flourish in an environment that combines music, song and hideously grotesque imagery in a way that would be infinitely more difficult and distasteful in a live-action setting.

At the time of writing, there is every indication that Burton is increasingly pursuing animation projects, with plans for an animated *Alice in Wonderland* in place for 2010 and a feature-length animated revisiting of *Frankenweenie* provisionally announced for 2011. Whether or not these evolve as animated *musicals*, both are likely to involve Elfman as composer and songwriter. This suggests that the side of their work which has thus far been the lesser area of activity in their overall collaborative output is likely to develop further in the coming years. The engagement of such internationally respected artists as film personnel – and the close collaboration of writer/director with composer – in such productions confirms the ongoing significance of animation as a creative format for feature films.

Notes

1. These words are among those particularly identified by critical analysts Bill Englehardt and Jeff Bond (1997).
2. For a more detailed account of Elfman's work as a pop musician and his route into film scoring, see Halfyard, 2004: 5–10.
3. There is a slight discrepancy between their accounts of how long this process lasted: one month according to Elfman (J. Schaefer, 'Interview with Danny Elfman', New York Public Radio, 28 September 2006, transcribed by Ian Davis, online at http://www.bluntinstrument.org.uk/elfman/archive/NYPublicRadio06.htm; accessed 23 June 2007), two according to Burton (Salisbury and Burton, 2006: 121).
4. Howard Shore scored *Ed Wood* (1994) during the brief period in which Burton and Elfman did not work with each other.
5. This information comes from an interview with Elfman by Andy Carvin in 1993, reproduced at http://ftp.ust.hk/edweb/nightmare.elfman.html, accessed 23 June 2007 (no longer available).
6. J. Schaefer, 'Interview with Danny Elfman'; see note 3 above.
7. Elfman also sang a lyrically altered version of this Calloway song in Richard Elfman's *Forbidden Zone*.
8. It is almost impossible for a harpsichord player to nuance a played note, as it is plucked by an internal plectrum in response to a key being pressed. This means that the note either sounds or it does not: how one presses the key makes no difference to its volume and cannot alter in any way how the plectrum plucks the string.
9. By non-diegetic song, I refer to situations where characters burst into song without displaying any awareness that it is not normal to be singing (or hearing someone sing) in this situation. The character is expressing emotion rather than performing to a (diegetic) audience, and the source of the accompanying music is not visible. 'What's This?' is a case in point. Diegetic songs occur where all characters are aware that a song is being performed, and the source of the accompaniment is normally visible to them, as in 'Remains Of The Day' in *Corpse Bride*.

10. Even in *Charlie and the Chocolate Factory*, the songs act as commentaries on what has happened. They are self-contained and arguably extra-diegetic moments, e.g., when the Oompa-Loompas step outside the main narrative and reflect on events. This comes from Dahl's original novel more than from Burton or Elfman's interpretation of the narrative

References

Englehardt, B., and Bond, J. (1997), 'The Never-ending Style Discourse', *Film Score Monthly*, 27 August, online at http://www.filmscoremonthly.com/articles/1997/27_Aug–Style_discourse.asp (accessed 6 December 2007).

Gorbman, C. (1987), *Unheard Melodies: Narrative Film Music*, Bloomington: Indiana University Press.

Halfyard, J. (2004), *Danny Elfman's* Batman*: A Film Score Guide*, Lanham, MD: Scarecrow Press.

Johnson, M. (2005), 'Corpse Bride: Puppet Pushing to New Heights', *Animation World Magazine*, 23 September, online at http://mag.awn.com/index.php?article_no=2633&ltype=columns (accessed 3 March 2007).

McMahan, A. (2005), *The Films of Tim Burton: Animating Live Action in Contemporary Hollywood*, New York/London: Continuum.

Salisbury, M., and Burton, T. (2006), *Burton on Burton*, rev. edn, London: Faber and Faber.

Thompson, F. (1993), *Tim Burton's The Nightmare Before Christmas*, New York: Disney Editions.

2 Halas & Batchelor's Sound Decisions

Musical Approaches in the British Context

Paul Wells

Between 1914 and 1939, European artists, architects and thinkers invested in designing the new world. Their works remain profoundly influential, even in the contemporary era, but they became especially significant in Britain during World War II and afterwards, during post-war reconstruction. 'Modernism', like many of the progressive movements in art and culture – Impressionism, Post-Impressionism, Cubism – had not significantly impacted on British art and society, which in general remained conservative and reactionary, rooted in its literary and theatrical traditions and the ghosts of empire. It was in this context that the Halas & Batchelor studio was established in 1940, defined by the sensibilities of a Hungarian émigré, John Halas, and Watford-born Joy Batchelor, whose talents in graphic design and animation were perfectly suited to the needs and challenges of the changing world, when finally Britain embarked on its own sense of 'modernity'.

Halas & Batchelor was effectively to define British animation for much of the studio's fifty-year existence, and among its innovations was a particular interest in, and focus upon, the use of music in films. Though the studio produced over 2000 pieces of work, most were shorts, ranging from public information and commercial work to art-house films; comparatively few longer films were made. The foremost of the feature films were *Animal Farm* (Joy Batchelor and John Halas, 1954), *Handling Ships* (Alan Crick and John Halas, 1944–45), an Admiralty training film, and a television adaptation of Gilbert and Sullivan's light opera, *Ruddigore* (Joy Batchelor, 1964). Amongst such a significant output, these long-form works must be contextualized in terms of their contribution to the body of work, as well as within an historical timeframe. The following discussion will explore Halas & Batchelor's responses to different animated musical forms over time and, most importantly, analyse the particular approach to animation soundtracks within the British context, set against its more well-known and acknowledged American cartoon counterparts.

Halas & Batchelor cartoons — a new approach

Halas & Batchelor first made commercials for the J. Walter Thompson agency and their major clients included Kelloggs and Lux. Early examples of the studio's work, like *Train Trouble* (Joy Batchelor and John Halas, 1940), scripted and storyboarded by Alexander Mackendrick (later of Ealing fame), showed a demonstrable influence of the Disney style, and this was even the case with the ways that the soundtrack was predicated purely on reinforcing the unfolding characteristics of the narrative. As the composer, Francis Chagrin, recalled:

> 'Train Trouble' had a passage where the main character, a squirrel who was a station master, was always late — before he was converted to cornflakes for breakfast. We wanted to convey the feeling of urgency, of fighting against time, of impending disaster, in the shortest possible space. Two trains were converging from two opposite sides and we first prepared, from records, a track which brought two trains nearer and nearer; inside his room the squirrel was pacing up and down impatiently listening to the trains coming nearer. We decided to emphasise the urgency further by having several types of watches and clocks, ticking more and more loudly, at different speeds. Finally, out of the rhythm of the train came the words "You're going to be late" repeated faster and faster, taken over by the kettle, etc., until the tension becomes unbearable. (Chagrin, in Halas and Manvell, 1958: 240)

This attention to detail coupled with a creative engagement with narrative that used the natural condensation in the animated form to persuasive and accessible effect won Halas & Batchelor attention from the British government's Ministry of Information (MOI). Their wartime propaganda and public information films, including *Dustbin Parade* (Joy Batchelor and John Halas, 1941), about recycling materials for munitions, and *Filling the Gap* (Joy Batchelor and John Halas, 1941), concerning the effective deployment of garden space for growing vegetables, are merely two examples of the seventy artful, yet highly engaging, cartoon films made by the studio that addressed domestic, government and military needs. These reflect the studio's movement away from the Disney model, the increasing influence of modernist art practices, and the studio's particular investment in distinctive musical scores.

Animation was perceived by Jack Beddington of the MOI as the ideal form to both educate and entertain. Acknowledging the popular appeal of Disney cartoons in Britain, and responding to concerns that live-action public information films were often viewed as tedious, or ignored altogether by the cinema-going audience, the MOI hoped that the apparent innocence and accessibility of the form would have persuasive effects. Halas also recognized that the general public was not merely enamoured by the sheer charm of the Disney output, but by the very 'difference' in the animated form per se. Films made by John Grierson's GPO (General Post Office) film unit, including work by Norman McLaren and Len Lye, for example, which were ostensibly abstract experimental films with a commercial 'tag' added at the conclusion, proved very popular, foregrounding the appeal of musical idioms which prompted and counterpointed dynamic improvisations in the representation of colour and form for its own sake, rather than 'comic' scores. Music was thus as important a factor in privileging this 'difference' in the cartoon, especially since British cartoons did not have the iconic presence of a Mickey Mouse or Donald Duck.

Government-supported work, coupled with the increasing number of promotional and instructional films made by the studio, effectively led to an acceptance of animation as a mode of expression which could engage with mature subjects and serious themes. Studio productions at this time included the Admiralty-sponsored *Handling Ships* (1944–45), a 70-minute tour de force of technical education, characterized by an authoritative voice-over; *Water for Fire Fighting* (Alan Crick and John Halas, 1948), a 3D model animation made for firefighter recruitment purposes; and promotional work for Shell, Esso and, later, academic publishers like Longman and Macmillan. Both Halas and Batchelor were instrumental in moving animation from juvenile premises to a more adult perspective on the world. In many senses, this was no surprise, as Halas had trained with the Dutch master animator, George Pal, and with Sándor Bortnyik at the Mühely ('little Bauhaus' workshop) in Hungary, and had been greatly influenced by the teachings and experimental work of Lázsló Moholy-Nagy at the Bauhaus, and the art of Paul Klee. Batchelor had trained at the Watford School of Art, and was well versed in state-of-the-art approaches to graphic design, the particularly 'British' idioms of expression and storytelling, and the slowly emerging animation industry in Britain.

The Halas & Batchelor studio, like its contemporary, the W. M. Larkins Studio, brought a distinctly European agenda to their work, which effectively redefined the cartoon aesthetically and reconstructed it as a serious medium for political, ideological and instructional purposes. Animation was the radical language of expression required by 'the new world', and Halas & Batchelor were its standard-bearers in Britain. This radicalism was most clearly seen, though, in the studio's musical soundtracks, predominantly composed by two major figures who worked with Halas & Batchelor for many years, Mátyás Seiber and Francis Chagrin, whose high-quality and distinctive work enhanced the originality of the studio's animated films.

Animating soundtracks

Valuing the scores of Seiber and Chagrin may be easier in the British context than, for example, in the United States, where 'cartoon music' has suffered from being dismissed as a less valuable artistic form and, even when subjected to analysis, has found itself addressed using inappropriate tools. As Daniel Goldmark observed:

> *A telltale sign that cartoon music is seen as a poor relation to film music is the application of film music terminology to cartoons. Such dichotomies as source/underscore, diegetic/nondiegetic, and iconic/isomorphic can be very useful in discussions of the music in live-action films. They all in some*

way gauge the degree to which music stays within the traditional bounds of the narrative. That is, the audience usually knows whether or not the music is coming from within the story or diegesis (thus, nondiegetic music is perceptible not to the characters on screen but only to the audience). Occasionally, these terms can be helpful for analyzing particular situations in cartoons, but they fail to take into account that music is far more integral to the construction of cartoons than of live-action films because the two forms are created in completely different ways. (Goldmark, 2005: 4)

This observation is important for a number of reasons, but not least because it notes the intrinsic difference in the ways animated films use music, and the significance of sound, in general, in the composition and construction of animation. Sound functions extend beyond the anchoring or illustrative model of narrative allusion, and act as an imperative for, and articulator of, the embedded literal, metaphorical and metaphysical conditions of the language of animation itself. Goldmark also draws attention to the profound significance of cultural context. Animated film was viewed and received very differently in Britain, in the sense that 'the cartoon' was very much seen as an American form, and Disney, its presiding agency. While there was later recognition that Warner Bros. cartoons were in some way different, this was largely marked out as a difference in character – these were effectively 'Bugs Bunny' cartoons, which seemed of a different order to 'Mickey Mouse' or 'Donald Duck' cartoons, and altogether different again from the aesthetic achievements of the Disney features.

The British public saw the cartoon in its British incarnation as something related to, but removed from, the American model (see Wells, 1998: 226–32), recognizing it as a film form much more akin to public information and experimental film than 'a cartoon' (meaning a humorous short vignette, featuring amusing animal characters). This enabled British animators to facilitate the British cartoon with more indigenous content, and to explore its terrain of expression in a more open, less questioned way than in the American model, which had already established itself as the benchmark in the form by virtue of its quality and wide distribution, and which, crucially, had very quickly established comic codes and conventions. British animated cartoons simply could not be made in the same way, and this included their music. American composers like Carl Stalling and Scott Bradley essentially created their scores in relation to an evolving medium, and ultimately their work was to define some of the core characteristics of the American animated cartoon, not least of which was the music's emphasis on pointing up gags or functioning as a gag in itself. While McLaren's or Lye's use of 'jazz', for example, may have been witty or whimsical in the British context, it was never about 'laugh out loud' amusement in the same way as in the American cartoon. This enabled composers like Seiber and Chagrin to compose with less restriction and, inevitably, more out of a European 'classical' music tradition, thereby determining a distinctiveness in British cartoon idioms that could be readily acknowledged and understood by the public.

The nature of this distinctiveness, then, is bound up with two key aspects of cartoon music as it was perceived in Britain. First, there was an expectation that American cartoons possessed their own emphatic, fragmentary, highly particular scoring – a style Goldmark has called "highly dissonant, contrapuntally labyrinthine, and rife with special effects" (2005: 45) – and which is intrinsically linked with the 'action' and 'events' of the cartoon, whether in Disney's more 'symphonic' model, or in Warner Bros.' or MGM's more 'cacophonic' compositions (see Brophy, 1991: 86–112). Second, and very much related to the anticipated tone and rhythm of British cartoons, the British public was more literally attuned to light music and music hall songs, which were to find their most celebrated place in Anson Dyer's 'Old Sam' shorts during the 1930s, featuring monologues by the popular entertainer Stanley Holloway. Arguably, and to some degree, orchestral scores in such cartoons displayed a neo-classicism of sorts and a relationship to the American cartoon. They often echoed some of the idioms of comic opera by using the relationship between lyrics and musical phrases to create a series of possible narrative events pertinent to visualization.

In this way Britain found its own possibilities for 'difference'. The less romantic, and more progressive, classically orientated works of Seiber and Chagin were grounded in an older tradition of composition and were 'not comic', even at their most witty. If American cartoon soundtracks – however clearly in error this may be – are seen as in some way an 'over-determined' construct, calling too much attention to the way that they underpin the cartoon narrative, then the Halas & Batchelor scores were seeking out a different response much more rooted in how the music evoked and suggested meaning and affect, rather than in directly supporting the action on screen. Crudely, such scores privileged a relationship with the choreographic principles of the animation before its more overtly dramatized or comic aspects. Further, if the American context was characterized by the ways in which the cartoon embraced jazz or played with popular classical melodies to provide a contextual or narrative charge to each short – mainly in the spirit of finding a vaudevillian comic or performative styling to a narrative – Britain, in general, even in its seemingly most popular forms, used music in a more abstract fashion, normally as a vehicle by which to accompany (not 'shadow') visual forms. This enabled audiences to necessarily interpret sound rather than being directed by it.

Halas identified that music in many Hollywood cartoons largely functioned as a 'cueing' device for jokes and dramatic climaxes, or prompted narrative – literally or metaphorically – by establishing locations or contexts, a particular mood or atmosphere, or provided information in some way. For his own work, however, he preferred to seek an emotional arc in the music that echoed the subject of the film. This was a pronounced difference from what he perceived as the literalness of the cartoon score, epitomized by Carl Stalling, and here described by Chuck Jones:

> [Stalling] *was a brilliant musician. But the quickest way for him to write a musical score – and he did one six minute score a week – was to simply look up some music that had the proper name. If there was a lady dressed*

in red, he'd always play 'The Lady in Red'. If somebody went into a cave, he'd play 'Fingal's Cave'. If we were doing anything about eating, he'd do 'A Cup of Coffee, a Sandwich and You'. I had a bee one time, and my God if he didn't go and find a piece of music written in 1906 or something called 'I'm a Busy Little Bumble Bee'. (Jones, cited in Goldmark, 2005: 22)

While this kind of literalness (and one might argue, literate-ness) did much to support the development of the gags, it was unappealing to Halas, who, while admiring the American cartoon, was nevertheless frustrated by the ways in which it cast animation as a comic form (see Halas and Wells, 2006). It was equally the case that in defining the structure of the gags in relation to a predetermined scenario, this very infrastructure of the piece all but ensured particular outcomes. As Ingolf Dahl noted:

Seeing old cartoons again we realize how much the medium has changed. The procedure used to be one of fitting humorous story and action to cheerful, zippy, bouncy music which hovered in style between Gilbert and Sullivan and Zez Confrey. The music was rhythmically defined, symmetrically constructed in eight bar phrases, somewhat on the order of a dance tune, and its changes of mood ('chases', 'danger', 'villain', 'heroism', etc) were modified by the structural symmetry of popular music and its inherent simplicity. The cartoons represented in essence a kind of humorous 'choreography' to catchy music. (Dahl cited in Prendergast, 1977: 171)

This is a long way from Halas's preferred role for music, which in the traditional American cartoon context, merely serviced a pre-determined script and a set of largely formulaic dramatic situations. In Halas's view, the composer was as significant, if not more so, in delineating the shape and tone of the visual narrative:

the composer is, in fact, frequently more essential to the animator than is the writer ... For the cartoon the composer must be able to respond exactly to the continuous movement which carries its own accents and responses in every second of the score. And yet he must develop an unfettered melody which will captivate an audience and rouse it through its atmosphere as well as through its wit. (Halas and Manvell, 1958: 69–70)

In arguing for the autonomy of the composer and the music itself, Halas fundamentally drew attention to animation's 'chicken or egg' question – should the music be written and recorded before the animation, or synchronized after? In the first instance, the soundtrack essentially delineates the nature of the visuals, as evidenced in more abstract works, which have often used music formally as a creative stimulus or as a kind of illustration, either of the lyrics of a song or of a popular, often narrative-based or symbolically charged, instrumental melody. In the latter instance, the soundtrack is always subservient to the needs of the visuals with regard to post-dubbed lip-synced dialogue, diegetic sound or atmospheric, mood-determining music. Prendergast has pointed out, though, that this decision may be predicated not particularly on aesthetic choices but on the talents of the personnel involved:

> The reason for scoring and recording music after the animation was done was that most cartoon directors were not musical and would have had some difficulty to build their action to fit musical patterns. Consequently, the music had to shift to the rapidly changing image. The composer's almost overwhelming task in this situation was to create some sort of coherence and structure to the music. (Prendergast, 1977: 178)

The Halas & Batchelor composers

Halas employed high-quality composers and animators in the studio, and could select relevant personnel on a case-by-case basis. His best-known collaborators were Mátyás Seiber and Francis Chagrin, who were key figures in the studio's output over several years. Seiber, born in Budapest in 1905 and a fellow Hungarian, and Chagrin, also born in 1905 but in Bucharest, Romania, shared Halas's émigré sensibility. Both were keen to embrace the indigenous contexts in which they worked while being eager to bring the breadth of their cosmopolitan knowledge and application to new fields. An admirer of Bartók, Schoenberg and Bach, Seiber was committed to the view that the composition of each note and musical configuration should perform a purpose in a piece, and this approach was especially suited to the specific choices necessarily made to create animated films. Having composed since his teens, Seiber arrived in England before World War II, became a tutor at Morley College in 1942, and completed his Schoenberg-

Figure 2.1   Mátyás Seiber. Image courtesy of the Halas & Batchelor Collection. Used by permission.

styled, yet jazz and blues inflected, String Quartet No. 2. He established the Society for the Promotion of New Music, an initiative which chimed with Halas's progressive approach in his own field. Seiber, initially taught by the ethnomusicologist Zoltan Kodály,[1] had introduced the formal study of jazz when teaching in Frankfurt, but this was opposed by the National Socialists and resulted in his emigration to Britain and association with Halas. Seiber's desire to educate as well as create became an important aspect of his attachment to the studio's ethos and enterprise.

Chagrin came to Britain in 1936, fleeing from the rise of both Franco and Hitler. Though his wealthy Jewish parents had expected him to participate in the family business, he wanted to pursue a musical career and, having funded his own training at the École Normale in Paris, he established himself there as a live performer and writer of popular songs. In London he studied with Seiber and, with the outbreak of war, was appointed musical adviser and composer-in-chief in the BBC French Service. Like Seiber, Chagrin was multilingual although his approach to composition was much more eclectic and populist, ranging from symphonies to folk songs, and this versatility was once more highly pertinent to Halas & Batchelor's needs and outlook. Further, Chagrin was committed to the advocacy of contemporary music and he championed a variety of musical idioms, insistent that these find purchase in the emerging cultures of post-war Britain. In the 1940s, when the two composers began working with the studio, Halas saw Seiber and Chagrin as extremely important in re-inventing the cartoon for British audiences encultured in the more 'vulgar' populism of the American form.

It is clear that Halas's overriding desire to refine the cartoon was less to do with classicism, in the first instance, and more to do with the class issues he perceived in British culture. The musical score was one barometer of how class could be addressed. Halas viewed 'wit', for example, not as a model of humour comparable to the 'gag' in the American animated cartoon, but as a sign of the cleverness or irony with which a composer used a particular motif or accent. This preoccupation is made overt in *The Cultured Ape* (1960), where a jungle ape is cast as a virtuoso musician who, like King Kong, is captured and brought back to 'civilization'. Ironically, civilization proves too uncouth for the cultured ape, who finds his art and ability rejected by three strata of British society – the upper class, who are both jealous and resentful of his musical talents; the middle class, who merely prefer his musical efforts 'in the background' of their chatter; and the working class, who prefer more popular, 'street' music like skiffle (a jazz and blues inflected folk idiom, often played with improvised and home-made instruments). It is perhaps only the British who could make a film that positions its satire about class in England in an address to musical taste. The rather arcane punchline to the film – "When the arts go out of fashion the artist must retire and wait", which accompanies the ape's retreat back to the jungle – suggests that the arts operate in a cyclic manner and the distinctiveness of the ape's talents will one day be pertinent. Halas was to return to the relationship between music, art and satire when Halas & Batchelor created *The Tales of Hoffnung* (1964) (discussed below), a telling point of comparison to the American model in mocking both the classical music tradition and its culture. The status of the music in its own right is really the subject of these films, and is intrinsically related to whether it was composed in advance of the cartoon – in essence, 'privileged' – or whether it follows the animation itself. In the contemporary era, the visuals and soundtrack to an animation can mutually evolve, since the technology allows for a greater degree of compositional flexibility. Nevertheless, the choice of 'which comes first' is both literally and metaphorically instrumental in determining how an animation will be made, and its likely creative intention.

On the one hand, Francis Chagrin argued that the animation soundtrack "is the only kind of film music that is – as a rule – always carefully planned ahead, usually before the actual art work, or at least the animation, is started; which is discussed in the greatest detail by producer and composer; where the musician has to work to specification", thereby determining the dynamics of the visualization. Nevertheless, Chagrin continues by observing:

> *The problem has always preoccupied me: how to find a way which will make everybody happy; how to write the music in such a way that it is not submerged when the spoken word invades the soundtrack. The solution was simply to do the polite thing and retire, submerging the music intentionally by altering the orchestration for as long as a word or a phrase is spoken and come back to normal as soon as it is finished. If the music is written around the words it comes down or up by itself much more naturally than if it is turned up or down by the sound engineer's knob, and without any loss of quality.* (Chagrin, in Halas and Manvell, 1958: 238–9)

Chagrin effectively articulates the difference between music that is responsive to animation's propensity for change and music that leads its metamorphoses. Halas was aware that music was an essential part of the armoury in reinventing the cartoon, and crucial in helping to privilege its language as a modernist art form.

Kevin Donnelly has suggested:

> *Film music is usually fragmentary and relies on a logic that is not an organic part of the music but a negotiation between the logic of the film and the logic of the music. Consequently, its analysis has to acknowledge this dual logic in merging the two main approaches.* (2001: 3)

The Halas & Batchelor animations demonstrate an understanding of this principle by embracing the creative intentions of the narrative, or the conceptual 'problem' they had been set by sponsors or government agencies, using the music or other aspects of the soundtrack to suggest the particular psychological or emotive axis related to the topic or story. The 'logic of the film' in the case of animation is a different kind of logic from that of traditional live-action cinema in the sense that animation can run the gamut from purely abstract metamorphoses to hyperrealist, quasi-live-action narratives. Furthermore, the sometimes 'oppressive' conditions that have been determined by, and for, the

American animated cartoon, both in its short form and at feature length, can operate as an unhelpful 'generic' model that determines how 'the logic' of a piece 'ought' to unfold. A ready example of this comes in Halas & Batchelor's best-known work, *Animal Farm* (1954), which set itself the unenviable task of creating a serious adaptation of George Orwell's acclaimed novella.

Animal Farm

By the early 1950s, the animated cartoon, particularly in its popular feature-length form, was characterized by 'funny' talking animals; anthropomorphized creatures who were the embodiment of gags and evacuated of their intrinsic animality. *Animal Farm* essentially recovered this animality in long sequences of non-anthropomorphized animal movement, scenes of death and conflict, and in a highly innovative reinvention of the song. Animal sound was used in the delivery of an anthem, not cultivated singing voices delivering the words of a song – Old Major leads the singing. This resistance to the conventions of the musical is reinforced by Mátyás Seiber's soundtrack, which conveys an increasingly oppressive mood as the pigs begin their careful takeover of the farm and betray their fellow animals. Even at the uplifting moment of the animals apparently fighting back against the pigs and their human allies – the film's key difference from the novella –

Figure 2.2   Still from *Animal Farm*. Image courtesy of the Halas & Batchelor Collection. Used by permission.

the music resists the notion of ultimate triumph and, rather, suggests that this action is more symbolically resonant of permanent revolution, not indisputable success. There is certainly an ambivalence in the final musical accompaniment, and a recognition that there should be not the resonant chords of a happy ending but rather a sudden denouement and a resistance to an uplifting conclusion that suggests easy resolution.

Though John Halas consistently argued that the studio's version of Orwell's fable was an anti-authoritarian piece, produced in a spirit of rejecting the kinds of oppressive government he had known in Eastern Europe before emigrating to Britain, it is equally clear that the more optimistic conclusion of the film suited the American outlook during the Cold War. Its producer Louis de Rochemont, who had been responsible for 'The March of Time' newsreels,[2] was also able to make the film on more economic terms and work with a studio that was free from the politically activist agenda of many of the US cartoon studios, while still having a philosophically engaged outlook that was left-leaning and utopian in tendency. Crucially, the studio was also modernist in its embrace of a more avant-garde scoring in support of a darker, more complex vision; a perspective that brought the themes of the piece to the fore, unrelieved by any clichéd comic 'sign-off'. Halas and Batchelor were quite clear that they wanted to liberate animation from its status merely as a vehicle for humour, and from its predominant identity – the association with the signature style of the Disney studio. To this end, in 1948 they had made *Magic Canvas*, an abstract narrative with a specially composed score, again by Mátyás Seiber, which anticipates some of the approaches in *Animal Farm*. He described his approach as follows:

> The film was an abstract project: consequently, I considered that a similarly 'abstract' chamber music piece would be the most appropriate musical equivalent. I chose the rather odd combination of one flute, one horn and a string quartet. The form of the piece is that of a rather free 'phantasy', consisting of several sections. A slow contrapuntal piece covers the first section. At the dramatic moment of the human shape breaking into two the horn enters for the first time. The speed increases, and at the moment when the bird breaks away the flute takes over. Now follows an 'allegro' moment which covers the storm sequence. The next section, the revival of nature, is expressed by a 'pastorale' in the music. This is followed by a 'scherzo', covering the play with the waves. Then a bridge section leads back to the recapitulation of the slow, first movement, as the bird returns to the human shape. But the slow movement returns transformed: instead of a low-pitched brooding mood as it appeared originally, it comes back now in a higher register, and a solo violin ends the piece as the bird disappears in the distance. (Seiber, in Halas and Manvell, 1958: 249)

Seiber's sense of the way the music itself should accompany not merely the narrative movement in the piece, but its implied shifts in psychological and emotional emphasis, was highly pertinent to Halas's outlook, and his intrinsic belief in the inherently metaphysical nature of animation as a form. Halas makes an important claim for the film as a reinvention of the cartoon, privileging abstraction in both a visual and aural sense. He stresses the metaphorical intention in depicting the tensions in the human spirit as it seeks to soar while feeling entrapped; the human condition as it seeks insight about a higher purpose while being abandoned to life's vicissitudes. Such abstraction, then, is not purely formalist but an approach that echoes the capacity for instrumental music to operate as a catalyst for suggestive symbolic tropes of possible meaning and affect. At one and the same time, the music can retain its seeming 'literalness' while prompting ideas, narrative and, most important of all, feeling.

It was this view that underpinned the studio's approach to the Poet and Painter (1951) series made for the Festival of Britain. This series confirmed Halas & Batchelor's affiliation with Britain's progressive arts culture in the post-war period, as they worked with artists of the calibre of Ronald Searle, Michael Ayrton, John Minton and Henry Moore in the creation of new moving-image works.[3] Halas & Batchelor continued to experiment and develop their work in *The Owl and the Pussycat* (Brian Borthwick and John Halas, 1952), Britain's first stereoscopic production; and *The Figurehead* (1953), a 3D stop-motion piece in the spirit of Halas's mentor, George Pal, but based on an old English folk narrative.

Animal Farm was effectively both a vindication of the studio's success in progressing animation as an art in the short form, and an opportunity to advance the studio's work further, fully aping the industrial model of feature production in the United States. As part of a statement made by John Halas and Joy Batchelor in *British Kinematography*, the couple stressed that only twenty-five full-length animated features had been made before their own, and this afforded the opportunity to move beyond the mickey-mousing of standard cartoons and to experiment with the role and function of the soundtrack. They described their approach in this way:

> To achieve a simultaneous and equal visual and auditory effect, the music and picture need not coincide at the same moment. The total effect should be fused into a perfect partnership but one should counterpoint the other, the story being the governing factor. The contribution of music to underline mood is unlimited; it can help tell the story and make situations clearer. In Animal Farm we have tried to use the music as a fully equal contributor to the partnership rather than as effects and illustrative accompaniment. (Halas and Batchelor, 1954: 110)

The music in *Animal Farm* is an undoubted contributor to the doom-laden and foreboding atmosphere of sequences when the audience is encouraged to feel more acutely the oppressive nature of the animal experience and, while never triumphal, Seiber's score also captures the inspiring aspects of moments of liberation and the brutal chaos of conflict. In a film predicated on its visualization, the formality of its narrative voice-over, its lack of Disneyesque sentimentality and 'cuteness', and its prioritization of seriousness in the depiction of animals, the sensitivity and vibrancy of the soundtrack become a profoundly influential storytelling idiom. The film's 'Tension Chart', a visual diagram created at the studio, noting the shifting moods across the film's narrative, reflects this readily as the score moves from 'subdued' to a 'sinister note' to 'determined' and 'jubilation' as the animals explore the farmhouse in one sequence, and encourages similar dynamics in others (see Halas and Wells, 2006: 126–7).

Music-culture satires

Halas & Batchelor remained progressive and pursued new contexts for expression and exhibition. Undaunted by the television era, which in the USA had been greeted in the first instance as 'the end' for animation as a form, and their own complex ownership issues when the Tyne Tees TV organization owned the company for a short period, the Halas & Batchelor studio created innovative works like *Foo Foo* (1960) and *Snip and Snap* (1960). These works most notably included the *Tales of Hoffnung* (1964), seven short films using Gerard Hoffnung's amusing caricatures of classical-music culture and, in its most famous instance, the voice of Peter Sellers as an embarrassed father seeking to tell his son the facts of life in *Birds, Bees and Storks*.

Born in 1925 in Berlin to Jewish parents, Gerard Hoffnung fled Nazi Germany when only thirteen, and ultimately became well known as a cartoonist, musician, raconteur and broadcaster in England. In this alone he found great empathy with Halas, but his illustrations and cartoons readily drew him into Halas's orbit, as the studio increasingly embraced a range of approaches in the desire to continually reinvent the cartoon, especially given its apparent demise in the United States. Working in the tradition of Wilhelm Busch, the creator of *Max and Moritz* (picture stories published in 1865), and Heinrich Zille, the pre-war chronicler of Berlin's social mores, Hoffnung became the master of the graphic pun, allying German tradition with English whimsy.

To those intimidated by the seriousness of classical music, Hoffnung offered a point of access, innocently and affectionately sending up the hopeless attempts to master an instrument physically and technically, and the often pompous culture associated with classical music and performance. In this, he echoes some Hollywood cartoons that also parodied the opera or more formal kinds of music, while responding to the deep respect accorded such culture in Disney's *Fantasia* (1940). Daniel Goldmark points out:

> *though* What's Opera, Doc? *and cartoons like it are often accused of under-cutting and weakening classical music's rightful place in the cultural hierarchy, in reality they do as much to maintain music's elevated status as do more worshipful representations. Just as* Fantasia *firmly places Bach and Beethoven in the temple of high culture, so too* What's Opera, Doc? *reminds us that classical music is high art; every time we see these cartoons, we are reminded that the object of their parody – opera – occupies a place of honor in our culture. By focusing on music and concert hall culture as worthy subjects for deflation, these cartoons more firmly set the music and spectacle in their high place.* (Goldmark, 2005: 159)

Figure 2.3   Gerard Hoffnung 1960. Image courtesy of the Halas & Batchelor Collection. Used by permission.

This degree of back-handed reverence, even in something as ironic and insightful as Chuck Jones's *What's Opera, Doc?* (1957), was accorded a different perspective in Britain. Halas and Batchelor undertook to make a series of Hoffnung cartoons with their long-time associate, Francis Chagrin, who had collaborated with Hoffnung in his Music Festivals, three concerts given at the Royal Festival Hall in 1956, 1958 and 1961, and described in publicity materials as "extravagant evenings of symphonic caricature".[4] Chagrin was to write specific scores for the series, to be played by a six-piece ensemble, each characterized by pieces from a range of composers in a variety of idioms. This in some ways directly echoed the Hollywood cartoon, not merely in poking fun at classical-music cultures, but in assembling a score of fragmentary pieces of music in the development of a narrative. Yet again, though, there are major differences. If the 'fragments' in US cartoons were in the service of defining both a narrative for the cartoon, and a method by which to privilege the dynamics of any gag, particularly those which were character-centred, the Hoffnung cartoons were specifically directed at playfully engaging with the music itself, and were unambiguously about the orchestra, the conductor, the musician, and their audiences. In the credits to each cartoon, it notes that the music is "composed, re-composed, arranged, disarranged and conducted by Francis Chagrin", and includes the coda, "with acknowledgement and apologies to" before listing the composers in the film's music track. This alone foregrounds the sustained respect for the culture that is being parodied but signals, too, that even if the graphic puns and exaggerated caricature that characterize the cartoons would appeal to children, there was nevertheless an intention to address a classical music-literate viewer. This might usefully be compared to the kinds of composers Goldmark has identified as being used in American cartoons:

> *Who, then, is in the cartoon canon? At the top of the list is Wagner, with both the greatest number of overall references and the greatest number of specific pieces cited. Other favorites include Rossini, Mendelssohn, Liszt, Chopin, Franz von Suppé, Brahms, Johann Strauss, Schubert, Schumann, Tchaikovsky, and Beethoven. Often just a fragment of a piece is used ... Chopin is represented in cartoons almost entirely by the opening four-note motif of his* Funeral March. (Goldmark, 2005: 109)

Most of the composers cited here are perhaps those who might be the most well known to a popular audience, each having almost a 'signature tune' which has been embedded in the public imagination by continued use and repetition. Chagrin also uses Chopin, for example – yet not his four-note 'Funeral March' – and the likes of Mozart, Wagner and Tchaikovsky, but his musical palette is much wider in its inclusion of more extended pieces from Boccherini, Borodin, Auber, Rimsky-Korsakov, Greig, Gounod, Delibes and Gruber. This is much more in a spirit of using a range of musical idioms and privileging an appreciation of the wit embedded in the music, rather than using the music to support 'the gag'. In *The Hoffnung Maestro* (1964), the various styles and approaches to musical form are used within a narrative that is underpinned by terms that sound like those traditionally used to describe particular phrases in musical form but which, here, more readily describe the attitudes invoked : 'diabolico', 'pomposo', 'religioso', 'furioso', etc.

In *Professor Yaya's Memoirs* (1964), the old professor looks back at his life through a photo-album featuring his musical relatives, each of whom evidences a different musical idiom. Instead of music merely supporting character animation and enabling the facilitation of cartoonal gags, this kind of work uses the premise of the narrative vignette to foreground the music. Though Hoffnung's musical caricatures are used to extend the humorous effect, no one character is privileged as the presiding focus of the stories. In focusing on the musician and the act of playing as a main theme, these cartoons largely enable the comic enactment of performance without undermining the qualities of the music. This is the crucial difference in the way Halas & Batchelor viewed their use

Figure 2.4   Hoffnung's 'Drummer' 1964. Image courtesy of the Halas & Batchelor Collection. Used by permission.

of classical scores: nothing in relation to the visualization should undermine or detract from them; all visualization had to enhance the music's features and characteristics. This became most explicit in the studio's version of *Ruddigore* (1967). Halas & Batchelor created a 55-minute adaptation of Gilbert and Sullivan's 1887 opera, commencing production in 1964, and finally completing it three years later. Written and directed by Joy Batchelor, it was the first opera to be adapted into an extended animated film, though its length was predicated on broadcast opportunities and so it was not planned as a traditional 'feature'. Plans to rework *The Mikado, Pirates of Penzance* and *H.M.S. Pinafore* were rejected by the D'Oyly Carte Opera Company on the basis that the notoriously particular and purist Gilbert and Sullivan audience would not be able to accept these classics in abridged form. Even *Ruddigore*, though less commercially successful than the other operas, was a risk. This was reflected in a problematic production process, subject to many delays, in which the musical and narrative continuity became subject to constant revision.

   Ruddigore, subtitled 'The Witch's Curse', was Gilbert and Sullivan's tenth collaboration, opening at the Savoy Theatre in 1887 and running for 288 performances. In typically witty style, Gilbert parodies melodramatic conventions by making his heroes less than heroic, villains more than successful, and a happy ending subject to many compromises. By the time it was made as an animation in the mid-1960s, it echoed the more ambiguous moral and social climate of the era, and works almost as a parody of a parody. The hero, Robin Oakapple, is deeply in love with the village beauty, Rose Maybud, but is too shy to pursue the virtuous heroine. No one is aware, however, that he guards a terrible secret. He is actually Sir Ruthven Murgatroyd, Baronet of Ruddigore, whose family has been cursed by a witch to commit a wicked crime every day or die a horrible death. Robin has feigned his own demise to escape the curse and it has been inherited by his brother, Despard. Robin's foster-brother, Richard, returns from his heroic sea voyages and encourages Robin's pursuit of Rose, though he secretly wants her for himself. Rose does choose Robin, however, and a vengeful Richard tells Despard that Robin lives. Despard confronts Robin, and transfers the curse back, prompting the ghosts of his ancestors to return and admonish him. Though Robin agrees to take ownership of the curse, he finds a clever solution to his problem.

Joy Batchelor embraced the challenge of the film – actually a one-hour television special – recognizing the profound difficulty of reducing the opera by over half of its original length, while responding to the condition that no words or songs could be altered or rewritten. This was a considerably different problem from creating scores for the short form, or even for the longer interludes in *Animal Farm*, and required a sensitive approach to choosing the pertinent music/lyrics to both tell the story and provide as much resonant emotional affect as possible through the music itself. Further, the story was hard to adapt because it contained numerous subplots, involving, for example, 'Mad Margaret' and Robin's loyal retainer, and changes of identity in the main characters. Usually a strong story relies on a sympathetic lead character and appropriate expositional dialogue but here, again, the story was in the song, making it harder to understand. This led Batchelor ultimately to employ voice-over to help with narrative clarity and continuity, and to emphasize the central role of Robin Oakapple. Crucially, though, the animation itself always works in the service of the expression of the emotion in the music, and enhances the narrative with close attention to the gestures and attitudes of the characters, especially, for example, when Robin metamorphoses back into Sir Ruthven. Batchelor herself admitted that the first half of the film took too long to establish character and situation but little could be done to change this in the light of the conditions imposed on her. Only in the second half of the film is there a genuine justification for animation in the more fantastical and supernatural sequences.

The story had sixteen sequences, some with as many as 72 scenes, and it relied a great deal on character animation. The D'Oyly Carte Opera Company, for all its prevarication and anxiety about the project, nevertheless saw the film as having cultural importance, particularly in reaching new audiences who might not have encountered Gilbert and Sullivan before. Batchelor herself was shocked that the film received its best reception in Pittsburg, New Hampshire. The 'limited animation' used in the film was akin to the minimalist, more cost-effective kind of cartoon that was being produced in the United States (such as those produced at UPA [United Productions of America]), or by independent artists in Eastern Europe (principally from the Zagreb Studio). 'Full animation' in the Disney style had essentially passed with the closure of Hollywood's studio animation units and the advent of the TV era. The film ultimately resembles a combination of the caricatural drawings of Ronald Searle and the more decorative work of the Fauvist Raoul Dufy, both of whom were central to some of the modernist idioms used in UPA cartoons. The exaggeration at the heart of this kind of caricature suits the performance style of the piece, dramatizing the often static aspects of traditional operas, and enhancing the parodic and melodramatic moments.

The sound for *Ruddigore* was recorded at Abbey Road Studios, featuring the voices of John Reed as Robin Oakapple, Ann Hood as Rose Maybud, and David Palmer as Richard Dauntless. The D'Oyly Carte Company also helped the animators with the choreography of the dances, and the proper integration of sound and image. In a logical step from this work featuring theatre music, Halas & Batchelor's preoccupation with the sound/image relationship continued into the popular music video era.

Conclusion

Music video was an inevitable progression from the Halas & Batchelor studio's investment in music, and in their use of music to prompt animation. The studio created visuals – initially based on experimental work in computer animation, though none survives in the final video – for Kraftwerk's *Autobahn* (1979). Though not the abstract suggestive scores of Mátyás Seiber, or the cleverly combinative arrangements of Francis Chagrin, Kraftwerk's electronic soundscapes and vocal parodies of the Beach Boys ("Wir fahr'n, fahr'n, fahr'n auf der Autobahn"; 1975) prompted a quasi-surrealist narrative featuring a blue, marine boy encountering abstract creatures and environments. Halas & Batchelor focus upon the timbre, tone, rhythm and melody as suggestive elements in the music, refusing to impose imagery upon the track and preferring to generate the most pertinent and resonant interpretation of it. A similar approach occurred in the Lee Mishkin-directed *Butterfly Ball* (1974), adapted from the children's story illustrated by Alan Aldridge, popularly known as a 'Beatle in Blue Jeans', and famed for his illustration of the Beatles lyrics. A rock band, led by Deep Purple bassist, Roger Glover, sings the signature song of Butterfly Ball called 'Love Is All', which is 'performed' on screen by the central character of a singing frog guitarist. The short employs the lush colours and designs of the book, but more significantly, suggests a countercultural psychedelic visualization. Interestingly, though *Yellow Submarine* (George Dunning, 1968) had been made some six years earlier, it proved less influential than expected due in part to the difficulties of animating graphic design-led styling, and it was only with a return to a more illustrative approach, here epitomized in Aldridge's work, that this quasi-surreal look was again preferred.

Although this has been a brief overview of a particular studio's address to musical forms, it clearly shows the respect John Halas and Joy Batchelor had for the way in which music essentially defined the very terms and conditions of animation itself. In their work this prompted an exacting investment in the animation to properly suggest the witty, affecting, and narrative qualities of the music, and the overall soundtrack in general. This investment in the synergy of sound and image informs the distinctiveness of the studio's oeuvre, and is a contributory factor in its longevity. No other British studio has survived through so many different periods, remaining responsive to changing trends and markets. It is only in recent years, with exhibitions of the studio's work, numerous retrospectives, increased research based on archive holdings, and acknowledgement of *Animal Farm* as a major work – praised by Hayao Miyazaki, for example, and part of an exhibition at Studio Ghibli – that the studio's influence has been properly recognized. There is little doubt that Halas & Batchelor's engagement with music remains one of the distinctive aspects of the studio's identity. Most significantly, the synergy between scores based on classical idioms and the dynamics of modern art spoke to new audiences, and enabled the studio to create highly distinctive and progressive works. These not merely modernized the cartoon and animated forms in Britain, but made a significant contribution to the art of animation per se.

Notes

1. A prominent Hungarian composer, linguist, and philosopher, who collected Hungarian folk songs.
2. 'The March of Time' newsreels were shown in US cinemas between 1935 and 1951, and featured 'pictorial journalism' of topical events worldwide, sometimes addressed on location, sometimes subjected to dramatic re-enactment. Lasting ten minutes, each newsreel had high production values, and cost over $50,000 to make. The brainchild of Time Inc.'s CEO, Roy Edward Larsen, the newsreels were produced by Louis de Rochemont, and were clearly left-leaning in ideology, and a consolidation of intrinsically American values during the periods of world war and insipient Cold War.
3. Halas approached Picasso to take part in the series, but was rejected on the grounds that some thousands of drawings were required for an animated film, and the fee for one of Picasso's would cost more than the whole production!
4. Publicity materials: private collection, Vivien Halas. The Concert series is now available on CD released on the EMI label, titled *The Hoffnung Music Festival Concert 1956; The Hoffnung Interplanetary Music Festival 1958*; and *The Hoffnung Astronautical Music Festival 1961.*

References

Brophy, P. (1991), 'The Animation of Sound', in A. Cholodenko (ed.), *The Illusion of Life*, Sydney: Power Publications, pp. 67–112.
Donnelly, K. (2001), 'The Hidden Heritage of Film Music: History and Scholarship', in K. Donnelly (ed.), *Film Music: Critical Approaches*, London & New York: Routledge, pp. 1–15.
Goldmark, D. (2005), *Tunes for 'Toons: Music and the Hollywood Cartoon*, Berkeley & Los Angeles: University of California Press.

Halas, J., and Batchelor, J. (1954), 'Producing "Animal Farm"', *British Kinematography*, 24(4), 105–10.

Halas, J., and Manvell, R. (1958), *The Technique of Film Animation*, London: Focal Press.

Halas, V., and Wells, P. (2006), *Halas & Batchelor Cartoons: An Animated History*, London: Southbank Publishing.

Prendergast, R. (1977), *Film Music: A Neglected Art*, New York: W. W. Norton & Co.

Wells, P. (1998), *Understanding Animation*, London & New York: Routledge.

3 An Animated Partnership

Joe Hisaishi's Musical Contributions to Hayao Miyazaki's Films

Kyoko Koizumi[1]

The early twenty-first century has seen major international recognition for Japanese animation cinema. In 2002, Hayao Miyazaki's *Spirited Away* (*Sen to Chihiro no Kamikakushi*[2]; 2001) received the Golden Bear Award at the 52nd Berlin Film Festival and in 2003 it won the Oscar for Best Animated Feature Film at the 75th Academy Awards. Among international fans of Japanese animation, Studio Ghibli has been known since the middle of the 1990s but, with these significant awards, the studio's name became recognized by general film audiences. Studio Ghibli was founded in 1985 after the domestic success of Miyazaki's film *Nausicaä of the Valley of the Wind* (*Kaze no Tani no Naushika*; 1984). According to studio producer Toshio Suzuki's history of Studio Ghibli,[3] animation films in Japan are usually extended from popular television series. Studio Ghibli is distinct by virtue of specializing in *original* animated feature films produced for *cinema* release.[4] The best-known examples of the studio's oeuvre are the animation films directed by Hayao Miyazaki (1941–), as they have achieved international critical and scholarly acclaim in the arenas of both cinema and Japanese studies. Although Susan Napier has analysed *Princess Mononoke* (*Mononoke-hime*; 1997) and *Spirited Away* in terms of Japanese cultural traditions (2001, 2005)[5] and other scholars have discussed the animation techniques (see McCarthy, 1999; Lamarre, 2002), Miyazaki's animated films have scarcely been examined from the perspective of their music and sound.

The original music for Miyazaki's main feature films was composed by Joe Hisaishi (1950–), whose collaboration with the director commenced with *Nausicaä of the Valley of the Wind* and continued to *Howl's Moving Castle* [*Hauru no Ugoku Shiro*] (2004).[6] The connection between Miyazaki's imagery and Hisaishi's music offers an identifiable stylistic approach to the point that Hisaishi's musical themes represent a significant element of Studio Ghibli films and the duo's creative partnership offers a distinctive body of work.

Hisaishi's approach was informed by his introduction to film composing as assistant to Masaru Satô (1928–99), a film composer highly regarded for his scores for Akira

Kurosawa's films. Hisaishi's scores for over fifty films, including those by Miyazaki and Takeshi Kitano, have earned him a reputation as the leading contemporary Japanese film composer and successor to Satô. In this chapter I investigate the musical styles and idioms of Hisaishi's scores for Miyazaki's animated films as a way of analysing them.[7] Hisaishi employs four identifiable musical approaches in Miyazaki's films, which are: his use of Dorian mode to create an historical European feel; western classical-styled music to suggest occidental themes; pentatonic scales, natural minor scales, and other 'Asian' musical elements to enhance Japanese and oriental images; and an eclectic style of Japanese popular songs in which Japanese and western musical approaches are mixed. This study shows how Hisaishi's four types of music contribute to the construction of narratives in Miyazaki's animated films.

The succession: Joe Hisaishi and Masaru Satô

From 1983 to 2007, Miyazaki and Hisaishi collaborated on eight films.[8] Of these, the most musically distinctive are *Nausicaä of the Valley of the Wind*, featuring prominent use of Dorian mode; *Princess Mononoke*, which emphasizes traditional Japanese musical elements; and *Howl's Moving Castle*, with its prominent use of leitmotivs. In Japan, Hisaishi's lyrical approach in Miyazaki's films is often referred to as 'Hisaishi melody' (*Hisaishi merodî*).

Hisaishi studied composition at a private conservatoire in Tokyo, the Kunitachi Music College, where he explored minimalist techniques and orchestration. Born Mamoru Fujisawa, he adopted a pseudonym when he began his career as a professional composer. 'Joe Hisaishi' was an adaptation of the name of Quincy Jones, an African American trumpeter turned record producer, film composer and music arranger whom Hisaishi admired.[9] After graduating in the early 1970s, Hisaishi composed for TV animation series such as *Primitive Human Family Gartles* (*Hajime Ningen Gâtoruzu*, 1974–76) and *Robotic Child Beaton* (*Robokko Bîton*, 1976–77).[10] Masaru Satô had also graduated from the Kunitachi Music College and appointed Hisaishi as his assistant when he was twenty-three. As Satô's assistant at a critical age, Hisaishi was conscious of inheriting Satô's significant role in film music; in 2000, he observed, "I now feel like a prodigal son who finally makes up his mind to succeed to his father's business" (Kaku, 2000: 34).[11]

Through his work on three of Satô's film productions (most notably *Je n'accuse* [*Kokuso sezu*], directed by Hiromichi Horikawa, 1975), Hisaishi learned about the process of composition and how to earn a living as a film composer, skills not taught in music school (Shimizu, 2000). Satô devoted himself to his job as a 'full-time' film-music composer, while his contemporaries prioritized composing and performing avant-garde music. They regarded film music as a 'part-time' job, merely a means to earn money or to experiment with sound (Kobayashi, 2007: 14–15). Satô was skilful in composing with many varied musical styles from jazz to bolero and was highly regarded for his soundtrack use of tone colours created through the combination of unexpected instruments.

Ironically, Satô did not think that his composition style was suitable for animated films (Satô, 1993). In 1980, he composed for an animated film (titled *To the Earth* [*Tera-e*], Hideo Onchi, 1980) for the first time in his career (and employed Hisaishi on synthesizer). Satô admitted that he did not find the task interesting as he considered that the role of music was to explain characters' expressions through sounds and compensate for the loss of live actor performances. Whereas Satô composed music for over 300 films using rough cuts in post-production, Hisaishi developed a new style of collaboration involving early intervention with the director of the animated film and used this working method to create an impact on animated film music.

Dorian modal music for European moods

An opportunity for Hisaishi to enter the world of film-music composition in his own right arose in 1983. In 1982, Hisaishi released his solo album titled *Information* through the Japan Record label, owned by the major entertainment publishing company Tokuma Shoten (Hisaishi, 1992). At that time, the Tokuma company was planning to produce an animated feature film, later known as *Nausicaä of the Valley of the Wind*. One of the members of this project listened to Hisaishi's *Information* and appointed him to make an 'image album' of the film. In the Japanese animated film industry, an 'image album' is devised for general release as a promotional vehicle for the film; it comprises ten to fifteen tracks that present the musical ideas that more or less suggest the film's themes and soundtrack. To compose the image album for *Nausicaä of the Valley of the Wind*, Hisaishi met the film's producer, Isao Takahata, and the director, Miyazaki, who was devising the screenplay from his original *manga* story. Hisaishi devised the musical pieces of the image album freely from the story of the film and his melodies were strongly connected to Miyazaki's original illustrations and key words, such as 'Nausicaä's glider' (*mêve*) or 'decayed sea' (*fukai*). Hisaishi's melodies in the image album suited Miyazaki's and Takahata's intentions to convey emotional depth. The success of the image album led to Hisaishi's employment as composer for the film soundtrack.

In his study of animation film, Ryohei Okada (2006) identifies a method of 'mixed-media' and 'cross-media' marketing using simultaneous and sequenced promotion of film, music and comic books (*manga*), and this was an approach successfully adopted for *Nausicaä of the Valley of the Wind*. For Okada, the Tokuma company's strategy of requesting Miyazaki to draw on the original graphic story of *Nausicaä of the Valley of the Wind* in the animation magazine (*Animage*) and asking Hisaishi to compose the image album of the film initiated a connection that bore fruit for subsequent successful films produced by Studio Ghibli when it was formed as an offshoot of Tokuma Shoten in 1985.

Nausicaä of the Valley of the Wind is based on an original *manga* written by Miyazaki, although the film storyline is a simplified extract.[12] Based on a science-fiction scenario, the film is set a thousand years after a major conflagration that destroyed much of humankind and Earth's ecosystem. Nausicaä, a princess of 'the Valley of the Wind', fights as a girl soldier to reconcile the remnants of warring species with the disrupted ecological order (the decayed sea) that threatens to overwhelm the planet. In a book on Japanese *manga*, Frederik L. Schodt argues that *Nausicaä* was different from other Japanese *manga* for its lack of 'Japaneseness', given that there are no Japanese characters or settings, and Miyazaki shows a preference for European style in the film (Schodt, 1996: 278). The name of the main character in the film is taken from Homer's *Odyssey*, Book vi, in which a princess named Nausicaä helps Odysseus after a shipwreck. However, the ecological concerns in this film relate to familiar Japanese themes. For example, Nausicaä's affection for a large insect-like arthropod (*ômu*) originates from a Japanese classic 'Mushi Mezuru Himegimi' ('The princess who loves insects') in *Tsutsumi Chunagon Monogatari* (ten short stories and one unfinished chapter), written in the last years of the Heian period (the twelfth century).

   If the ecological concerns of the film originate from the relationship between human-ity and nature present in traditional Japanese life, then how does *Nausicaä of the Valley of the Wind* suggest 'Europeanness' or a lack of 'Japaneseness'? I suggest that Hisaishi's music confers the image of ancient Europe in the film. As Hisaishi says, "Rather than composing music for each scene, I put an emphasis on making decisions for 'this music for this film' as the core" (Yoshioka, 1998: 131), suggesting that he worked from the broad musical ideas already devised in the production of the image album. The opening title music of *Nausicaä of the Valley of the Wind* is composed in Dorian mode (C-mode; see Figure 3.1) and this music dominates the overall impression of the film.

Figure 3.1   The opening title music of *Nausicaä of the Valley of the Wind* (transcribed by present author)[13]

   The Dorian mode is a Christian church mode used since the medieval period in Europe. It comprises seven notes in an octave, in which the musical interval between the second and third, and the sixth and seventh, notes is the minor second. Of church modes, the Aeolian and Ionian modes have predominated as major and minor scales because they can be easily harmonized with tonic (I), subdominant (IV) and, in the case of Ionian, dominant (V) triads. Other church modes became less common as they proved difficult to modulate or transpose. The employment of such church modes in a soundtrack context suggests European history. In the contemporary musical world, jazz musicians use church modes to broaden the expressive palette available for improvisation, and Paul McCartney composed 'Eleanor Rigby' (1966) as a ballad using Dorian mode to suggest an oral traditional form once used in England or Scotland.

Hisaishi uses Dorian mode in his composition of the opening title music (Figure 3.1) for *Nausicaä of the Valley of the Wind* to suggest a past European period, as he explained:

> My music is based on a pentatonic scale. But when I use the 'yona-nuki'[14] pentatonic scale, I treat it like a mode such as the English-like Dorian mode. When I composed the music for Nausicaä of the Valley of the Wind, I thought it was influenced by elements of Scottish or Irish folk music. Mr. Miyazaki also likes those kinds of elements. It is obvious that Scottish folk music is based on the 'yona-nuki' pentatonic scale too. But if I use a pentatonic scale, my music might become 'enka'.[15] So I adopt a defensive stance to keep my music within a frame of western-style music but also to refrain from making 'enka'. This is a characteristic of my music. (Agawa, 1999: 157; author's translation)

Hisaishi emphasizes the main thematic melody by threading it throughout the film (Hisaishi, 2006: 87–8). The opening title music changes in sound texture to follow Nausicaä's feelings and the audience is led to empathize with the heroine of the film through the main Dorian mode melody that recalls ancient Celtic rather than modern European culture. The music also employs sub-thematic melodies that derive from western-style music. Besides the main orchestral melody in Dorian mode, Hisaishi uses musical elements such as minimal music, sitar (a fretless microtonal instrument from India) and rubbed glass (making sounds by tracing the edge of a glass with a wet finger) to provide aural exoticisms suitable for the science-fiction context. These elements are essentially incidental colorations, and Hisaishi designed the film music so that the main thematic melody in Dorian mode offers a coherent representation of the heroine's inner world.

A little girl's song titled 'Nausicaä Requiem' is used as a sub-thematic melody to suggest Nausicaä's nostalgic recollections of her early childhood and her realization that she could not return to this secure and happy time of her life. The song is based around a simple syllabic style of singing (la-la-lala-la-la-la) structured in a binary form (a-a'-b-a') that is characteristic of nursery rhymes or some folk songs. For the soundtrack record-ing, Hisaishi recorded his (then) four-year-old daughter's performance of the song. In his analysis of *Nausicaä of the Valley of the Wind*, Okada claims that this little girl's song is the most significant music in the film (2006: 22). However, I argue that Hisaishi's use of Dorian mode for the thematic melody is more important in conveying an impression of European orientation, a notable aspect of Miyazaki's work as early as the 1980s.

The next collaboration by Miyazaki and Hisaishi was *Castle in the Sky* (1986), a 'boy meets girl' adventure story based on the floating island of Laputa that features in *Gulliver's Travels* by Jonathan Swift (1726).[16] The theme music of *Castle in the Sky* (1986) is also composed in Dorian mode (see Figure 3.2). This theme is similar to the main thematic melody of *Nausicaä of the Valley of the Wind*, and these two Dorian

Figure 3.2 The theme music for *Castle in the Sky* (transcribed by present author)

mode-based melodies from Miyazaki's film soundtracks established an emphasis on European style together with a lack of Japaneseness that characterized Miyazaki's early films. However, this had changed by the mid-1990s and in *Princess Mononoke*, while the opening thematic melody, 'The Legend Of Ashitaka' ['Ashitaka Sekki'], is written in Dorian mode (F-mode; see Figure 3.3), the overall musical style is orientated to Japaneseness.

Figure 3.3 'The Legend Of Ashitaka' from *Princess Mononoke* (transcribed by present author)

Bars 1 and 2 in Figure 3.3 seem to be written in F natural minor scale, as they lack D, the key sixth note of Dorian mode (F-mode). Only when the melody appears in bar 3 can we identify that it is based on the Dorian mode. The pentatonic scalelike movement in bar 2 (C, E♭, F) originates from Japanese traditional folk songs (*min'yô*) and precedes the use of Dorian mode in bar 3, thereby giving precedence to the 'Japaneseness' of *Princess Mononoke*. This film combines folklore and animistic perspectives from early periods of Japanese history. Setting it in medieval Japan, Miyazaki depicts a war between the animal kingdom and humans. The main girl character, San, is raised by and lives with wolves. After the war, the main boy character, Ashitaka, invites her to live with him but eventually she opts to stay with the wolves. Moving between the natural minor scale and Dorian mode, the melody of 'The Legend Of Ashitaka' suggests San's vacillations between Ashitaka and her brother animals. The melody also symbolizes the (disputed) evolution of Japan from ancient ecological to modern militarized nation.

Western-classical styled music for occidental impressions

As Miyazaki's early films were set in European countries rather than in Japan or other Asian countries, Hisaishi composed many melodies for his films in the western classical orchestral style. *Kiki's Delivery Service* (*Majo no Takkyûbin*; 1989) is based on a book by Eiko Kadono in which a thirteen-year-old girl named Kiki leaves her home and trains herself to be a fully fledged witch. In this film (for which Isao Takahata was music director), Hisaishi avoids minor scales but uses what he terms 'light melodies' because the story follows the girl's growth in a northern European country (Hisaishi, 1992: 69). 'On A Clear Day' ('Hareta-hi ni') is written as a waltz (Figure 3.4). In this cue, Hisaishi effectively uses the chromatic progression common to western operetta. He also consciously employs Mediterranean-flavoured instruments like the guitar and accordion in the soundtrack (*ibid.*: 71).

Figure 3.4 'On A Clear Day' from *Kiki's Delivery Service* (transcribed by present author)

The underscore of *Porco Rosso* (*Kurenai no Bura*; 1992) is basically an extension of *Kiki's Delivery Service*. 'Adoriano's Window' ('Adoriano no Mado') uses the kind of 'easy-listening' strings and keyboard-based concert orchestration heard in the music of Raymond Lefevre or Paul Mauriat[17] (Figure 3.5). After making the somewhat 'too realistic' animation film *Only Yesterday* (*Omoide Poroporo*, Isao Takahata, 1991), Miyazaki stated that he wished to make a film that was more lighthearted and easy-going (Mori, 1992). Reflecting the director's wishes, Hisaishi composed cues for *Porco Rosso* that ranged from march to mood music to flavour the story of a middle-aged pig aviator who hunts pirates in the Depression era near the Adriatic Sea and who loves a beautiful widow, Gina, owner of the Hotel Adoriano.

Figure 3.5 'Adoriano's Window' from *Porco Rosso* (transcribed by present author)

In a film made twelve years later, Hisaishi adopts a further western-style technique. As a film composer, he rarely uses the tool of leitmotiv to portray characters and reflect their actions in the storyline, arguing that this method is typical of Hollywood film soundtrack and is not appropriate to his musical aims. Hisaishi criticizes character-related leitmotiv compositions that to him are too obvious, and he prefers to compose music that emphasizes the director's broader message and themes for the film (Hisaishi, 2006: 93–4). *Howl's Moving Castle* is the only film in which he does use leitmotiv on the soundtrack. The theme music of this film is called 'The Merry-Go-Round Of Life' ('Jinsei no Merî-gô-rando') (Figure 3.6).

Figure 3.6 'The Merry-Go-Round Of Life' from *Howl's Moving Castle* (transcribed by present author)

Based on a novel with the same title (2001) by UK fantasy and science-fiction author Diana Wynne Jones, *Howl's Moving Castle* centres on Sophie, who, under a spell, shifts in age from eighteen to ninety years old. Miyazaki required a central musical theme to support Sophie's change and to draw the story together. According to the composer, Hisaishi was asked by Miyazaki to write the soundtrack of *Howl's Moving Castle* around one leitmotiv. As a result, the main theme 'The Merry-Go-Round Of Life' appears in 18 of 33 cues in the film's soundtrack. Throughout their collaboration, Miyazaki's film soundtracks were generally composed from the basic musical ideas in the image albums that Hisaishi devised before the film went into production. However, in making *Howl's Moving Castle*, Miyazaki broke with custom and rejected the use of items from Hisaishi's image album titled *Image Symphonic Suite: Howl's Moving Castle* (Hisaishi, 2006: 89–92; 2007: 32–5). Maejima explains that Miyazaki did not believe that the image album adequately represented the work-in-progress of the film sketches but seemed like an autonomous work. Ultimately, from among other pieces presented by Hisaishi, Miyazaki chose the simplest waltz as the main theme, despite having previously rejected both this item and the image album (Maejima, 2004: 140).

Maejima analyses in detail Hisaishi's use of leitmotiv in *Howl's Moving Castle* and points out the 'circular' characteristic in this waltz-style main theme. The leitmotiv of 'The Merry-Go-Round Of Life' is varied following the growth of love between Sophie and Howl, a beautiful young wizard who owns the mysterious moving castle (*ibid.*: 140–4). In terms of orchestration, in *Howl's Moving Castle*, the waltz style of 'The Merry-Go-Round Of Life' is highly sophisticated compared to Hisaishi's previous waltz 'On A Clear Day' in *Kiki's Delivery Service*. It is ironic that the more sophisticated Hisaishi's orchestration becomes, the closer his soundtrack resembles the dense orchestral style often associated with Hollywood cinema music, a style generally disliked by him.

'Asian' musical elements for 'oriental' images

As Miyazaki's films shifted to representations of Japaneseness, Hisaishi's music also changed in style. *My Neighbor Totoro* (*Tonari no Totoro*, 1988) was the first film in which Miyazaki fabricated the fantasy of little children and verdant countryside in 1950s Japan. The narrative adopts the viewpoint of two young sisters, Satsuki and Mei. The film's feature melody, 'The Path Of Wind' ('Kaze no Tôrimichi'), is written in C minor pentatonic scale (Figure 3.7).

Figure 3.7 'The Path Of Wind' from *My Neighbor Totoro* (transcribed by present author)

This pentatonic scale is also called *niroku-nuki*, literally meaning 'lacking the second and sixth', that is, five notes that lack the second and sixth notes in the diatonic scale. The ethnomusicologist Fumio Koizumi notes that *niroku-nuki* was the most important pentatonic scale in Japan prior to the influence of China (Koizumi, 1984: 21). Many Japanese popular songs named *kayôkyoku* in the 1970s were based on this scale. From the *My Neighbor Totoro* soundtrack, other songs like 'Stroll' ('Sampo') and 'My Neighbor Totoro' ('Tonari no Totoro') became more widely recognized than 'The Path Of Wind'. Specifically, 'Stroll' has become a new nursery rhyme sung in kindergartens and primary schools in Japan. Nevertheless, 'The Path Of Wind' is the most significant thematic melody in this film, as both 'Stroll' and 'My Neighbor Totoro' are written in the western style, and the tone of 'nostalgia' throughout the film comes from the minor pentatonic scale of 'The Path Of Wind'. It is the use of this scale that strongly suggests ancient Japanese traditional songs, and supports the Japanese-styled storyline.

In *Spirited Away*, 'One Summer's Day' ('Natu no Hi') takes the role of the main thematic melody (Figure 3.8). At the opening, 'One Summer's Day' is played on solo piano to express the loneliness of the main character, ten-year-old Chihiro, who has just left her friends and moved with her parents to a new suburban home. After her parents stumble on an abandoned theme park, they disappear into a magic kingdom and Chihiro has to work for the middle-aged landlady Yubâba at a large bathhouse for millions of gods. Through this Japanese variation of an *Alice in Wonderland*-like adventure, Chihiro finds new friends and matures. 'One Summer's Day' is written in the natural minor scale,[17] one that is also heard in many Japanese popular songs. Added to this, Hisaishi places importance on notes from the pentatonic scale (E, D, A, C, G in Figure 3.8), giving the impression of nostalgia through this melody.

Figure 3.8 'One Summer's Day' from *Spirited Away* (transcribed by present author)

On the soundtrack of *Spirited Away*, a commonly used Okinawan scale (the *niroku-nuki* that lacks the second and sixth notes in the C major scale) is used in 'Procession Of The Spirits' ('Kamisama-tachi') (Figure 3.9). Okinawa is thought to be exotic in Japan for both historical and cultural reasons (see Mitsui, 1998; Pope, 2005) and Okinawan scales are considered to sound exotic, as they resemble Indonesian music more than that of Japan's adjacent regions. In the soundtrack of *Spirited Away*, an Okinawan-styled melody is used in 'Procession Of The Spirits' to effectively draw a line between Chihiro's life in Japan and the mysterious magic kingdom, a world *somewhere else* from everyday space.

Figure 3.9 'Procession Of The Spirits' from *Spirited Away* (transcribed by present author)

Eclectic-styled theme songs

As usual for animated films in Japan, Miyazaki's films also feature 'theme songs' that stand apart from the main thematic music discussed above. These songs are commonly heard at the film's conclusion and, while he left many musical decisions for the soundtrack to Hisaishi, Miyazaki devoted considerable time to devising appropriate theme songs. In some films, the songs were written by Hisaishi, but other composers (Yumi Kimura in *Spirited Away* and *Howl's Moving Castle*, for example) also provided theme songs to Miyazaki's films. Here I briefly outline the theme songs from *Castle in the Sky* and *Princess Mononoke*, as both were written by Hisaishi.

Since westernization began in Japan during the Meiji Era (1868–1912), Japanese composers have tried to devise new songs by accommodating Japanese traditional musical elements to western musical harmonization or forms. In the area of popular music, they composed songs such as *kayôkyoku* or *enka* as an indigenous *uta* (song) to be part of everyday life in Japan. While the former song style appears 'fashionable' to young Japanese for its orientation towards western popular music, the latter is thought to be more 'traditional' for its use of melismatic vocalization and the expression of vernacular and familiar Japanese sentiments in song lyrics.

This 'western-style popular song made in Japan' is relevant to the theme songs for Miyazaki's films. In the 1960s and 1970s, the Japanese version of the 'folk song' was in its heyday. Based on western-style folk songs, these songs generally included guitar accompaniment and were composed and performed in the style of western artists of the 1960s and 1970s such as Bob Dylan, Joan Baez and Peter, Paul and Mary.[19] Miyazaki enjoyed the western-style folk songs popular in Japan and Hisaishi followed Miyazaki's musical tastes for the theme songs for his films. Hisaishi's theme songs characteristically adopt western stylistic elements but feature the minor scales and lyrical aspects that were typical of Japanese folk song in the 1960s and 1970s.

In *Castle in the Sky*, the theme song 'Carrying You' ('Kimi o Nosete') exemplifies this approach (Figure 3.10). 'Carrying You' is based on a natural minor scale but the harmonization sometimes employs the melody with the leading tone (D) in E-flat harmonic minor scale and the sixth note (C) in E-flat melodic minor scale (ascending). This is a typical melodic and harmonic progression of Japanese folk song.

Figure 3.10 The theme song of *Castle in the Sky*, 'Carrying You' (transcribed by present author)

In *Princess Mononoke*, the theme song of 'Princess Mononoke' (Figure 3.11) was sung by the countertenor Yoshikazu Mera. The high register and melodic sweeps of the countertenor's voice suggest the feminine in this song, and the boundary between Japanese and western-style music is blurred. Musically, while this melody is written in a natural minor scale typical of many Japanese popular songs, it also suggests the Aeolian mode, the notes for which are the same as those used in the natural minor scale. The melody is also linked to 'The Legend Of Ashitaka', written in Dorian mode, and these two melodies are connected. On Miyazaki's film soundtracks, usually the main thematic melody and the theme song are composed separately and the two seldom meet. However, in *Princess Mononoke*, the main thematic melody and the theme song are successfully interwoven through the fabric of the film, and influence each other. This union of melody and song itself suggests the successful collaborative encounters between Miyazaki and Hisaishi.

Figure 3.11 Vocal ending theme song of 'Princess Mononoke' (transcribed by present author)

Conclusion

In this chapter I have shown how Hisaishi's music in Miyazaki's films can be categorized into four approaches based on the use of musical scales: Dorian mode to create ancient European moods (*Nausicaä of the Valley of the Wind* and *Castle in the Sky*); western-classical styled music to suggest occidental impressions (*Kiki's Delivery Service, Porco Rosso* and *Howl's Moving Castle*); pentatonic scales, natural minor scale, and other Asian musical elements to enhance Japanese and oriental images (*My Neighbor Totoro* and *Spirited Away*); and an eclectic style of Japanese popular songs in which Japanese and western musical approaches are mixed (*Castle in the Sky* and *Princess Mononoke*). These musical approaches parallel Miyazaki's changes in thematic emphasis and narrative features.

Several prominent Japanese composers have employed avant-garde musical approaches to devise soundtracks for Japanese films, using traditional instruments such as the *shakuhachi* (bamboo flute) or *shamisen* (Japanese three-stringed fretless lute) to experiment with the integration of a Japanese 'sound' with European orchestration and composition style. Hisaishi's mentor, Masaru Satô, was also innovative in his use of various elements from Japanese folk songs and other types of traditional Japanese music. In contrast, Hisaishi's soundtracks for Miyazaki's films do not conspicuously use Japanese traditional instruments but rather suggest 'Japaneseness' through the use of musical scales. When compared to Satô's film music, Hisaishi's scores seem straightforward in both melodic development and instrumentation. However, the two composers are comparable in two respects, that is, they both viewed their film-music work as their principal occupation (rather than being concert or experimental composers) and both aimed to compose familiar and memorable melodies for general viewers, rather than artistic or enigmatic melodies for intellectual stimulation or anime fans.

I have provided an overview of Hisaishi's compositions in Miyazaki's films that shows the significance of the music for the narratives and atmospheres. A detailed analysis of each film soundtrack and the cues themselves could provide fruitful extensions of this study. My analysis has emphasized the collaborative process between Miyazaki and Hisaishi in the construction of these film soundtracks. Their working method and the resulting soundtracks offer a model that is unique for animation film production in Japan, providing a bridge between the Japanese industry and an international audience.

Notes

1. All Japanese names will follow the English convention of family name after given name.
2. Throughout this chapter, the English-language release titles of the films are used, with the Japanese titles included in brackets at the initial mention.
3. The name derives from an Italian nickname for scouting planes used over the desert, and is used to suggest a fresh approach to animation for the Japanese anime industry.

4. Toshio Suzuki, 'Sutajio Jiburi no rekishi [The history of Studio Ghibli]', online at http:// www.ghibli.jp/30profile/000152.html (accessed 26 September 2006) [in Japanese].
5. Napier (2005) is the updated version of Napier (2001), adding analyses of Miyazaki's *Spirited Away* and *Howl's Moving Castle* (2004).
6. In contrast to this partnership, Isao Takahata, a Studio Ghibli producer, long-time Miyazaki collaborator and significant animation-film director in his own right, is knowledgeable about music and chooses different appropriate composers for each of his films. As a result, Takahata's films lack the overall musical impression evident in Miyazaki's oeuvre.
7. I will analyse Hisaishi's music for Miyazaki's films using the following DVDs [all in Japanese with English subtitles]:

   Nausicaä of the Valley of the Wind (1984) (Buena Vista Home Entertainment)
   Castle in the Sky (Japanese version, 1986) (Buena Vista Home Entertainment)
   My Neighbor Totoro (1988) (Buena Vista Home Entertainment)
   Kiki's Delivery Service (1989) (Buena Vista Home Entertainment)
   Porco Rosso (1992) (Buena Vista Home Entertainment)
   Princess Mononoke (1997) (Buena Vista Home Entertainment)
   Spirited Away (2001) (Buena Vista Home Entertainment)
   Howl's Moving Castle (2004) (Buena Vista Home Entertainment)

8. If the US version of *Castle in the Sky* (2002, distributed by Disney) is included – for which Hisaishi rearranged and in part newly created the soundtrack – their collaboration amounts to nine films. However, in this paper I analyse the original Japanese version of *Castle in the Sky* [*Tenkû no Shiro Rapyuta*] (1986).
9. The Chinese character of Hisaishi's 'hisa (久)' is also pronounced as 'ku', which is close to Quincy's 'qu' pronunciation.
10. Hisaishi continued to work on television anime after his success with *Nausicaä of the Valley of the Wind*, and since 2000 he has worked on commercials and documentaries for television. However, his main work is on feature films and concerts of light orchestral music in the style of the Boston Pops Orchestra. He continues to live in Japan but since 2005 he has also composed for live-action Korean and Chinese films.
11. Satô himself inherited a significant film-composition role when he took over the unfinished scores by his mentor, Fumio Hayasaka, who had composed for several of Kurosawa's early films.
12. The *Nausicaä* screenplay was originally rejected. Mayazaki wrote the *manga* version over thirteen years and the film represents a simplified version of only the first quarter of the *manga* chapters, those devised at the time of the film production.
13. In this chapter I have notated Hisaishi's main melodies with code names by listening to the DVD soundtracks as listed above.
14. In *yona-nuki* ('lacking the fourth and seventh'), the pentatonic scale is composed of five notes without the fourth and seventh notes of the diatonic scale.
15. *Enka* is a traditional Japanese popular song, often based on sad stories about unrequited or unfulfilled love, with melodies indigenous to Japan.

16. From the original Japanese version of *Castle in the Sky* [*Tenkû no Shiro Rapyuta*] released in 1986, rather than the 2002 US version.
17. Both French composers and arrangers had several chart hits in the 1960s. Paul Mauriat attracted a large following in Japan and a Japanese branch of the international Paul Mauriat club maintains a website at http://www.pluto.dti.ne.jp/%7Epmclub/.
18. The natural minor scale has the same tones as the major scale but the pattern of intervals is different, commencing on the sixth tone, giving it a different feeling.
19. For an overview of Japanese popular music, the 26-page publication by IASPM-Japan (International Association for the Study of Popular Music), *A Guide to Popular Music in Japan* (1991), provides a helpful summary (available on request from IASPM-Japan). See also Hosokawa (1999).

References

Agawa, S. (1999), 'Agawa Sawako no konohito ni aitai: Hisaishi Joe' [Those who I want to meet: Interview with Hisaishi Joe], *Shûkan Bunshun*, 41(34), 156–60. [In Japanese]

Hisaishi, J. (1992), *Ai am: Harukanaru ongaku no michi e* [*I Am: To the Long Way of Music*], Tokyo: Media Factory. [In Japanese]

Hisaishi, J. (2006), *Kandô o tsukuremasuka?* [*Can You Make Impressions?*], Tokyo: Kadokawa Shoten. [In Japanese]

Hisaishi, J. (2007), *Hisaishi Joe 35 miri nikki* [*Joe Hisaishi 35-mm Diaries*], Tokyo: Takarajima-sha. [In Japanese]

Hosokawa, S. (1999), 'Soy Sauce Music; Harumi Hosono and Japanese Self-Orientalism', in P. Hayward (ed.), *Widening the Horizon: Exoticism in Post-War Popular Music*, Sydney: John Libbey & Co., pp. 114–44.

Kaku, T. (2000), 'Hisaishi Joe intabyû' [Interview with Hisaishi Joe], *Kinema Junpô*, 1311, July, 31–5. [In Japanese]

Kobayashi, A. (2007), *Satô Masaru: Ginmaku no Kôkyôgaku* [*Satô Masaru: Symphony of Screen*], Tokyo: Wides Shuppan. [In Japanese]

Koizumi, F. (1984), *Kayôkyoku no Kôzô* [*The Structure of Popular Songs* (*kayôkyoku*)], Tokyo: Tôjusha. [In Japanese]

Lamarre, T. (2002), 'From Animation to Anime: Drawing Movements and Moving Drawings', *Japan Forum*, 14(2), 329–67.

McCarthy, H. (1999), *Hayao Miyazaki: Master of Japanese Animation: Films, Themes, Artistry*. Berkeley: Stone Bridge Press.

Maejima, H. (2004), ' "Eiga ongaku no kakushin" eno kaiki: "Jinsei no merì-gô-rando" no imisuru-mono' ['Return to "the Centre of Film Music": The Meaning of "The Merry-Go-Round Of Life" '], *Eureka*, 36(13), 137–44 [In Japanese]

Mitsui, T. (1998), 'Domestic Exoticism: A Recent Trend in Japanese Popular Music', *Perfect Beat*, 3(4), 1–12.

Miyazaki, M. (1999), 'Miyazaki Midori no kirikomi tôku: Hisaishi Joe-san' [Miyazaki Midori's Point-blank Questions: Hisaishi Joe], *Shûkan Yomiuri*, 58(51), 148–52 [In Japanese]

Mori, T. (1992), 'Miyazaki Hayao rongu intabyû' [Extended Interview with Miyazaki Hayao], *Kinema Junpô*, 1079 (April), 106–11. [In Japanese]

Napier, S. J. (2001), *Anime from Akira to Princess Mononoke: Experiencing Contemporary Japanese Animation*, New York: Palgrave Macmillan.

Napier, S. J. (2005), *Anime from Akira to Howl's Moving Castle: Experiencing Contemporary Japanese Animation*, New York: Palgrave Macmillan.

Okada, R. (2006), '"*Kaze no Tani no Naushika*" ni okeru Miyazaki Hayao to Hisaishi Joe no deai' [Encounter of Hayao Miyazaki and Joe Hisaishi in *Nausicaä of the Valley of Wind*: Generation of Movie Music], *Japanese Journal of Animation Studies*, 7(1A), 17–28. [In Japanese with an English abstract]

Pope, E. (2005), 'Ekizochizumu to nihon popurâ ongaku no dainamizumu: Tairiku merodî o chûshin ni' [Exoticism and Dynamism of Japanese Popular Music: Centred on Continental Melodies]', in T. Mitsui (ed.), *Popurâ ongaku to akademizumu* [Popular Music and Academism], Tokyo: Ongaku-no-tomo-sha, pp. 161–82. [In Japanese]

Satô, M. (1993), '300/40: Sono e, oto, hito, 15' [300/40: My image, sound and person, no. 15], *Kinema Junpô*, 1101 (March), 142–5. [In Japanese]

Schodt, F. L. (1996), *Dreamland Japan: Writings on Modern Manga*, Berkeley: Stonebridge Press.

Shimizu, A. (2000), 'Watashi o eiga ni michibiita hito, kotoba: Hisaishi Joe-shi [People and words which have led me to films: Hisaishi Joe]', *Sankei Shimbun* (Tokyo Edition), 27 May, p. 24. [In Japanese]

Yoshioka, A. (1998), 'Hisaishi Joe intabyû' [Interview with Hisaishi Joe], *Kinema Junpô*, 1247 (February), 128–31. [In Japanese]

Part II
Musical Intertextuality

4   Something Old, Something New, Something Borrowed ... Something Blue

The Beatles' Yellow Submarine

Ian Inglis

Yellow Submarine (George Dunning, 1968) is a remarkable film in many ways. Its integration and presentation of a wide range of visual styles, the impetus it provided for the synthesis of art and pop, its legacy for subsequent generations of animators, its prototypical place in the evolution of music video, the part it played in the narrative of the Beatles, its early exploitation of film-related merchandise and memorabilia, and the position it occupies as popular music's first, and only, full-length animation feature are all important elements of the film's overall significance.

Given the visibility of these attributes, it is, perhaps, not wholly surprising that its musical components have been rather overlooked. Much of the responsibility for this rested with the Beatles themselves, who showed little initial interest in the project. Their lack of enthusiasm was easy to understand. In 1963, United Artists had contracted with their manager Brian Epstein for a three-picture deal with the group and had appointed the London-based American Walter Shenson as producer. *A Hard Day's Night* (Richard Lester, 1964) and *Help!* (Richard Lester, 1965) had been enormous commercial successes, but by 1967, the group – wearied by the demands of movie-making and largely unimpressed by the potential scripts they had been offered – was unwilling to co-operate with the studio's increasingly aggressive demands for the promised final film.

However, in the intervening years 39 half-hour episodes of *The Beatles* cartoon series, produced by King Features and networked on US television by ABC, had been broadcast over three seasons in the autumn schedules of 1965, 1966 and 1967. Lacking any input from the group itself (the animators simply produced stories loosely inspired by, and performed to, Beatles songs; speaking voices were provided by actors), the series was dismissed by the group as one more example of the many (often bizarre) spin-offs that had accompanied the first wave of Beatlemania in North America.

When Al Brodax (Head of TV & Motion Pictures at King Features) approached Epstein to propose a full-length animation feature, to be directed by George Dunning, who had produced many of the cartoon episodes, Epstein reluctantly agreed, recognizing that such a movie could satisfy United Artists' demands for a third film. However, when the Beatles, newly retired from touring in order to concentrate on creativity in the studio and buoyed up by the extraordinary critical response to *Sgt Pepper's Lonely Hearts Club Band* (June 1967), learned that they were now to be depicted as animated characters in a film based on Ringo Starr's nursery rhyme-like song from *Revolver* (August 1966) and produced by those responsible for the television series, they refused to co-operate or contribute. Having abandoned the imagery and ideology of the 'Fab Four', the group feared that any association with a project likely to be (wrongly) perceived as 'a cartoon movie for children' would be an unwelcome and inappropriate regression at this stage in its career.

These unpromising beginnings played a decisive part in determining the musical soundtrack of *Yellow Submarine*. With no new songs forthcoming, the film's score was, of necessity, assembled from an assortment of familiar tracks, a number of unreleased songs recorded but discarded by the group, and several incidental sequences composed and orchestrated by George Martin, who, in addition to being the Beatles' producer, was the film's musical director. The group's apparent disdain for *Yellow Submarine* was further demonstrated by the decision to delay the release of the soundtrack album until January 1969, some six months after the film's UK premiere. Even its sleevenotes sought to deflect attention from the music by reproducing a review of the group's previous album *The Beatles* (conventionally known as the White Album), released in November 1968.

The team of screenwriters (Brodax, Lee Minoff, Erich Segal and Jack Mendelsohn) created a plot that combined elements and themes from the lyrics of 'Yellow Submarine' and the magical-mythical world of Pepperland, as apparently revealed in the elaborate sleeve design of *Sgt Pepper*. When the tranquil world of Pepperland is invaded by the Blue Meanies, 'Young Fred' – actually very old – escapes and journeys to Liverpool in his yellow submarine to recruit the help of the Beatles; on their return, they use the power of their music to defeat the invaders, and restore peace and harmony. Although somewhat simplistic, the contours of the narrative are, in fact, central to the musical content. The film does not merely *use* music; it is *about* music and the transformative nature of music – in this case, quite literally, the capacity to save the world. The trajectory of the film thus echoes the conclusions of the many contemporary biographers, musicologists and cultural critics who had pointed to the unique abilities of the Beatles and the multiple functions of their music:

> The Beatles' significance … is inseparable from the ambiguity of their function. As pop musicians, they are simultaneously magicians, priests, entertainers and artists … the Beatles in particular have reinstated magic.
> (Mellers, 1973: 183–4)

> The four ... were beings such as the modern world had never seen. Only
> in ancient times, when boy Emperors and Pharaohs were clothed, even fed,
> with pure gold, had very young men commanded an equivalent adoration,
> fascination, and constant, expectant scrutiny. (Norman, 1981: 264)

> The Beatles are divine Messiahs. The wisest, holiest, most effective avatars
> that the human race has yet produced. I declare that John Lennon, George
> Harrison, Paul McCartney and Ringo Starr are mutants. Evolutionary agents
> sent by God, endowed with mysterious power to create a new human
> species. (Leary, 1968: 44)

Whether depicted as magicians, emperors or messiahs, it was the persistent belief that
the Beatles wielded unprecedented powers far beyond their music – although, crucially,
their music was the vehicle through which those powers were expressed – that underpins these, and many other, accounts. And what *Yellow Submarine* accomplished,
through its specific depiction of the Beatles as heroes, was to reflect and articulate that
belief and, at the same time, to focus yet further attention on their music. Indeed, the
characteristics of the Beatles and the plight of Pepperland display an almost symmetrical
correspondence with the archetypal hero-myth described by Campbell:

> the composite hero of the monomyth is a personage of exceptional gift ...
> frequently, he is honored by his society. In apocalyptic vision the physical and
> spiritual life of the whole earth can be represented as fallen, or on the point
> of falling, into ruin. (1949: 37, emphasis added)

The music of *Yellow Submarine* – the music that rescues Pepperland from physical
and spiritual ruin – falls into three categories, whose creative rationales can be characterized as engagement (with familiar songs), employment (of unfamiliar songs) and
experiment (in the composition of an original score). These categories break down in
the following way:

(a) Engagement (previously released Beatles songs): 'Yellow Submarine'; 'Eleanor
     Rigby'; 'When I'm Sixty-four'; 'Nowhere Man'; 'Lucy In The Sky With Dia-
     monds'; 'Sgt Pepper's Lonely Hearts Club Band'; 'With A Little Help From My
     Friends'; 'All You Need Is Love'; 'Baby You're A Rich Man'.
(b) Employment (previously unreleased Beatles songs): 'All Together Now'; 'Only A
     Northern Song'; 'Hey Bulldog'; 'It's All Too Much'.
(c) Experiment (instrumental score): George Martin provided an original instrumen-
     tal score of 55 minutes. The most substantial pieces were condensed into
     seven tracks included on the soundtrack album: 'Pepperland'; 'Sea Of Time';
     'Sea Of Holes'; 'Sea Of Monsters'; 'March Of The Meanies'; 'Pepperland Laid
     Waste'; 'Yellow Submarine In Pepperland'.

In addition, there are numerous references to dialogue taken from the lyrics of 'Help',
'When I Get Home', 'A Day In The Life' and 'Getting Better'; and musical quotations
from 'Within You Without You', 'A Day In The Life', 'Love You To' and 'Think For

Yourself'. Running for a mere 87 minutes, the movie is, therefore, saturated with music (in addition to a bombardment of stylized and exaggerated sound effects during the action sequences).[1]

Music and image: engagement

The animation film – more than any other type of movie – is characterized by its construction of worlds in which the audience routinely encounters the unpredictable, the surreal, the illogical, the impossible, and around which the opportunities for imagination and invention are infinite. In such circumstances, a reliance on existing tracks seems undesirable since, as Wright has commented, "pre-recorded music is, in essence, a 'prefabricated' element ... it enters the process already formed, and the options for manipulating it are limited" (2003: 9). And yet, as was demonstrated in Walt Disney's *Fantasia* (James Algar *et al.*, 1940) the crafting of images to music, rather than music to images, can be successful and memorable. Indeed, rather than any prior knowledge of the music serving to diminish an audience's appreciation of images, it can be argued that the greater the familiarity of audience members with what they are hearing, the deeper their engagement with what they are watching.

It is this factor that illuminates the union of music and animation throughout much of *Yellow Submarine*. An early example is the use of 'Eleanor Rigby', heard as we are introduced to the Beatles' Liverpool of the 1960s. Gloomy images of the skyline are revealed as the sun rises over the terraced roofs of the city. Factory hooters blare out, announcing the start of another working day. Scores of dispirited workers trudge listlessly through the monochrome streets. And as this happens, McCartney's voice urges us to consider the loneliness and isolation of the characters he describes. As the song continues, its themes of estrangement, sadness, alienation and anomie are emphasized in the accompanying images. In contrast to the Edwardian refinement of Pepperland (and, more obliquely, to the actual prosperity of Liverpool itself in the nineteenth century), we now see a melancholy landscape of neglected churchyards, grey cobbled streets, decaying buildings. Just like Eleanor Rigby and Father McKenzie, those who live in the city are trapped, despairing, frustrated, and unable to escape from the repetitive and pointless routines of their daily lives. The countless faceless men in their bowler hats from René Magritte's surrealist paintings are there; so too are the unidentifiable footballers from the city's two clubs, Liverpool FC and Everton FC. Like everyone else in the city, they are anonymous. McCartney's explanation of the song, as "stream-of-consciousness stuff ... the lonely old person opening her tin of catfood" (Miles, 1997: 282), presents another, equally poignant image of isolation.

'When I'm Sixty-four' had originally been written by McCartney as a teenager in the 1950s, and was revisited (and partly rewritten) for *Sgt Pepper*. It too considers old age, but in a playful way that the singer described as his "rooty-tooty variety style" (*ibid.*: 319). The context in which the song is introduced is crucially dependent upon the audience's prior knowledge of it as a music-hall pastiche. Now on board the yellow submarine with Young Fred, and travelling towards Pepperland, the Beatles enjoy an atmosphere of light-hearted excitement as they play with the controls, joke, and tease each other. Thus, the onset of sudden ageing as they pass through the Sea of Time, recognized by the assortment of clocks, timepieces and hourglasses on the ocean floor, is not a cause for concern, but an opportunity for fun that the tempo and delivery of the song effectively complement (the original vocal track was speeded up to raise the pitch). Their hair turns white and beards sprout at an alarming rate, but – away from Liverpool and en route to Pepperland – the mood is positive and old age is no longer perceived as something to be feared. The re-creation of a pre-war, vaudeville style of music was common in the 1960s, in the music of groups like The Temperance Seven, The Bonzo Dog Doo Dah Band, and The New Vaudeville Band. 'When I'm Sixty-four' not only cheerfully confirms that musical tradition, but provides a specific link to the visual elements of Pepperland itself. As the clock ticks away on screen to take the Beatles (and Young Fred) one minute nearer to their destination, and the audience one minute nearer to old age, the song's status as "an affectionate satire regarding old age from a young man's point of view" (Martin, 1994: 38) is equally valid inside and outside the film.

The theme of loneliness emerges again when, after escaping from the Sea of Monsters, the Beatles come across the multi-talented polyglot, Jeremy Hillary Boob Ph.D. His isolation, however, derives from difference rather than anonymity. An obsessive scholar, alone in a blank terrain lacking colour or form, he sits typing books and reviews that no one will read (rather like Father McKenzie's sermons that no one will hear). Searching for a way to describe him, the group performs 'Nowhere Man', mocking the groundless intellectualism typified by his persistent complaint, "so little time, so much to know". Their performance not only directs attention to Boob's plight, but brings waves of psychedelic colour to the empty seascape. After Boob repairs the submarine's faulty motor, Ringo invites him to join them on their journey; he gratefully and tearfully accepts. This outcome is, of course, expected, given the audience's knowledge of the insight contained in Lennon's lyrics that the 'Nowhere Man' of the title is, in fact, representative of us all. In allowing a 'nowhere man' to accompany the world's most famous musicians, the Beatles are implicitly inviting all of us aboard their yellow submarine, and emphasizing that it is our similarities, not our differences, that define us.

The observation that the film is "filled with … the hallucinatory rainbow of psychedelia" (Carr, 1996: 141) is best illustrated in the animation that accompanies 'Lucy In The Sky With Diamonds', which is itself widely regarded as among the group's most psychedelic songs (O'Grady, 1983: 124–5; Brown and Gaines, 1983: 213–14; Kozinn, 1995: 155–8). Stranded on the seabed – "the foothills of the headlands" – the Beatles and Boob are confronted by hundreds of human heads whose inner thoughts are exposed to reveal an extravagance of colours, patterns, figures and emotions. As in many conceptual music videos, there is no explicit correspondence between music and image, nor is there any clear input into the film's narrative. However, the delicate, meandering lyric, which presents an assortment of surreal visions, is complemented by a 'brushstroke' animation in which dancers, horses and acrobats float or leap across landscapes that constantly shift and re-form. The supple, unresolved artwork stands in contrast to the consistency and clarity that characterize the rest of the film's images. The sequence thus exemplifies psychedelia through its musical and visual disruptions to meaning, logic and iteration.

Yellow Submarine's final utilization of previously released music is in an extended sequence of four songs, when the Beatles, having arrived in Pepperland via the Sea of Holes and the Sea of Green, confront the Blue Meanies. Taking up the instruments and uniforms of Pepperland's original musicians, their performance of 'Sgt Pepper's Lonely Hearts Club Band' begins to free the grey, frozen figures from their imprisonment. Members of the crowd regain colour and movement; the Blue Meanies retreat from the music. As on the album, the track segues directly into the opening bars of 'With A Little Help From My Friends', its applause amplified by the cheers of the liberated residents, who join the advance against their oppressors. In many ways, this stands as the definitive moment of the film, demonstrating conclusively the charismatic abilities of the Beatles against an enemy who hates and fears their music. The appearance and nomenclature of this enemy is doubly significant. On the one hand, it alludes to a repressive political agency:

> The wicked Blue Meanies ... can be read as simplistic symbols of the ultimate grassroots manifestation of state power, the police. Like the police, they carry weapons, wear blue uniforms, and use ferocious dogs. (Neaverson, 1997: 88)

The other pertinent reference is to the blues as a musical form:

> It is ... an abbreviation of 'blue devils' or melancholia. The blues is also a basic emotional response to an oppressive environment, a song of the alienated ... a music of accommodation, of coping with the realities of living in a socially and economically segregated society. The battering the human spirit takes when it strains to ascend towards its true purpose: this is the subject matter of the blues. (Palmer, 1976: 55–6)

The Beatles' victory is therefore political *and* musical. Blue is at the heart of the Meanies' tactics: the chief Blue Meanie's assertion that "heaven is blue", the deadly powers of the Blue Flying Glove, the blue glass dome in which Sgt Pepper and his band are imprisoned, the command to "oblueterate" the citizens. All testify to the suffering and desolation implicit in a blue world.

As the Beatles perform 'All You Need Is Love', Pepperland's liberation is concluded. The lyrics themselves form a barrier that the remaining Blue Meanies, and the Glove, cannot penetrate; they scatter and flee in confusion. The population rallies and marches to reclaim its territory, while the Beatles themselves lead the victory parade through what is once again a green and pleasant land. To John's observation that "nothing is

Beatle-proof", Ringo frees Sgt Pepper's band from its glass prison. As 'Baby You're A Rich Man' plays, the congratulatory lyrics speak directly to the freed inhabitants of Pepperland. The musical and political transformations are thus complete: the Beatles (in the guise of Sgt Pepper's Lonely Hearts Club Band) have, with a little help from their friends, shown that love is all that is needed to bring personal freedom and understanding. Their songs have told "a classic fairy tale, a modern morality story, and the final expression of the whimsical side of 'love and peace' " (Evans, 1984: 84).

The film's exploitation of these songs (plus 'Yellow Submarine', which plays over the opening credits) to guide its narrative is contingent upon the audience's familiarity with the Beatles' music. By 1968, the music released by the group over the previous five years was arguably the most instantly recognized and celebrated that the popular music industry had yet produced. While this imposed upon the makers of *Yellow Submarine* a requirement to observe some kind of schematic connection with the songs' broad themes, it nonetheless provided a huge advantage to their ability to make use of the affective experience of popular music:

> *By condensing meanings already in circulation through their intertextual relationship to a particular style of music, performer or historical moment, the soundtrack can evoke emotions and associations without having to produce those elements directly through narrative. The back catalogue thus becomes a cultural bank with instant access.* (Tincknell, 2006: 134)

In this case, a successful engagement with narrative by the film's audience was triply strengthened – through its relationship to the Beatles' music, to the performers themselves, and to the historical moments to which the group had contributed.

Music and image: employment

As with the batch of songs discussed above, the availability of four previously unreleased Beatles songs brought with it opportunities and constraints. Clearly, the presence of *any* additional music from the group was a strong marketing point in the promotion of the film and the soundtrack album. However, the Beatles themselves had considered the songs inferior examples of their music that were unworthy of public release. They grudgingly consented to their inclusion in order to fulfil the requirement to supply four new songs for the film, as stipulated in the production contract agreed between Brian Epstein, King Features and United Artists, before Epstein's death in August 1967 (Spitz, 2006: 768–9). Furthermore, the audience's lack of familiarity with the tracks made it difficult to slot them into a narrative broadly determined by the familiar lyrics of the nine previously released songs. In the end, two of the songs – 'All Together Now' and 'Hey Bulldog' – were employed in ways that (loosely) reflected, or contributed, to plot development, and two – 'Only A Northern Song' and 'It's All Too Much' – were used as little more than incidental or functional bridges.

'All Together Now' is heard as the Beatles and Young Fred begin their voyage from Liverpool to Pepperland. If anything, its repetitive (the title is repeated forty-nine times), childlike vocabulary is even more suggestive of the nursery rhyme than 'Yellow Submarine'. Each new letter or number in the lyrics cues a corresponding visual shift inside or outside the submarine. Each new colour signals the appearance of shoals of fluorescent fish and underwater plants. In place of their typical black, inky fluid, startled octopuses pump out bright blue, red and yellow clouds of liquid. Shoals of luminous tropical fish swim rhythmically through the clear water. The Beatles are in high spirits at the prospect of their adventure and, coming at the start of their journey, the song is usually interpreted as a simple holiday singalong. However, Turner has pointed to its "dual meaning ... which could be either a music hall-style invitation to participate, or a slogan for world unity" (1994: 179), both of which are equally plausible, given the nature and outcome of the Beatles' quest. The song is also repeated during the closing credits, at which point the on-screen translation of its title phrase into numerous foreign languages might well suggest a global slogan.

The description of 'Hey Bulldog' as "a great, growling rocker, [its] tight ferocious intensity whiplashing its simple groove to a fever pitch ... barking and maniacal laughter" (Hertsgaard, 1995: 229) also serves as an apt summary of the accompanying animation. Among the remnants of the Blue Meanies' army, the Beatles are suddenly confronted by four snarling and ferocious dogs. They take refuge behind (and inside) a stranded pianola which, when operated, produces the piano introduction to the song. The dogs become increasingly agitated, in response to the growing urgency of the song and their own chaotic inability to corner the Beatles, and they eventually collapse in exhaustion, thus allowing the group to escape. The opportunistic use of a single word in the song title to create an episode in the movie was reflected in Lennon's comment that in the making of *Yellow Submarine*, "they lifted all the ideas for the movie out of our heads and didn't give us any credit ... it's a good-sounding record *that means nothing*" (Sheff and Golson, 1981: 172, emphasis added).

Although there is no correspondence between song and narrative, the lyrics of 'Only A Northern Song' unequivocally determine the animation. As the Beatles leave the Sea of Time and enter the Sea of Science, Harrison's droning vocal and an overlapping instrumentation introduce the idea of an altered state in which the normal rules of perception are no longer valid. This sense of unease is continued through what is, essentially, a music video. Built around a series of central images that freely recalls Richard Avedon's enhanced photographs of the group members, the sequence is drenched in optical and musical distortion – impulses of static electricity, multiple waves of interference, high- and low-frequency signals that connect and disconnect the faces, and ears, of the four Beatles. Its overall attempt to "emphasise a higher reality than that of the objective world and ... simulate a hypnotic 'psych-out' of epic proportions" (Neaverson, 1997: 85) may explain the fusion of music and animation, but its place in the movie

– and its specific location in the Sea of Science – remains confusing, and it is best approached as incidental rather than integral.

During the making of *Yellow Submarine*, the Beatles had been encouraged to lend their active support to the movie by filming a brief post-animation, pre-credits appearance. The chief function of 'It's All Too Much' is to provide a transition from the Beatles in Pepperland to the Beatles in the studio. Following their defeat, the Blue Meanies are persuaded to cease hostilities and join Pepperland's residents. The festivities continue amid the bright and glorious colours of the restored Pepperland: flowers bloom, sunbeams glow, the words YES, OK and LOVE are prominent across the landscape, and the song celebrates the exuberance and power of love. Although it has been dismissed as "a cosy nursery rhyme in which the world is a birthday cake" (MacDonald, 1994: 208), Harrison's description of his song as "written in a childlike manner from realisations that appeared during and after some LSD experiences" (1982: 106) demonstrates its compatibility with the generic and specific objectives of *Yellow Submarine*. Derived from Lennon and McCartney's contemporary nursery rhyme, produced by those who had created the television cartoon series, distinguished by an innocent belief that music and love can change the world, filled with surreal and hallucinatory references, and driven by a conviction that good will triumph over evil, *Yellow Submarine* is above all a modern fairy tale, and the jubilant, if somewhat naïve, message of 'It's All Too Much' is, in fact, an appropriate song with which to close it.

Image and music: experiment

The soundtrack was completed by a series of incidental pieces composed and arranged by George Martin; it was the only genuinely new music in the movie. In 1964, Martin had provided 47 seconds of original linking music for *A Hard Day's Night*; his subsequent Academy Award nomination for Best Original Score was almost certainly the shortest ever to be considered (Yule, 1994: 16–19). However, disagreements between Martin and director Dick Lester during the making of *A Hard Day's Night* led to Martin's exclusion from *Help!* and the appointment of Ken Thorne as its musical director. His participation in *Yellow Submarine* was much more substantial, and he provided 55 minutes of music. But whereas the Beatles' music had preceded, and largely defined, the animation, Martin's orchestral contributions followed, and were largely determined by, that animation:

> There was no room for mistakes. Everything had to be tailor-made to the picture. If a door opened or a funny face appeared at a window, and those moments needed to be pointed up, it was the musical score that had to do the job. (Martin, 1979: 227)

An important distinction between an audience's response to pre-existing songs and scored music is that it is more likely to *listen* to the former, and *hear* the latter. This is not to say that scored music is any less important; indeed, Brown has emphasized three essential roles that such music performs: "a wallpaper soporific, an aesthetic counterbalance to the iconic/representational nature of the cinematic signs, a cogenerator of narrative affect" (1994: 32). However, such music is seldom remembered in itself, and is often devalued in audience recollections; as Donnelly has noted:

> incidental film music can often seem to lack something without [its] image counterparts. The context of the music is crucial and is the cradle of its power ... such music can work outside the film, but its full potential is realised only in the space of the cinema. (2005: 14)

The perception of George Martin's music for *Yellow Submarine* is that it certainly suffers from these disadvantages – especially when compared to the energy and variety of the Beatles' songs. It is no coincidence that the original soundtrack release, which featured the group's songs on Side 1 and Martin's (re-recorded) score on Side 2, has the poorest sales figures of any Beatles' album. But when assessed in conjunction with the film, his music is a plausible and effective narrative catalyst. It anticipates and illustrates the Blue Meanies' invasion of Pepperland; it charts the Beatles' progress through the various seas en route to Pepperland; it introduces and describes key characters, from Ringo Starr to Jeremy Boob. In turn comic, plaintive, jaunty, chaotic, menacing and mysterious, Martin's music also relies on extensive and novel sound effects to achieve its objectives. A telling example comes when the Beatles, stranded in the Sea of Monsters, are threatened by the Vacuum Cleaner Monster, which uses the suction power of its funnel-like trunk to devour its victims:

> How to do it with an orchestra? Suddenly, I hit upon the obvious – backwards music. Music played backwards sounds very odd anyway, and a trombone or cymbal played backwards sounds just like a sucking-in noise. So I scored about forty-five seconds for the orchestra to play, in such a way that the music would fit the picture when we played it backwards. (Martin, 1979: 228)

This sense of experimentation runs throughout Martin's score: his expropriation from the Western movie of stylized war-drums to herald the first appearance of the Blue Meanies; his choice of "avant-garde and weird sounds" (*ibid.*) to accompany the Bridget Riley-derived optical distortions to geometry and perspective in the Sea of Holes; his post-production insistence that "in some places we cut out the music because sound effects worked better, in others we eliminated the sound effects because what I had written sounded better" (*ibid.*: 229). Several decades on, his variegated score stands as an early example of what Kassabian has called "the evaporating segregation of sound, noise and music" (2003: 92).

In a film widely applauded for the vibrant and colourful qualities of its visual invention, Martin's account of his musical strategy contains some remarkable parallels:

> The essence of arranging and orchestrating is first having the necessary vivid imagination to know what kind of sound you want to achieve, and then having the ingenuity and experience to know how to achieve it. Never have we had

> *such a vast range of colours in our musical palette. All the more important to be able to paint with taste.* (Martin, 1983: 83)

When it was first released in 1968, the critical reaction to *Yellow Submarine* was mixed, and its early box-office returns were considerably less than those achieved by *A Hard Day's Night* or *Help!* The Beatles, however, had become increasingly positive about the project, and were easily persuaded to appear as themselves in a brief sequence at the end of the movie, in which they seek to draw attention to the preceding soundtrack, refer explicitly to the redemptive power of music, and urge the departing cinema audience to "go out singing".

Conclusion

Undoubtedly, *Yellow Submarine*'s apparently haphazard assembly of musical items – some old songs from the group's previous records, some 'borrowed' and recycled from its store of discarded material, some new instrumental segments composed by George Martin – was at the time difficult for a general popular-music audience to recognize as an authentic Beatles product. Furthermore, its collection of nursery-rhyme, music-hall, Indian-derived, rock, pop, psychedelic and orchestral styles defied any attempts at easy categorization. However, although audiences may have been deterred by these apparent inconsistencies, there is little doubt that for those involved in its production, the interplay between music and animation was, in fact, far from haphazard, but crucial to its eventual 'classic' status. As animator Tom Halley has confirmed, both were regarded throughout as equally vital and deliberate components of the creative process:

> *The creative look of it, I'm sure, is inspired as much by the music as by those of us who developed the characters and laid out the particular situations. I think* Yellow Submarine *is unique. There have been pretenders and copiers who have failed miserably because they don't understand the philosophy of the design, the graphic qualities, and that superb sense of colour. I think* Yellow Submarine *will always be unique for its time. And the genius of it is that the Beatles' music was both a catalyst for what happened but also linked the whole film together.* (Pritchard and Lysaght, 1998: 262)

There are two important observations that flow from this assertion. First, it must be pointed out that the film itself is constructed around an unusually wide range of visual styles, including op art, pop art, art nouveau, surrealism, comic-book art, photo montage and Dadaism. Such an extravagant miscellany requires an equally varied musical contribution that can reflect in sound the breadth of its artwork. This demand is amplified by the differentiation of locations through which the story travels (from Pepperland to Liverpool via the Seas of Time, Science, Monsters, Heads, Holes and Green) and by the diversity of performative genres from which the journey borrows (vaudeville, pantomime, dance, marching band, rock concert). The musics of *Yellow Submarine* do not therefore detract from its multifarious images, but support and balance them.

Second, there are strong grounds for assessing *Yellow Submarine* as an early example of a postmodernist text. Whether we focus on the *motivation* of postmodernism as "an aesthetic of disturbance which seeks to disrupt the presupposed expectations between reader and text" (Whitley, 2000: 106) or on the appearance in the 1960s of a postmodernist *style* when "artists in many fields began mixing media and incorporating *kitsch* and popular culture into their aesthetic" (Best, 1991: 10), the music and animation of *Yellow Submarine* present a compelling case for inclusion in its developing trajectory. The film explicitly, and persistently, contains many of the strategies associated with the postmodernist project. These include: bricolage (multiple quotation from earlier styles and periods); fragmentation (paradox, contradiction, incongruity); pastiche (imitation of another work, artist or period); parody (imitation for comic or satirical effect); reflexivity (self-conscious reference or attribution to itself); plurality (the absence of a single preferred meaning); irony (the deliberate juxtaposition of meaning); exaggeration (abnormal enlargement or intensification); anti-representation (the deflection of attempts to define 'reality'); meta-art (the admission that all art is constructed). Indeed, although the film's pre-occupation with identity (who are John Lennon, Paul McCartney, George Harrison and Ringo Starr? The Beatles? Sgt Pepper's Lonely Hearts Club Band?) is repeated and re-stated, musically and visually, it is left unresolved, thereby justifying the postmodernist assertion that the only certainty (either here or in Pepperland) is that there are no longer any certainties.

Yellow Submarine thus stands as a pivotal early example of the ways in which an integrated deployment of the aural and the visual throughout a film's production can be mutually advantageous for both mediums. Its animation continues to act as a memorable visual vehicle for its music; the music remains a major catalyst in shaping the public recognition and critical status of the animation. Furthermore, the crucial fact that both songs and images are anchored around the distinctive presence of the Beatles provides a specific historical and cultural signature to its innovative explorations of music and animation.

Note

1. I do not propose to explore the aesthetics and practices of cinema sound and sound effects in this chapter. There is, however, a substantial and relevant body of literature, including: Weis and Belton (1985); Chion (1994); Brophy (1999); Sider (2003); Horn (2006).

References

Best, S. (1991), *Postmodern Theories: Critical Interrogations*, New York: Guilford Press.
Brophy, P. (ed.) (1999), *Cinesonic: The World of Sound in Film*, Sydney: AFTRS.
Brown, P., and Gaines, S. (1983), *The Love You Make*, London: Macmillan.
Brown, R. S. (1994), *Overtones and Undertones: Reading Film Music*, Los Angeles: University of California Press.

Campbell, J. (1949), *The Hero with a Thousand Faces*, Princeton, NJ: Princeton University Press.

Carr, R. (1996), *Beatles at the Movies: Scenes from a Career*, London: UFO.

Chion, M. (1994), *Audio-Vision: Sound on Screen*, New York: Columbia University Press.

Donnelly, K. J. (2005), *The Spectre of Sound: Music in Film and Television*, London: BFI.

Evans, M. (1984), *The Art of the Beatles*, New York: Beech Tree.

Harrison, G. (1982), *I Me Mine*, London: W. H. Allen.

Hertsgaard, M. (1995), *A Day in the Life*, New York: Delacorte.

Horn, G. M. (2006), *Movie Soundtracks and Sound Effects*, Milwaukee: Gareth Stevens.

Kassabian, A. (2003), 'The Sound of a New Film Form', in I. Inglis (ed.), *Popular Music and Film*, London: Wallflower, pp. 91–101.

Kozinn, A. (1995), *The Beatles*, London: Phaidon.

Leary, T. (1968), 'Thank God for the Beatles', in E. E. Davis (ed.), *The Beatles Book*, New York: Cowles, pp. 44–55.

MacDonald, I. (1994), *Revolution in the Head*, London: Fourth Estate.

Martin, G. (1979), *All You Need Is Ears*, New York: St. Martin's Press.

Martin, G. (1983), *Making Music*, London: Pan.

Martin, G. (1994), *Summer of Love: The Making of Sgt Pepper*, London: Macmillan.

Mellers, W. (1973), *Twilight of the Gods: The Beatles in Retrospect*, London: Faber.

Miles, B. (1997), *Paul McCartney: Many Years from Now*, London: Secker & Warburg.

Neaverson, B. (1997), *The Beatles Movies*, London: Cassell.

Norman, P. (1981), *Shout! The True Story of the Beatles*, London: Hamish Hamilton.

O'Grady, T. J. (1983), *The Beatles: A Musical Evolution*, Boston: Twayne.

Palmer, T. (1976), *All You Need Is Love: The Story of Popular Music*, London: Weidenfeld & Nicolson.

Pritchard, D., and Lysaght, A. (1998), *The Beatles: An Oral History*, Toronto: Stoddart.

Sheff, D., and Golson, G. B. (1981), *The Playboy Interviews with John Lennon & Yoko Ono*, New York: Playboy Press.

Sider, L. (ed.) (2003), *Soundscape: The School of Sound Lectures 1998–2001*, London/New York: Wallflower.

Spitz, M. (2006), *The Beatles: The Biography*, New York: Little, Brown & Company.

Tincknell, E. (2006), 'The Soundtrack Movie, Nostalgia and Consumption', in I. Conrich and E. Tincknell (eds), *Film's Musical Moments*, Edinburgh: Edinburgh University Press, pp. 132–45.

Turner, S. (1994), *A Hard Day's Write*, London: Carlton.

Weis, E., and Belton, J. (eds) (1985), *Film Sound: Theory and Practice*, New York: Columbia University Press.

Whitley, E. (2000), 'The Postmodern White Album', in I. Inglis (ed.), *The Beatles, Popular Music and Society: A Thousand Voices*, London: Macmillan, pp. 105–25.

Wright, R. (2003), 'Score vs Song: Art, Commerce and the H Factor in Film and Television Music', in I. Inglis (ed.), *Popular Music and Film*, London: Wallflower, pp. 8–21.

Yule, A. (1994), *The Man Who 'Framed' the Beatles*, New York: Donald I. Fine.

5 Polar Grooves

Dance, Music and Musicality in Happy Feet

Philip Hayward

Australian director George Miller established an international reputation through his post-apocalyptic *Mad Max* trilogy (1979, 1982 and 1985) and enjoyed further success with his two live-action + animatronics features *Babe* (1995) and *Babe: Pig in the City* (1998). *Happy Feet* – co-directed with Judy Morris and Warren Coleman – was Miller's first digital animation project. Released in 2006, the film more than delivered on its US$100-million production budget, earning US$385 million in cinema income alone.[1] The film was also a significant critical success, winning Best Animated Feature at the 79th Academy Awards.

Happy Feet is (mainly) set in the Antarctic and concerns a community of Emperor penguins (*Aptenodytes forsteri*), the largest living species of the flightless bird. Popular interest in polar fauna has risen in recent years, as manifested by documentaries such as John Weiley's IMAX film *Antarctica* (1991), the acclaimed BBC/National Geographic series *Life in the Freezer* (1993) and Luc Jaquet's Academy Award-winning documentary *La Marche de l'empereur* (2005) (released as *March of the Penguins* in anglophone markets). However, despite its popularity with media audiences, the species has experienced a significant decline in numbers since regular surveys commenced, with the current population estimated to be at only 50 per cent of the levels observed in the mid-twentieth century. Researchers such as Barbraud and Weimerskirch (2006) have identified a particularly sharp reduction in numbers since the 1970s and attribute this to an increase in southern oceanic temperatures that has depleted the penguins' key food source, oceanic krill. While the evidence is inconclusive, Barbraud and Weimerskirch and other researchers point to global warming as a likely cause of this temperature shift.

In press interviews accompanying the film's release in the USA and Australia, Miller stressed the manner in which the film's theme arose from his discovery that Emperor penguins use their voices to identify each other in crowded colonies. As he has explained:

> When I saw that they sang to each other – to differentiate each other and find a mate – I said, "OK, we've got penguins and they'll sing"... Suddenly, I found myself in the middle of a musical. And there's a penguin who can't sing, but can dance. It became what I call an accidental musical.[2]

Miller's characterization of the penguins' vocal communication as "singing" – and its interpretation in *Happy Feet* as human vocal singing – are of course anthropomorphic. This is within the classic cinematic tradition of endowing animated animal characters with human attributes in order to make them appealing to (human) audiences, a tradition that runs from early Mickey Mouse cartoons through to the present. In *Happy Feet*'s narrative the penguins' distinctive vocal utterances are further romanticized as "heart songs" that act as expressions of core identity. As *Happy Feet* composer John Powell has commented:

> Scientists have recorded their sounds and determined that each squawk is unique. When they're wandering around looking for each other, they're squawking and listening, and if they like the other person's squawk and it's mutual, they come together for mating. In our movie, they happen to be singing iconic songs. (quoted in Ball, 2006)

Against this background of concentrated vocality, the plight and narrative progress of the film's only non-singing penguin (the appropriately named 'Mumble', voiced by Elijah Wood) is central to the film as he attempts to establish tap-dancing as his personal identity marker. Intertwined with this is a narrative concerning human pollution of Antarctic environments. After scenes depicting human detritus, such as plastic waste and abandoned machinery, the film culminates with Mumble, then a massed ensemble of penguins tap-dancing in front of human observers to convey the impact of human activity on the fragile polar ecosystem. In the film's finale this novel form of communication is shown to have paid off as governments agree to a moratorium on Antarctic fishing.[3]

This chapter analyses the operation of the "accidental musical" text of the film. It considers the nature of the 'iconic' songs presented, the role of tap-dancing in relation to these and – in conclusion – how these relate to the eco-political messages that are heavily inscribed within (sections of) the text.[4]

Musical components

In a process that is increasingly common in larger-budget films that combine popular-song material and orchestral scoring, the audio product components of the multimedia *Happy Feet* package (which also includes a lavish website[5]) comprise two CDs (both released in 2006 on Atlantic/WEA). The first release was *Music From The Motion Picture Happy Feet*, featuring extended versions of the popular-music tracks from the film (together with a tokenistic 5-minute medley of the orchestral score as the final track). The second CD, released after the film, was a CD of orchestral sequences entitled *Happy Feet Original Score – Music By John Powell*. The music present in the film and CDs can be divided into three main categories – original score, popular-song material and tap-dance sequences – all of which overlap to a significant extent (as discussed below).[6]

Original score

John Powell trained at Trinity College of Music in London and performed in British rock and jazz bands before establishing a company to produce music for European TV advertisements, TV programmes and films. Following freelance work with the prolific Hollywood composer Hans Zimmer in the late 1980s (when he worked on music programming for Zimmer's contributions to the score of Randal Kleiser's *White Fang* [1991]), Powell moved to the USA in 1997 and began work with Zimmer's Media Ventures production house. This employment familiarized him with the company's and (in particular) Zimmer's trademark combination of orchestral and digital scoring to create high-impact soundtracks, typified by his Academy Award-winning scores for *The Prince of Egypt* (Brenda Chapman, Simon Wells and Steve Hickner, 1998) and Ridley Scott's *Gladiator* (2001). Powell was approached by George Miller to work on *Happy Feet* in 2001, largely on the strength of his collaborative work with fellow Media Ventures composer Harry Gregson-Miller on soundtracks for the animated films *Antz* (Eric Darnell and Tim Johnson, 1998), *Chicken Run* (Peter Lord and Nick Park, 2000) and *Shrek* (Andrew Jameson and Vicky Jenson, 2001). One aspect of his work on these films that particularly attracted Miller's interest was Powell's ability to combine original scores with popular-song material.

Powell's contribution to the final score for *Happy Feet* combined original material (including orchestral, choral and popular-music compositions) and arrangements and medleys of popular-song material.[7] The high production budget for *Happy Feet* allowed him the luxury of writing several sequences for large musical ensembles (performed by the Sydney Symphony Orchestra and Sydney Philharmonic Choir for the recording). One of the most striking of these occurs early in the narrative during the long, bleak winter period when the male penguins huddle together to incubate eggs while the female penguins leave in search of fish. This sequence works effectively with its score to provide a sense of the masculine fortitude and solidarity that enables the group to survive the experience. Powell emphasizes these aspects with a composition for choir and orchestra (referred to on the *Original Score* CD as 'The Huddle'). The piece begins with unaccompanied massed male voices chanting unintelligibly; a drum part is then added to the mix before the orchestra enters, creating a rich and highly dense passage that continues with variations in density and intensity to the conclusion. The alternation of staccato, guttural passages and more conventional choral harmonies evokes Carl Orff's cantata *Carmina Burana* (1935). A second notable use of this chant pattern occurs at the end of the film as the older Emperor penguins resist Mumble's attempts to get the colony tap-dancing. The internal conflict is represented by the younger penguins tapping while the older birds stand on the slopes above them chanting the old chants in an attempt to sonically repel the blasphemous innovation that Mumble promotes.

The most extended orchestral passage in the film occurs during the trek by Mumble and his companions across mountains and ice sheets to find the 'alien' base. The sequence (referred to on the CD as 'Fun Food Storm', Track 21) has a number of the trademarks associated with Music Ventures (and ultimately derived from orchestral works such as Stravinsky's *Rite of Spring* [1913]), including alternating atmospheric high string and brass parts (and occasional choral vocables) with orchestral stabs and sustained ostinati. Prominent digital drum patterns are used to enhance rhythmic drive and intensity. This sequence is succeeded by another equally dramatic one – using similar musical ingredients – as Mumble and his companions are menaced by killer whales near the base. To accompany this, Powell provides a musically busy and varied passage of (often dissonant) brass parts, urgent string patterns, militaristic snare-drum sounds and frequent intensifications of volume and rhythms, before ending with the incongruous sound of an electric organ as the penguins make good their escape.

In addition to short 'functional' cues and the featured compositions discussed above, several of Powell's popular-music compositions support and extend the musical association of place and characters established by non-original tracks. This is most evident during Mumble's visit to the Adele penguin colony, which is given a strong Latino flavour through the prominent presence of an arrangement of Catalan–Cuban bandleader Xavier Cugat's composition 'Cui Cui' (1955)[8] and Powell's musically similar 'Adeleland' during the initial sequences.

Popular song

In addition to Powell's original instrumental compositions in a contemporary idiom, there are three types of popular song used in *Happy Feet*:

   a)   original songs;
   b)   versions of previously recorded songs represented as being performed by animated characters;
   c)   previously recorded music that features (non-diegetically) during particular sequences.

The first category refers to one particular number, 'The Song Of The Heart', written and performed by Prince.[9] The composition was one of the key tracks used to promote the film and it appears as the first track on the *Original Soundtrack* CD. The song features rich instrumentation of brass, keyboards and guitar around powerful funk percussion, together with Prince's signature falsetto yelps and clipped melodic lines. Its success in expressing the film's theme and popularizing it was recognized by a Golden Globe Award for Best Original Song in a Motion Picture. Illustrating the manner by which even major Hollywood productions are less than meticulously planned enterprises, the song was a last-minute addition to the film (explaining its position under the end-credits rather than any incorporation into the narrative). Powell has identified that Prince was originally approached to allow a lyrical revision of his 1986 song 'Kiss' rather than contribute new material:

> It was a very last minute thing – the score was finished, and everything else was finished. But he [Prince] came up with this great song, and George

> listened to it and was very happy with it. Prince was [initially] shown the film
> to try to get him to approve a lyric change. And he discovered he liked the
> film, and was inspired by it – and he came up with this song almost
> immediately. But it was very much a last minute thing, so unfortunately I
> didn't get to have any collaboration with him.[10]

As the late inclusion of Prince's track suggests, there was also a substantial element of
fortuity in the selection of the second category of popular songs identified above. The
selection process involved Miller and Powell identifying material for possible inclusion
in the score, with the latter attempting to adapt and weld disparate elements into a
whole that served the narrative and characterization:

> if it wasn't going to work, it wasn't because I hadn't tried. If the lyrics were
> good, but the song sounded (in its original form) opposite to what we
> wanted, I always made sure that I could give it a go and turn it around into
> something completely different – if that's what we needed. Sometimes that
> worked, and sometimes it didn't. We tried it with a lot of numbers … We
> discarded a lot, obviously, because you probably end up with a 5% success
> rate – it's such a mad endeavour… I think I have about five CDs full of
> arrangements of just some of the song numbers, which ultimately only make
> up about 25 minutes in the film. There are lots of things we tried, where some
> were close, some definitely didn't work, and some ended up in the movie.

While not specifically identified by Powell, this serial experimentation provided major
difficulties for music supervisor Christine Woodruff and her team, requiring them constantly to research ownership and seek permissions for use of copyright material. Since
clearances were not always successful, several songs planned for inclusion had to be
withdrawn from early versions of the film, necessitating fresh choices, negotiations and
then new arrangements and recordings of successfully cleared material. The somewhat
haphazard nature of the score's assemblage emphasizes the considerable time and
money available for big-budget productions.

   Given that the majority of the pre-written music used in the film was featured in
adapted, abbreviated and/or medley contexts, new recordings were made of most of the
film's song material. Initial versions of these songs were made using experienced Los
Angeles-based demo singers (incurring further facilities and personnel costs) and these,
in turn, were used to select and try out well-known actors whose (vocal) presence
could boost box-office appeal. This approach draws on two models. The first is the
practice of using recognizable star actors to voice characters in animation films that was
pioneered by Jon Lasseter's *Toy Story* (1995) (which featured Tom Hanks and Tim Allen
in key roles) and honed in *Shrek* (2001) (utilizing such luminaries as Eddie Murphy,
Mike Myers and Cameron Diaz). The second (allied) element was utilizing the vocal
talents of screen actors in conjunction with digital post-production facilities (such as
pitch-fixing[11]) to allow performers with less than fully developed singing abilities to
deliver creditable song performances. The specific inspiration for *Happy Feet* in this

regard was fellow Australian director Baz Luhrmann's 2001 feature *Moulin Rouge!*, with actors such as Ewan McGregor, Richard Roxburgh and *Happy Feet* performer Nicole Kidman.

Many of the songs featured in *Happy Feet* are assembled as medleys interweaving different song texts. The earliest example of this establishes the manner by which songs operate to bring penguin couples together. Norma Jean, a young female penguin, voiced by Nicole Kidman (doing a Marilyn-Monroe vocal impression that befits her character's name[12]), is shown singing her heart song 'Kiss' as she walks through a crowd of ardent male penguin admirers. Unconvinced by her suitors, she turns away, only to be arrested by the sight of Memphis (voiced by Hugh Jackman) singing Elvis Presley's 1956 hit 'Heartbreak Hotel'. Attracted to each other, the two penguins signal their intention to become romantically involved by interweaving their performances into a duet that ends with them represented as a couple.

The scene was intended to represent the vocal exchange and acceptance that mark long-bonded male–female relationships in Emperor penguin colonies. Powell has indicated that Miller originally intended to include more sequences of this kind but that, in an intertextual media environment, this proved unnecessary:

> When we started, we thought we were going to have to do a lot more of these coming together songs, but since [the documentary] March of the Penguins, a lot more people have been educated on what's going on and we don't have to hammer the point home so much. (Powell, quoted in Ball, 2006)

As the presence of Kidman emphasizes, this sequence, and many others in the film, shows the influence of *Moulin Rouge!*[13] and, in particular, its use of disjunctured, 'mashed-up' song dialogues between romantically aligned characters to address and resolve tensions. The clearest point of comparison in this regard is to Kidman (Satine) and Ewan McGregor (Christian) in *Moulin Rouge!* as they exchange snippets of seminal popular love songs during an attempted rooftop seduction (in the sequence called 'Elephant Love Medley' on the CD soundtrack). Extending beyond a call-and-response style medley, these numbers have rearranged instrumental parts and interwoven melodic and lyrical lines from original songs, and they provide an appropriate format for use in several key scenes.

One of the central narrative threads of *Happy Feet* concerns the interaction and eventual coupling of Mumble and the young female penguin Gloria, voiced by Brittany Murphy. As an actress not previously known as a singer, much attention was given to Murphy's singing performances in promotional material for the film. Gloria/Murphy's first feature song in the film is a version of Queen's 1976 hit single 'Somebody To Love', sung as the climax of the young penguins' graduation celebration. The version featured in *Happy Feet* further emphasizes the gospel element of the original (which was written and sung by Freddie Mercury, reputedly in tribute to soul singer Aretha Franklin).[14] Murphy provides a spirited rendition within the contemporary soul-pop style (derived from elements of Mariah Carey's and Whitney Houston's repertoires) that has come to signal 'soul' in TV programmes such as *American Idol*. This involves strong dynamics, featured high notes, showy vocal melismas and prominent vibrato on sustained notes.[15] Murphy uses a similar vocal approach in her performance of Gloria's heart song, Earth Wind and Fire's 1979 dance hit 'Boogie Wonderland' (discussed below).

Disdained by both his peers and his elders for his lack of vocal skills, and unable to consolidate his attraction to Gloria by providing a convincing heart song, Mumble is depressed and wanders from home. Chancing across a colony of (Latino-accented) Adele penguins, he is befriended by a posse of young males led by Ramon (voiced by Robin Williams), who appreciate his dancing. Upon learning about his romantic plight, Ramon offers to solve the problem, and the Adele posse accompany him back to the Emperors' area. During his absence Gloria has still not found her lovemate and, in an echo of his father's courtship of his mother, Mumble strikes a pose on the ice and (apparently) delivers a rousing Spanish-language version of 'My Way' ('A Mi Manera'). Not falling for the ruse, Gloria discovers that Ramon, hidden behind Mumble, is the actual vocal source. Hurt and disappointed by the attempted deception, Gloria turns away. In desperation, Mumble taps out a rhythm (Figure 5.1), and invites Gloria to sing to it. After an initial refusal, Gloria eases her way into his groove and begins delivering a rousing version of 'Boogie Wonderland' featuring Mumble's tap patterns as a polyrhythm. Here I'm using the term 'groove' in the expanded sense offered by John Miller Chernoff (1979) of the groove being a pattern, a system of logic and flow, that animates and orientates those who 'get into' it and allows them to share a feeling of communal 'grooviness'.

Figure 5.1   Mumble's initial tapped rhythm pattern (transcribed by present author)[16]

The song serves as an anthem for both Mumble's belief in his rhythms and Gloria's growing belief in him, as its lyrics preach faith in the power of the 'boogie wonderland' as an affirmation of love and passion. Incorporating a range of rhythms, the song base progressively unites the younger penguins in the colony. Initially, the Adeles dance along with Mumble while the Emperors sing back-up. Unable to resist the rhythms, the young Emperors also join in the dance, following Mumble's dance leads in a call-and-response pattern until he taps out such a fast, complex break (Figure 5.2) that the mass acknowledge his dexterity by simply answering with a single stomp.

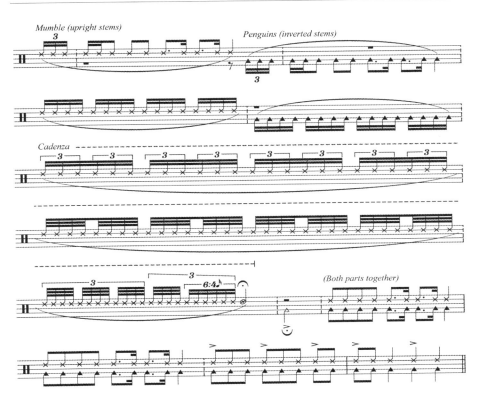

Figure 5.2 Mumble's final virtuoso tapped rhythm pattern and the response (transcribed by present author)

This triumphal moment is, however, abruptly cut short as the old penguins intervene, identify Mumble's dancing as an abominable deviance, and banish him from the colony. This exile switches the film into its second stage, Mumble's journey in search of confirmation of alien (human) existence and their disruption of the environment. After an unsuccessful attempt to board a fishing ship, Mumble swims north and ends up interned in an American zoo, where he manages to attract children's attention through dancing. He returns to the colony at the end of the film, leading a team of scientists to visit the Emperors' territory. Persuading even the elders of the need to dance in order to communicate, he leads a triumphant finale that also sees the scientists themselves tapping along in inter-species communication and harmony.

In terms of those songs used in the score (in relatively unmodified forms) that are *not* voiced by on-screen characters, perhaps the most significant are the paired tracks 'Jump And Move', by the Brand New Heavies (1994), and the Beach Boys' 'Do It Again' (1968). The former track, featuring rapid ragga toasting by Jamalski, gives a Caribbean carnival feel to the young penguins' procession to the shore, where they gather in nervous anticipation of their first swim. Sliding down by accident, Mumble shoots through the crowd into the water. The music pauses and, when he emerges unscathed, 'Do It Again' (brightly remixed for Dolby 5.1 sound) bursts onto the soundtrack. Originally recorded and released in mid-1968, the song is a rhythmically insistent, mid-tempo number, featuring Mike Love on lead vocals and harking back (both lyrically and thematically) to the Beach Boys' 'surf and fun' singles of the early 1960s (as opposed to their late-1960s neo-psychedelic phase). Accompanying images of exhilarating fun activities and joyous young animals under blue skies, in sparkling light and crystal-clear seas, the song 'California-izes' the Antarctic, casting it (literally) in a warm, summery glow. In this context, the graceful ease and spectacle of the underwater synchronized moves the penguins perform is more appropriately represented via the film's knowing nod to Busby Berkeley's aquatic routines in *Million Dollar Mermaid* (1952) than by the more challenging oceanic environment represented in *Life in the Freezer* (1993).

Tap-dance music

As previous sections have emphasized, tap dance is a central aspect of *Happy Feet*'s narrative and score. The form is an American vernacular performance practice that is commonly regarded as having its origins in traditions as diverse as European clog dancing, Irish jigs and African American shuffle dances and to have emerged in its present form in the 1900s in vaudeville theatres (see Frank, 1995, and Stearns and Stearns, 1994). Early synch-sound films used the talents of established vaudeville performers such as the African American actor-dancer Bill 'Bojangles' Robinson, who had a cameo dance role in Luther Reed's feature *Dixiana* (1930). One of the most successful performers to cross over in the 1930s was Ruby Keeler, who starred in *42nd Street* (Lloyd Bacon, 1933) and *Dames* (Ray Enright and Busby Berkeley, 1934), two productions that paired her with production/choreographic designer Busby Berkeley. Many early tap performers stayed more or less on a single spot, concentrating on rhythmic impact and dexterity rather than the more free-travelling style of the later 1930s that was influenced by dance forms such as 'Lindy Hopping'. Since its heyday in the 1930s and 1940s tap-dancing has undergone periodic revivals and has been championed by notable individual performers such as Gregory Hines (1946–2003), who starred in the 1989 feature film *Tap*, along with veteran performer Sammy Davis Jr and (then) rising dance star Savion Glover. Outside the United States, tap-dancing also received a significant image and associative 'makeover' in Australia in the 1990s. Dancer Dein Perry, who had become familiar with tap styles through his role in the stage revival of *42nd Street* in Sydney, achieved this in 1994 when he designed *Tap Dogs*, an award-winning stage show featuring muscular, proletarian-styled dance routines. He choreographed a similar sequence for the 2000 Sydney Olympics opening ceremony and also adapted the approach to film in his 2000 feature *Bootmen*.

Animating character movement in precise synchronization to sonic rhythms is a major task for cinema animators (analogue *or* digital) and the effectiveness of *Happy Feet*'s animation sequences is due in large part to the use of human dancers whose movements were motion-captured (through body sensors) and digitized. Sound recordist Simon Leadley has described how:

> a low-res version of the penguins' movements [appeared] *on screen* while the performers danced, walked and moved during the scenes. In this way it was exactly like a real shoot, with the ability to change virtually anything in post-production. It was actually quite similar in concept to Midi, where a performance is captured then manipulated and/or refined later in the production process. (2007: 52)

The lead dancer, used to provide Mumble's dance routines, was the accomplished US tap performer Savion Glover. In order to make the task easier for digital animators, Glover – and dancers employed for other characters – studied penguins and learnt to affect their posture (such as straight arm/flipper movements), under the guidance of Australian choreographer Kelley Abbey.

Writing in the *New York Times*, dance critic John Rockwell (2006) both argued that Glover's contribution to the film had been understated in publicity and identified that Mumble's on-screen performances are "unmistakably Savion – the widely spaced feet brushing the floor (ice), the dazzling ornamental flourishes, the spot-on musicality that distinguishes all of Mr. Glover's performances". While detailed discussion of the choreography featured in various sequences is beyond the scope of this chapter, Rockwell's reference to musicality is salient. While often considered as essentially choreographic (via its specification as 'dance'), tap-dancing produces sonic and spatial rhythmic patterns simultaneously, with both activities enhancing the other and contributing to a combined aesthetic effect.

Contemporary tap-dancing utilizes different patterns of striking steel-tapped shoes to produce rhythms, often featuring syncopation, acceleration and deceleration (and associated rises and falls in volume and sonic attack). *Happy Feet*'s lead 'dance modeller', Glover, is commonly acknowledged to be the most adept and ambitious contemporary tap-dancer and is known for his ambition (designing tap performances to accompany the music of classical composers such as Vivaldi and Bartók and jazz greats such as John Coltrane and Thelonius Monk) and for his perception of his work *as* musical.[17] This musical identity also informs his participation in the jazz band The Otherz, in which he features as foot percussionist, alongside saxophonist Patience Higgins.

For *Happy Feet*, the sounds of his taps were recorded simultaneously with the dance routines and then post-produced to provide the tap-dance sounds heard in the final film mix. Sound designer Wayne Pashley and his crew captured the sound of Glover's tapping shoes through a combination of microphones fixed in his shoes and a boom mike that followed his actions. Given that the analogue sound habitually created by Glover is produced by the interaction of his steel-capped shoes with a wooden floor, post-production of these sounds required a degree of imaginative modification to approximate what tapping might sound like on polar surfaces. This was attempted through a digital combination of the original tap sounds and samples of impact upon the different polar surfaces where the dances occur, i.e., hard ice, firm snow, slush, etc.[18] These married sounds were then forwarded to Glover for approval and they "became the whole premise of the percussion track of the musical numbers. From there the composer took those taps and built the music around it" (Pashley, quoted in Cohen, 2006).

The musical invention in these routines (such as the 'Boogie Wonderland' sequence notated earlier) confirms director George Miller's description of Glover: "He's a dazzling percussionist ... His rhythms are so complex and sophisticated. Tap-dancing is music you make with your body, and Savion is a virtuoso."[19]

In these regards, Mumble's eschewal of singing the fairly standard western popular songs that comprise the core repertoire of 'heart songs' for Emperor penguins in the film is less a rejection of musicality in favour of dance than an expansion of musical expressivity beyond the predictable fare offered in the film. Empowered with Glover's musical dexterity, the *sound* of Mumble's dancing embodies a greater musical accomplishment and originality than the (karaokesque) signature songs that emanate from other characters. Indeed, throughout the film it is through dance that individuality and cultural plurality are most manifest. In the finale, in particular, difference is celebrated through diversity. As ensemble choreographer and principal motion-capture performer Kelley elaborates:

> everyone finally lets themselves go, the penguins are expressing themselves in different ways, so we have some flamenco, some tango, some Riverdancing. Then there's Zulu, gumboot, Navajo and Samoan slap dancing ... When the penguins come together in this universal language of dance, it becomes part of the larger message of the film.[20]

Conclusion

As a film produced in the early twenty-first century, *Happy Feet* developed during a period of rising debate and controversy over environmental issues, particularly global warming, which was made manifest in media products such as Roland Emmerich's apocalyptic fiction film *The Day after Tomorrow* (2004) and *An Inconvenient Truth*, Davis Guggenheim's 2006 film version of former US vice president Al Gore's illustrated lecture on climate change. In this regard *Happy Feet* can be seen as a successful commercial media product that expresses (one side of) the zeitgeist of the times and can – from an Eco-Green viewpoint at least – be seen as a positive contribution to increased awareness of environmental issues and human impacts on non-human species. That it achieves this through anthropomorphism of its animal protagonists is hardly surprising. However, what is more arresting is the film's extreme 'Americanomorphism' of the animal population of the Antarctic. In this regard, it is precisely through performances of styles and specific repertoires of US popular music and the adoption of the vernacular US dance form of tap that the animals become sufficiently 'Americanomorphized' to merit audience sympathies. At a time when the USA is afflicted with a severe global image problem, in which the nation is perceived as intolerant of alternative political views and/or religious affiliations (let alone inter-species issues), this creates a disturbing undercurrent to *Happy Feet*'s narrative and narrative resolution.

This undercurrent also manifests itself in another way. One of the most unfortunate things about *Happy Feet* – as a notionally liberal, eco-progressive film – is how easily it can be read in terms of (and as representative of) entrenched racial stereotyping in US society. This is particularly evident in the sonic text. The Emperors (note the name) can easily be imagined as representing the WASP mainstream (with its fundamentalist and progressive wings) while the tricksy but carnivalesque Adele penguins are overtly signified in vocal and musical tracks as (parodic) Hispanics. Representations of African Americans are more opaque. Musically, many of the featured songs originate from African American performers and/or genre traditions, yet the most prominent vocal performers are Euro-Americans, such as Brittany Murphy, whose vocal imitation of soul singers provides the musical lead opposite Mumble's dancing. The latter is another opaque element, produced by Glover – the unseen human agent of the percussive tap-dance music that provides the film's sonic and choreographic highlights. His percussion music is also invisible in another sense. Despite the fundamental role that George Miller and Wayne Pashley have attributed to Glover's tap routines in the composition of music for the dance sequences, these do not register in the film's copyright music credits. His work is heard but invisible, rendered incidental, unheralded and unremunerated by royalties despite its central role in the film and its soundtrack – an unfortunate endnote to a film about tolerance, inclusivity and equality of creative expression.

Acknowledgements

Thanks to Jerome Maludid for his transcription assistance and comments on rhythm and to Rebecca Coyle for her discussion of an earlier draft of this chapter. This chapter originated from Australia Research Council Discovery Project Grant DP 0770026 'Music Production and Technology in Australian Film: Enabling Australian Film to Embrace Innovation'.

Notes

1. Box-office figures are taken from trade press information summarized at http://boxofficemojo.com/movies/?id=happyfeet.htm (accessed August 2007).
2. See D. Maddox (2006), 'Baby it's cold outside', *The Age* online, 24 December (http://www.the age.com.au/news/film/penguin/21/116629068158.html).
3. Thereby implying this is a major factor in penguin depletion – an aspect not emphasized by scientific researchers in the field.

4. While dialogue and sound effects play an important role in the production, detailed discussion of these is beyond the scope of this specific chapter. See Leadley (2007) for an insider's account of the sound design and production of the film.
5. *Happy Feet* official website at: http://www2.warnerbros.com/happyfeet/.
6. My triple characterization differs from accounts such as Leadley (2007), which identifies three primary production components: original score, adapted songs and sourced material. My categorization is a critical-strategic one, isolating tap-dancing as a conceptual and musical focus of the film.
7. Together with arrangers John Ashton Thomas, James McKee Smith and Gavin Greenaway.
8. Co-composed with Fausto Curbelo and Albert Stillman for the soundtrack of Daniel Mann's 1955 film *I'll Cry Tomorrow.*
9. Prince's engagement with the film and his ability to quickly produce a song acceptable to the producers reflect both his song-writing skills and his familiarity with the medium of film. He has previously written material for productions such as Tim Burton's *Batman* (1989) and directed his own films, such as *Under the Cherry Moon* (1986).
10. This and the following quotation from Powell are taken from D. Goldwasser, 'Toe Tappin' and Knee Slappin', interview with John Powell, 11 November 2006 (online at: http://www.soundtrack.net/features/article/?id=211).
11. Where individual notes and/or sequences can be pitch altered in final mixes.
12. Norma Jean Baker being Monroe's original name.
13. Norma Jean/Kidman's Monroesque version of 'Kiss' also clearly evokes Satine/Kidman's performance of 'Diamonds Are A Girl's Best Friend'/'Material Girl' in *Moulin Rouge!* as she bedazzles a room full of men.
14. In Queen's original version Mercury was backed by rich choral harmonies provided by multi-tracking band members' vocal lines.
15. Mumble points to exactly this formulaic aspect of her performance in an exchange where he dissuades her from accompanying him on his quest for the humans. Deliberately trying to upset her, he refers to her vocal style as "showy", "flashy" and "frou-frou". These comments have the desired effect and Gloria departs. (N.B. 'Frou-frou' is a term originally used to describe a dress that was overly ornamented and/or frivolous; in this context, it refers to the ornamentation and artifice of her habitual performance style.)
16. No time signature is given as the sequence uses various rhythmic patterns.
17. In a recent interview in *Jazz Times*, for instance, Glover asserted his musicality in the statement "I'm falling in love with the fact that I really have a chance to express myself as a percussionist" (Chinen, 2006).
18. See Cohen (2006) and Leadley (2007) for further discussion.
19. Quoted in HJ (2006), 'It's all in the dance', *HollywoodJesus.Com*, online at: http://www.hollywoodjesus.com/dvdDetail.cfm/i/8E7DE100-9045-D3AF-F548C1EDCDCA9649/ia/E42AFCEB-DA34-3509-95390EB8D80F4A06.
20. *Ibid.*

References

Ball, R. (2006), 'Happy Feet Composer John Powell', *Animation Magazine*, 17 November; online at: www.animationmagazine.net/article.php?article_id=6162

Barbraud, C., and Weimerskirch, H. (2006), 'Antarctic Birds Breed Later in Response to Climate Change', *Proceedings of the National Academy of Sciences of the United States of America*, 103(16), 00–00 (online at www.pubmedcentral.nih.gov/articlerender.fcgi?artid=1458863).

Chernoff, J. (1979), *African Rhythm and African Sensibility: Aesthetics and Social Action in African Musical Idioms*, Chicago: University of Chicago Press.

Chinen, N. (2006), 'Before and After with Savion Glover' (interview), *Jazz Times*, September, 00–00 (online at: www.jazztimes.com/columns_and_features/before_and_after/index.cfm?artist=36&action=about_the_artist).

Cohen, D. (2006), 'Feet Team Taps New Techniques: Glover's Movements, Sound Recorded on Motion-capture Stage', *Variety*, 4 January (online at: http://www.variety.com/awardcentral_article/VR1117956689.html?nav=soundvision07).

Frank, R. E. (1995), *Tap! The Greatest Tap Stars and Their Stories: 1900–1955*, New York: Da Capo.

Leadley, S. (2007), 'Happy Feet', *AudioTechnology*, 52, 52–8.

Rockwell, J. (2006), 'Penguin, Shmenguin! Those Are Savion Glover's Happy Feet!', *New York Times*, 28 December (online at: http://www.nytimes.com/2006/12/28/movies/28happ.html?ex=1324962000&en=f9b032638343ede9&ei=5090&partner=rssuserland&emc=rss).

Stearns, M., and Stearns, J. (1994), *Jazz Dance: The Story of American Vernacular Dance*, New York: Da Capo.

6 Minstrelsy and Musical Framing in *Who Framed Roger Rabbit*

Neil Lerner

In observing that "*Who Framed Roger Rabbit* is both time machine and time capsule" (Cholondenko, 1991: 217), Alan Cholondenko draws attention to that film's ambivalent chronological status. The film points on the one hand back to the past – drawing as richly as it does on the so-called golden age of US animation in the earlier part of the twentieth century – while also looking ahead to a desired (and indeed resultant) resurgence of interest in animation as a cultural and commercial form. (When *Who Framed Roger Rabbit* first appeared in 1988, *The Simpsons* and Disney's *The Little Mermaid* [Ron Clements and John Musker, 1989] were both still a year away from re-energizing their respective genres and audiences, to cite but two examples.[1]) That paradoxical blend of nostalgia and prophecy, mixed with a dash of historical white-washing, characterized Robert Zemeckis's earlier film, *Back to the Future* (1985), and its Reagan-era worshipping of the 1950s as a golden age of suburban bliss, sock hops, and oedipal complications. As a time capsule, *Who Framed Roger Rabbit* (Zemeckis, 1988; henceforth *WFRR*) situates its narrative in the year 1947 – unlike Gary K. Wolf's contemporaneously set 1981 novel, *Who Censored Roger Rabbit?*, on which the film was based – although it has much to tell us about 1988, the film's year of release. Much of the initial (and persistent) response to *WFRR*[2] rhapsodized about its remarkable fusion of live-action and animated filming and the historic on-screen meeting of characters like Mickey Mouse and Bugs Bunny. Aiming our gaze only at those compelling visions, however, can misdirect us from the film's problematic subtexts.[3]

The 1942 Warner Bros. cartoon *Fresh Hare* (Friz Freleng, 1942), which one is unlikely to find appearing on television in its original form, begins with the familiar narrative trope of Elmer Fudd in hot – and of course inept – pursuit of Bugs Bunny. After Bugs toys with him for the first six and a half minutes, he suddenly surrenders to Elmer, allowing himself to be handcuffed to him (in certain ways not unlike the future handcuffing of Roger Rabbit and Eddie Valiant) and then led to the place where he is to be executed. Standing blindfolded (and munching a carrot) in front of a firing squad, Bugs is offered one last wish by Elmer. He appears to ponder his options before responding "I wish ... I wish ..." and then singing "I wish I was in Dixie, hooray, hooray". Suddenly the five members of the firing squad, Elmer, and Bugs all appear as blackface minstrels (Elmer with the tambourine and Bugs picking at a banjo), a cotton plantation appears in the background, and the song changes to 'Camptown Races'. As they conclude their finale, Bugs looks to the audience and declares, "Fantastic, isn't it?" That blackface minstrelsy, the uniquely North American form of performance that originated in the mid-nineteenth century (see Lott, 1993) should erupt at the end of a Bugs Bunny cartoon – indeed, the appearance of the minstrels delivers the violent rhetorical punch leading up from the intended execution – may be shocking to some today, but the antebellum minstrel show bubbles up in many examples of US animation throughout the twentieth century. Mickey Mouse does not wear white gloves because he has sensitive hands, but because of their iconic link back to the minstrel stage.[4] The central tension of the minstrel show identified by Eric Lott – the paradox that minstrelsy allowed whites to indulge their hatred of black people together with their desire for African Americans' supposed hypersexuality – re-emerges in *WFRR*, which continues in that tradition.[5]

Michael Cohen reads *WFRR* with particular attention to "what at best can be called an insensitive attitude to marginal or minority groups" (Cohen, 1999: 147), finding strong similarities in the situation of the film's Toons with that of Asian and African Americans. The Toons, as Cohen writes,

> *bungle work because of shiftlessness and incompetence; they cannot get the simplest thing right, but they work very cheaply. Physically they are strong, practically indestructible, but they are also unpredictable and emotional. They are more affected by liquor than sober whites. They are colorful and interesting, vibrant and alive, but also threatening and dangerous. The danger and the fascination come together in the sexiness that is part of the stereotype as well.* (ibid.: 144)

Living apart from humans in Toontown, the Toons appear to be treated similarly to how African Americans were in the United States under the Jim Crow laws of segregation; for example, access to the bar where Jessica Rabbit performs, the Ink and Paint Club, is "strictly humans only". Mark Winokur moves further in his critique of the film, finding at the film's "center an anxiety about passing and tokenism" (1991: 204) and goes on to "compare the behavior of Roger to the behavior of antebellum minstrels" (*ibid.:* 205). Winokur's argument can be extended, though, by looking beyond Roger and the Toons for evidence of minstrelsy. The music in the film advances and deepens these readings. Closer scrutiny of the music framing the film – Alan Silvestri's quixotic instrumental score as well as the pre-existing songs quoted throughout – reveals further components of the film's reactionary positioning regarding both race politics and latent homophobia in the age of HIV-AIDS. While the appearance of subtle strains of racism and homophobia may come as no surprise in a big-budget Hollywood film from the age of Reagan, discerning their cloaked presence requires both close listening and attentiveness to the film's effective use of misdirection.

Tooning up?

Although *WFRR* purports to embrace a broad history of US animation in its references and allusions, in its gags and visual iconography, the Disney and Warner Bros. cartoons and characters claim most of the limelight. In comparing the feature-length animated films of Disney with the comedy shorts of Warner Bros., Paul Wells turns to Raymond Durgnat and his delineation of their respective "Republican" and "Democratic" attitudes. Wells points to

> *a clear dialectic here between Disney's Small Town Republicanism and Warners' Big City Democratic position, and the self-evident opposition between Disney's moral certainty and Warner Bros.' more ambivalent and, arguably, more "realistic" stance.* (Wells, 2002: 54)

That meeting, then, of Mickey Mouse and Bugs Bunny (literally the trademark characters for Disney and Warner Bros.) marks more than a calculated effort to command attention but rather one of several moments of structural, ideological and representational convergence. In addition to Republican Disney meeting Democratic Warner Bros., live action meets animation, feature length meets short cartoon, human characters meet animal characters, and mystery meets musical, to name only four. That so much transgression occurs in this film reminds us that boundaries were in place to be transgressed. For that reason, a focus on borders and framing – especially musical framing – can illuminate what gets shifted as well as what does not, because in this cynical blend of Republican and Democratic surfaces (cynical because the triangulation sacrifices integrity for market share), the more things change, the more things stay the same.

Warner Bros.' much-beloved *Looney Tunes* cartoons[6] frequently open and close with Carl Stalling's arrangement of 'The Merry-Go-Round Broke Down', the melody operating as a kind of frame setting the boundaries between the cartoon and its world and the non-cartoon world. The musical borders of the cartoon would have differed from the musical language delineating the feature film that would follow it in an original theatrical screening. Similar musical frames appear in *WFRR*, including the presence of a faux-Stalling score for the Baby Herman and Roger Rabbit cartoon that opens *WFRR*, 'Somethin's Cookin''. This musical introduction, however, does not reach its intended conclusion but falls apart mid-story because Roger sees birds instead of stars as a refrigerator crashes on his head, drawing shouts of "Cut! Cut!" and an angry upbraiding from the cartoon's director, a non-animated human.[7] The frame thus left open, the cartoon world and live-action world intermingle as we then watch Baby Herman storm off the set and interact with some of the humans blocking his way. Besides the brief film-within-a-film that opens *WFRR*, the entire film gets musically framed in notable ways.

Figure 6.1 Opening bass motive: first eight measures (transcribed by present author)

Silvestri accompanies the opening frames, featuring two screens of credits for Touch-stone Pictures, with a jazz trio. Beginning with a ride pattern on the cymbal, the bass then enters (Figure 6.1) with a melody featuring pitch-bending on scale degree three.

The modal ambiguity created here – will it be minor? will it be major? – introduces in subtle ways the film's tensions between binary oppositions, such as the dialectic between Human and Toon. After the trio reaches a major cadence – an answer to the modal ambiguity – a solo saxophone plays a melody with a descending contour that bends the third, fifth, and seventh scale degrees. Even more than with the initial musical cue in the trio, this sax melody employs the blues scale in a way meant immediately to invoke jazz.

Understanding that opening cues conventionally work to establish time period, place and atmosphere, what does Silvestri's faux-jazz signify here? Considered broadly, it helps to recall Krin Gabbard's observation that, in the 1950s, jazz in Hollywood scoring "was becoming the preferred and even appropriate music to express contemporary urban disaffection and turbulence" (Gabbard, 1996: 134). Stylistically, it resonates more closely with the cool sound of the later 1950s than with swing or bop from the late 1940s. Later in the film, when Jessica Rabbit performs at the Ink and Paint club, a band of black crows backs her up (Figure 6.2), further connecting the cartoon characters with notions of blackness and particular musical styles.[8]

Figure 6.2 Jessica Rabbit and her black band

If not there to fix time period, what about place or mood? Perhaps the urban space of Los Angeles calls for a jazz-inspired sound, and cool does have strong West Coast roots.[9] Still, it seems most likely that the music here functions within Hollywood's limited and limiting roles for jazz: it suggests fun, whimsy and sensuality. Silvestri's jazz cues relate to the music of someone like Miles Davis just as Stephen Foster's plantation songs resonate with African oral historians: what both Silvestri and Foster produce follows the original from the position of an outsider. Ultimately, the use of jazz, faux or otherwise, falls within a long tradition of jazz in cartoons that Daniel Goldmark surveys; he concludes that it forms a "large" and "essential" part of cartoons and their sound from the late 1920s through the 1940s (2005: 106). This chapter will unpack some of these elements to offer an interpretation of the film text through its music.

Silvestri's recurring themes

Alan Silvestri's score carefully negotiates and revives the earlier traditions of short comedy cartoons (Warner Bros.) while blending that tradition with the somewhat different musical conventions of feature-length narrative films (Disney). There is, then, a constant tension between, on the one hand, shorter cues, closely connected to visual gags on the screen (as with Carl Stalling's protean underscores), and, on the other hand, lengthier cues that hark back to the feature-length practices of distinctive recurring melodies (for example, the use of 'When You Wish Upon A Star' in Disney's *Pinocchio* [Hamilton Luske and Ben Sharpsteen, 1940]). Goldmark has posited that "Stalling's scores [for Warner Bros.' cartoons] have no emotional arc, instead carefully complementing and conveying whatever joke is being perpetrated at a given moment in the narrative" (2005: 16). Silvestri, in contrast, brings an emotional arc to *WFRR* through some recurring musical motives, most notably a wistful, almost melancholic, theme (Figure 6.3) that accompanies Eddie Valiant during some of his more reflective moments – a love theme? but, if so, for whom? his brother? – and also a related motive that often occurs as he engages in his professional sleuthing (Figure 6.4).

Figure 6.3 Eddie's wistful theme (transcribed by present author)

Figure 6.4 Eddie's sleuthing theme (transcribed by present author)

Even the playful bass melody in Figure 6.1 recurs, generally during transitions and establishing shots, although it becomes the basis for an extended cue (that runs just over a minute, from 8:43 to 9:45) as Eddie leaves Maroon's office. Maroon has just assigned to Eddie the job of investigating Jessica Rabbit. The exchange ends with Maroon bragging about how the Toons "work for peanuts", but Eddie declares he does not, asking about the other half of his payment (Maroon has advanced half his fee for the job). Maroon tells Valiant to think of the other half of the payment as a carrot, prompting Valiant to say "you been hangin' around rabbits too long". The cymbals enter just as Valiant finishes the joke, punctuating the punchline in a manner reminiscent of the live vaudeville shows that played such an important early influence on the cartoon tradition in the USA. We see Valiant leave Maroon's office and observe the Toons on the studio lot, where he watches a human saxophone player accompany a group of animated brooms (Figure 6.5) with the melody from Paul Dukas's 'The Sorcerer's Apprentice', made famous in *Fantasia* (James Algar and Samuel Armstrong, 1940). Indeed, the allusion takes on particular significance right after Maroon's line about the Toons serving as a cheap source of labour. Here, the human (and white) sax player appears to be using music to control the animated labourers (they are sweeping trash). The diegetic sax melody clashes with the non-diegetic faux-jazz music; the rhythm, metre and melodic phrasing of the faux-jazz music comes into question with the forced juxtaposition of the 'Sorcerer's Apprentice' melody, which has a different metre, phrasing and harmonic orientation.

Figure 6.5 Visual and musical allusions to *Fantasia*

The wistful theme of Figure 6.3 (which first appears at 10:20 mins, right after the scene in the studio lot, as Eddie praises the public transportation in Hollywood) serves as a signifier of Eddie's sadness over the loss of his brother (murdered with a falling piano by an unidentified Toon) but also his presumptive romantic interest in the film, Delores. The melody, with its sequencing and rich harmonization, evokes noir themes like the one Jerry Goldsmith wrote for *Chinatown* (Roman Polanski, 1974) – and *WFRR* emerges in several ways from the example of that film – but also an even earlier one, David Raksin's famous music for *Laura* (Otto Preminger, 1944).[10] The first four notes of the melody, indicated in the second example (Figure 6.3) as motive *x*, also appear (marked as motive *x'* in Figure 6.4) in the melody that accompanies Eddie's sleuthing. Figure 6.4 comes from a moment of especially close music and image co-ordination, as it follows Eddie and his shadow in an alley in Toontown; the hint of canonic writing, of one melody following the next, parallels the human figure following its shadow. As Eddie creeps along, he sneezes, prompting his shadow to turn to him and utter "Gesundheit". This visual gag of a figure and its shadow beginning in unison but then falling out of sync appears in earlier cartoons like the Fleischer Brothers' *Bimbo's Initiation* (1931). Bimbo, of Betty Boop fame, fights initiation into a secret society and his resistance brings a series of tortures. "Wanna be a member? Wanna be a member?" ask the hooded characters in the secret society. Bimbo blurts out "No" until the end of the film, when one member reveals herself as Betty, at which point Bimbo yelps "Yes". During one of the chase scenes, Bimbo's shadow has its head cut off, and Bimbo seems as shocked as the headless shadow, once it notices (Figures 6.6 and 6.7).[11]

Figure 6.6 Eddie and his shadow

Figure 6.7 Bimbo and his shadow

Silvestri shows an adroitness for musical jokes and at catching visual gestures in the music through some carefully nuanced compositional decisions (such as the imitative writing in Figure 6.4). At several points, his quickly shifting score follows the jokes at the pace of a Stalling score, if not with the same timbral and stylistic variety that occurs in the Warner Bros. shorts from the 1940s. Another connection to these cartoons appears in the way that Silvestri sets up a musical frame for the film, in this case, the longer songlike cues with the earnest melody in Figure 6.3, which returns in an upbeat version during the closing credits. Toontown receives a musical frame as well. When Eddie first drives into it, the same twangy guitar portamento that we hear at the start of 'Somethin's Cookin' ' returns, leading into the song 'Smile, Darn Ya, Smile!', which returns at the end of the film (notice the sly blending between the boundary of Toontown and the framing of the film, as the animated world and the 'real' world have bled together). The guitar portamento here parodies the familiar opening to Warner Bros.' *Looney Tunes*, and *WFRR* goes even further by positioning the song 'The Merry-Go-Round Broke Down' (the tune framing *Looney Tunes* cartoons) as diegetic within the film. First, Roger sings it in the bar, repeatedly breaking plates over his head while singing the words "no pain". When Judge Doom appears later in that scene and finds the record, he identifies the song's title and declares it "quite a loony selection for a group of drunken reprobates". In the film's climactic showdown between Eddie and the weasels, Eddie sings 'The Merry-Go-Round Broke Down', one of several ways he signals his larger acceptance of Toon culture to Roger as well as to the audience. To distract the weasels, Eddie engages in the same sort of masochistic gags that we saw Roger perform earlier with 'The Merry-Go-Round Broke Down' in the bar scene: he hits himself with a broomstick, he drops heavy round bombs on his head, he pogo-sticks into a light fixture and gets an electric shock. With Eddie's adoption of Toon behaviours, the non-diegetic musical score shifts into a series of mickey-mousings. As each weasel dies and in turn their souls float upwards, sometimes the funeral march from Chopin's Piano Sonata No. 2, a stock musical cue from the early days of film accompaniment and from later cartoons, accompanies the death. Eddie kicks a weasel and its ascending and descending arc is synchronized with a melody that rises and falls with a similar contour; the weasel's landing in the vat of cartoon-dissolving poisonous dip brings a climactic chord from the orchestra. As conveyor belts and machinery begin to operate, the music adopts hints of Raymond Scott's well-known repetitive machine music ('Powerhouse'), further channelling the musical world of *Looney Tunes*.

Framing and queer subtexts

The overt mention of framing in the film opens up other questions connected with boundaries and transgression, particularly questions of containment. Anxieties over a number of breached boundaries, of contamination from close physical contact, appear in the dialogue: for example, Eddie tells Maroon, "You been hangin' around rabbits too long", and Doom tells Eddie, "I see working for a Toon has rubbed off on you". Perhaps most obviously, coming into contact with Judge Doom's deadly dip can destroy the otherwise invulnerable Toons. Any number of boundaries that had previously been sacrosanct get violated in *WFRR*. Besides seeing Warner Bros. and Disney characters together on screen for the first time (for example, Bugs Bunny and Mickey Mouse, or Porky Pig and Tinkerbell), the film also brings together pairings sometimes considered as binary opposites: live action/animation and human/animal. Roger and Eddie transform these either/or binaries into a spectrum, as the cartoon character Roger takes on human attributes while the live-action human Eddie takes on more Toon attributes as the film progresses. Jessica Rabbit, in fact, further complicates the binary by being not simply a cartoon of a female human, but actually "more of a sex symbol in the movie than Eddie's live-action girlfriend Dolores" (Rosenbaum, 1988: 34). That she draws the romantic interest of both Roger and Eddie brings them together into a tenuous love triangle, one that causes the film, at the surface at least, to present an ostensibly heteronormative outcome, with Jessica and Roger paired up next to Dolores and Eddie.[12] Alan Nadel sees these fears over a loss of containment as a principal reason to read *WFRR* in the context of the AIDS epidemic of the 1980s, arguing that:

> Who Framed Roger Rabbit? is one of the earliest films to deal with the themes of the AIDS epidemic employing codes that have become somewhat conventional: the community at risk, facing extinction from some inexplicable

evil; the breakdown in the normal social and personal defense systems; the association with sexual ambiguity; the mystery of origins, connected with the sexual history of the suspects; the destructive power of an uncanny twin, sibling, or self-as-mutant Other; the threatening liquid (in this case dip, but more often blood); and, as the "framing" of Roger suggests, the blaming of the victim. (Nadel, 1997: 179–80)

Nadel pays close attention to Roger's explanation that "If you don't have a sense of humour, you're better off dead", seeing humour as a central element of Toonitude; Judge Doom, the Toon who passes as human (like a gay passing as straight in allegorical terms), hates laughter (he chastizes the weasels for laughing in the bar scene) and thus possesses a flaw, a sickness, that causes him to harm others and ultimately himself (*ibid.*: 177). Like human blood infected with the AIDS virus, Doom's dip is also liquid and lethal.[13]

"I see working for a Toon has rubbed off on you," Judge Doom says to Eddie Valiant shortly after their first meeting, just after Valiant has surprised Doom with the handshake buzzer. Silvestri's musical underscoring of Doom's response reveals key elements of Doom's character: after he is 'buzzed' (and the buzz gets punctuated by a pizzicato), the strings hold a dissonant pitch cluster as Doom's face is first blank, but then the music changes into a higher-pitched consonance with harp as he presents a smile. Initially a mystery, Doom then gives a surface answer of a smile (smiles and humour are closely associated with Toonitude here, and we learn later in the film that his smile was false, an example of his passing strategies). "I wasn't working for a Toon," Valiant defiantly responds. Though Eddie's hostility to Toons at this point in the story refutes Doom's assertion, Doom does, however, predict what will happen to Eddie: working for Roger Rabbit and Jessica Rabbit will indeed rub off on him, so much so in fact that the film's supposedly happy resolution hinges on Eddie's adoption of Toon behaviours. Eddie has adopted the Toons' capacity for slapstick humour but has also learned how to pass as humourless.

Marvin Acme's "biggest seller", the handshake buzzer, appears at key moments of male interaction throughout the film. At their first meeting, Acme buzzes Eddie's hand, to his evident chagrin. Later in the film, when Eddie first meets Doom, Eddie buzzes Judge Doom's hand, to the latter's closeted chagrin. Finally, at the end of the film, Roger buzzes Eddie's hand, to his feigned chagrin. When Roger buzzes Eddie, saying "Don't tell me ya lost your sense of humour already," Eddie grabs him by the throat and asks "Does this answer your question?", planting a big kiss on Roger's lips. The kiss causes the Toons to cheer and begin singing 'Smile, Darn Ya, Smile' (a song already heard in the film, during Valiant's entry into Toontown). The brief moment of male physical intimacy gets quickly overpowered by the next line, Jessica Rabbit saying, "Come on, Roger, let's go home. I'll bake you a carrot cake." Roger looks out at us, reminiscent of Bugs Bunny's occasional glances to the audience, and Jessica then rubs Roger's face down her breasts while a sort of reverse mickey-mousing effect happens in the score: a glissando rushes up to a trill, so, as we see Roger's face being lowered down the screen, the accompanying musical gesture quickly rises to a climax. An obvious and crude visual gag is matched to an extremely subtle, yet equally crude, musical one.

Along with the hand-buzzers, kissing forms another recurring (and related) motif in the film. Jessica Rabbit plays at kissing Eddie when he first sees her in the Ink and Paint Club, singing the words "Why don't you do right, like some other men" and then pauses and purses her lips. Instead of kissing Eddie, however, she sings the word "do" while tugging his tie into a stiff, upright position as she pulls away from him and then releases it.[14] At the end of the film, Jessica again teases Eddie: after being saved by him, she seems poised to kiss him, but instead pushes by to kiss Roger (the beginning of the scene has the love theme from Figure 6.3 playing, but with the kissing of Roger, the opening jazz melody in the bass returns for the final time). When Roger hides from Judge Doom's weasels in Eddie's office/apartment (and with Eddie's dual work/living space there is yet another example of ambiguous boundaries), Roger kisses Eddie and says, "You saved my life ... How can I ever repay you?" Eddie angrily responds, "For starters, don't ever kiss me again", asserting the appropriate heteronormative response, although the level of his hostility may suggest more conflict beneath the surface. When Eddie and Delores share a tender moment in the movie theatre, accompanied by the wistful love theme, their kiss is interrupted by Roger's heavy sigh. Yet another attempt at kissing happens when Eddie, thinking he has found Jessica Rabbit in Toontown, discovers instead a crazed character (presumably Lena the Hyena), who shrieks with pleasure "A man!" and proceeds to chase and try to kiss the horrified Eddie. Eddie almost kisses Dolores in the final scene, after discovering Acme's will and learning that the Toons will have possession of Toontown in perpetuity, but Roger yanks Eddie away from Dolores, leading to the final example of kissing in the entire film, where Eddie ends up kissing Roger.

Why all this rubbing off, buzzing and kissing? Why don't we ever see a female character using the buzzer on a male character? It may be helpful to consider *WFRR* as a buddy movie. Robin Wood observes in the 1970s buddy movies a

> threatening, antipatriarchal bisexuality ... Then, of course, one or both of the male protagonists had to die: patriarchy could not safely contain their relationship. Today, the explicitly gay couple can be permitted to survive and even be designated happy (though the happiness is never dramatized) – provided they accept their place. (2003: 218)

The film closes with the typical heterosexual pairing – Roger with Jessica, Eddie with Dolores –but that final kiss may open up the possibilities to more than just Eddie's future career in stand-up comedy. Eddie's progression from troubled Toon-hater to Toon-loving jokester may implicitly signal his embrace of a coy bisexuality. Ultimately, though, the most telling element may be that, at the end of *WFRR*, the wall separating

Los Angeles and Toontown literally comes crashing down. The rupture allows all of the Toons to come out, even if their coming out is only for the brief euphoric moment when they learn about the deed to Toontown. Coming out in *WFRR* may bring the illusion of security, but that security appears to be limited to a ghetto, even if it is accompanied by a quasi-utopic musical number ('Smile, Darn Ya, Smile').

Conclusion: *Who Framed Roger Rabbit* as minstrel show

Paul Wells argues that "America has produced four indigenous art forms. The Western (in film and fiction); jazz; the Broadway musical and the animated cartoon" (2002: 1). While not considered an art form, the minstrel shows of the nineteenth century (and later) are also indigenous to the United States. Peter Stanfield views Hollywood's repeated use of blackface as a central part of American culture:

> *Hollywood's representation of blackface as a signifier of nostalgia helped to undercut whatever relevance the form still had for a contemporary audience, but, in doing so, it also made blackface an essential element in the evocation of an American vernacular, a cultural miscegenation at once recognized and denied...* [Blackface's] *time has apparently long passed, yet it refuses to disappear, returning whenever American culture needs to express a vernacular tradition.* (1997: 438)

WFRR brings these traditions of cartoons and minstrelsy together, although it is hardly the first example of animation to indulge in the imagery and racism of minstrelsy. The film contains several elements of minstrel performances: singing, dancing, telling jokes, even ending with a large production number that included the whole cast (here, instead of a song like 'Dixie', or 'Camptown Races' as in *Fresh Hare*, it ends with 'Smile, Darn Ya, Smile'). While there is no direct representation of blackening the face with burnt cork, some more implicit vestiges of that part of minstrelsy may remain in *WFRR's* use of ape imagery. When looking at the history of animation, it becomes apparent that apes have frequently been used in US cartoons to signify people with dark skin.[15] The ape who serves as the bouncer at the Pen and Ink Club appears to be *WFRR's* most overt invocation of these earlier racist visual codes. When Eddie walks into the club, he looks at the bouncer and says "Nice monkey suit". After the show, as Eddie spies on Jessica, the bouncer interrupts him by saying "Whaddya think you're doing, chump?" "Who you callin' a chump, chimp?" responds Eddie, tilting towards minstrel dialect in the way he drops the verb "are." After the bouncer then throws Eddie out into the alley, Eddie shouts back at him "ooga booga" while scratching under his arm in imitation of an ape gesture. Eddie in effect apes the ape.

Apart from the bouncer and the clear symbolism of a segregated Toons-only nightclub, the film represses race as an issue. (Changing the 'T' of Toons into a 'C' may bring the allegory into sharper focus, though.) Because they continue to circulate so widely and pervasively, in so many forms of media (an argument Spike Lee makes in

Bamboozled, 2000), these vestiges of the minstrel show may lose their potency at both ends – their ability, that is, to titillate the racist in search of fantasies of black inferiority and to shock the non-racist into rejecting these images and their history. "Things are never black as they are painted," we're told in the song at the end of the film. It's a complicated, multivalent statement (like so much of this allegorical film), reminding us that, despite the declaration to the contrary, sometimes things are painted black, like Elmer Fudd in blackface, even if they are not black underneath. Does that not also open up the possibility that things not painted black can be set up to signify blackness? In the end, though, the song hurries us past such questions, insisting that we smile; the audience is told, to quote one of the most popular US songs (by Bobby McFerrin) from 1988, to "don't worry, be happy". *WFRR* does not encourage us to wake up from the fantasy dreams presented by Hollywood; instead, it treats us to the illusion that we have awakened from a dream only to weave us ever more tightly into it.

Acknowledgements

Besides thanking Rebecca Coyle for her insightful and generous editing of this essay, I also wish to acknowledge Daniel Goldmark, Andrew Oster, and the audience at one of Davidson College's Center for Interdisciplinary Studies lunch presentations for their helpful feedback on earlier versions of this essay.

Notes

1. Eric Smoodin is one of several who have noted that the release of *Who Framed Roger Rabbit* in 1988 marked a moment when cartoons became more acceptable as adult entertainment (1992: 130).
2. For instance, Stanley Kauffmann complained that "the film's only interest is in wondering how they did it – the mix of animation and live action" (Kauffmann, 1988: 34), while the film was described as "an amazing feat of entertainment engineering" in the *New Yorker* (Rafferty, 1988: 74). The review in *Variety* declared it "an unparalleled technical achievement where animation is brilliantly integrated into live action" (22 June 1988, p.12). François Chevassu raved that "les trucages sont pratiquement parfaits ici et, surtout, les Toons s'intègrent totalement à l'action, partenaires à part entière réels" (1988: 91). In the *Village Voice* J. Hoberman summarized the initial buzz surrounding the film before addressing the ghettoization of the Toons:

    > As everyone within TV range surely knows, Who Framed Roger Rabbit *is this summer's eighth wonder of the world – an animated epic, a* Newsweek *cover story, a* New York Post *page one, the Disney studio's $40 (or is it 50) million gamble, a technological marvel, a masterpiece of vulgar postmodernism, the greatest film Frank Tashlin never made but a triumph for director Robert Zemeckis and presenter Steven Spielberg, the Looneytune to top all Looneytunes.* (1988: 57)

Mark J. P. Wolf would later report that the film "broke the effects industry record for the largest number of process shots used in a film and for the most elements ever composited together within a single shot" (1995: 45).

3. In ways both similar to and prophetic of *WFRR*, Disney's (much) earlier live-action/animated hybrid film, *Song of the South* (Harve Foster and Wilfred Jackson, 1946), employed the strategy of "dazzl[ing] uncritical audiences with the technological 'attraction' of integrating cartoon characters with live action", as Matthew Bernstein has observed (1996: 220). Later, Disney's box-office success *Mary Poppins* (Robert Stevenson, 1964) included hybrid live-action and animation sequences.

4. Norman M. Klein notes,

   Mickey himself started out with touches of black caricature in his first cartoon, wearing tattered pants, with bare, black legs and saucer eyes. But these signifiers were never labelled simply as black. They were part of the generic vaudeville costume, even though many veteran animators of the era (for example, Freleng and Jones) identify them as obviously influenced by black slapstick. (1993: 192)

5. See, in particular, Chapter 2, 'Love and Theft: "Racial" Production and the Social Unconscious of Blackface'.

6. A series widely screened in US cinemas in the period 1930–69 and featuring the beloved characters Bugs Bunny, Bosko and Bunny, Wile E. Coyote and Road Runner, and many others besides Elmer Fudd. In its musical and directorial approach, *Looney Tunes* can be contrasted to the Disney *Silly Symphonies* series that ran approximately concurrently.

7. Spielberg would return to a falling refrigerator twenty years later in 2008's *Indiana Jones and the Kingdom of the Crystal Skull*, as Jones improbably finds refuge from a nuclear detonation within the confines of a refrigerator (thus prompting the phrase 'nuke the 'fridge' as the cinematic equivalent of television's 'jumping the shark').

8. These crows provide an intertextual link back to the crows in Disney's *Dumbo* (1941). The *Dumbo* crows (their leader is named Jim Crow) speak and sing in minstrel dialect: "I'd be done see'n about everything, when I see an elephant fly."

9. *Coal Black and de Sebben Dwarves*, a 1943 cartoon immersed in the jazz culture of its day, from the music accompanying and inspiring it to the demeaning caricatures littered throughout it, has been censored for its blackface depictions while at the same time Terry Lindvall and Ben Fraser have pointed to director Bob Clampett's "integration of marginalized jazz music into the low cartoon as a celebration of black culture rather than an exploitation of it" (1998: 133). As several other scholars have noted, Clampett took his animators to a black nightclub in downtown Los Angeles and attempted, unsuccessfully, to have only black musicians recorded on the score (see Goldmark, 2005: 100).

10. In her discussion of Raksin's score for *Laura*, Kalinak observes, "for white audiences of the era, jazz represented the urban, the sexual, and the decadent in a

musical idiom perceived in the culture at large as an indigenous black form" (1992: 167).

11. Does 'shadow' equal 'spook'? It may appear in an earlier Zemeckis film with a racist hostility. In *Back to the Future* (1985), an African American character (Marvin Berry) gets called a "spook" and that incites him and his band to fight the white character who uttered it. *Back to the Future* goes beyond harmless nostalgia for the 1950s into some insidious revisionism when it suggests that the rock-and-roll sound of Chuck Berry, Marvin's cousin, actually originated from Marty McFly.

12. Nadel hints that Eddie's brother may have been homosexual because "we do see photos of him in which he lacks any female companion, whereas Eddie is paired with his girlfriend" (1997: 178). That Eddie's brother was killed by a piano, a musical instrument, may support Nadel's suspicions; if being musical carries homosexual codes ("Are you musical?"), the brother's death by a musical instrument could support his involvement within musical and/or homosexual circles.

13. Nadel draws attention to Doom's red eyes, which he notes are

> *revealed to be blood when the eyes turn into menacing daggers ... Like the dip shooting out of phallic hoses at the bound-up Roger and Jessica, the blood at the tips of Doom's eyes suggest the dangerous fluid that not only threatens to destroy all the toons but also is capable of killing Eddie's brother or Eddie himself.* (1997: 179)

14. The words are from the eponymously titled 'Why Don't You Do Right', originally written by Kansas Joe McCoy, which was an early jazz hit for Lillian Green but gained particular popularity through the version recorded by Peggy Lee with Benny Goodman in 1942. In *WFRR*, the song (extract) is performed in a bluesy style by Amy Irving.

15. As Terry Lindvall and Ben Fraser point out about Bosko, an early cartoon character coded as black:

> In Congo Jazz *(1930)*, *Bosko appears in the jungle with a chimpanzee on one side and a gorilla on the other. What makes the scene eerie is that there is virtually no difference between the faces of the three. Bosko is only identifiable as human in two ways: he is midway in size between the chimp and the gorilla, and he is the one wearing clothes. The monkeylike face conjures up an animalistic genesis, not a transcending* imago dei, *and constitutes one of the most racist and demeaning representations of blacks in film.* (1998: 126)

References

Bernstein, M. (1996), 'Nostalgia, Ambivalence, Irony: *Song of the South* and Race Relations in 1946 Atlanta', *Film History*, 8(2), 219–36.

Chevassu, F. (1988), 'Review of "Qui veut la peau de Roger Rabbit" ', *Revue du cinema*, 35(442), 91.

Cholondenko, A. (1991), 'Who Framed Roger Rabbit, or, the Framing of Animation', in A. Cholodenko (ed.), The Illusion of Life: Essays on Animation, Sydney: Power Publications, pp. 209–42.

Cohen, M. (1999), 'The Detective as Other: The Detective Versus the Other', in K. Klein (ed.), Diversity and Detective Fiction, Bowling Green, OH: Bowling Green State University Popular Press, pp. 144–57.

Gabbard, K. (1996), Jammin' at the Margins: Jazz and the American Cinema, Chicago: University of Chicago Press.

Goldmark, D. (2005), Tunes for 'Toons: Music and the Hollywood Cartoon, Berkeley: University of California Press.

Hoberman, J. (1988), 'Name That Toon', Village Voice, 5 July, p. 57.

Kalinak, K. (1992), Settling the Score: Music and the Classical Hollywood Film, Madison: University of Wisconsin Press.

Kauffmann, S. (1988), 'Love and Other Diversions', New Republic, 199(5), 34–6.

Klein, N. (1993), Seven Minutes: The Life and Death of the American Animated Cartoon, London: Verso.

Lindvall, T., and Fraser, B. (1998), 'Darker Shades of Animation: African-American Images in the Warner Bros. Cartoon', in K. Sandler (ed.), Reading the Rabbit: Explorations in Warner Bros. Animation, New Brunswick, NJ: Rutgers University Press, pp. 121–36.

Lott, E. (1993), Love and Theft: Blackface Minstrelsy and the American Working Class, New York & Oxford: Oxford University Press.

Nadel, A. (1997), Flatlining on the Field of Dreams: Cultural Narratives in the Films of President Reagan's America, New Brunswick, NJ: Rutgers University Press.

Ohmer, S. (1988), ' "Who Framed Roger Rabbit": The Presence of the Past', in J. Canemaker (ed), Storytelling in Animation: The Art of the Animated Image, Los Angeles: American Film Institute, pp. 97–105.

Reese, M. (1988), 'The Making of Roger Rabbit', Newsweek, 111(26), p. 54.

Rosenbaum, J. (1988), 'Review of Who Framed Roger Rabbit? by Robert Zemeckis', Film Quarterly, 42(1), 33–7.

Smoodin, E. (1992), 'Cartoon and Comic Classicism: High-Art Histories of Lowbrow Culture', American Literary History, 4(1), 129–40.

Stanfield, P. (1997), ' "An Octoroon in the Kindling": American Vernacular & Blackface Minstrelsy in 1930s Hollywood', Journal of American Studies, 31(3), 407–38.

Wells, P. (2002), Animation and America, Edinburgh: Edinburgh University Press.

Winokur, M. (1991), 'Black Is White/White Is Black: "Passing" as a Strategy of Racial Compatibility in Contemporary Hollywood Comedy', in L. Friedman (ed.), Unspeakable Images: Ethnicity and the American Cinema, Urbana and Chicago: University of Illinois Press, pp. 190–212.

Wolf, M. (1995), 'In the Frame of Roger Rabbit: Visual Compositing in Film', Velvet Light Trap, 36 (Fall), 45–59.

Wood, R. (2003), Hollywood from Vietnam to Reagan ... and Beyond, New York: Columbia University Press.

7 An Aesthetic of Ambiguity

Musical Representation of Indigenous Peoples in Disney's Brother Bear

Janice Esther Tulk

Throughout its history, the Walt Disney company has produced animation that appeals broadly to both children and adults, with stories of epic journeys, fated love, and magical places, objects and events. Its films regularly feature talking animals, often in the role of the protagonist's sidekick, and they have represented a variety of different (sometimes imaginary) cultures and related geographic locations, including Arabian in *Aladdin* (Ron Clements and John Musker, 1992), African[1] in *The Lion King* (Roger Allers and Rob Minkoff, 1994), Native American in *Pocahontas* (Mike Gabriel and Eric Goldberg, 1995), Chinese in *Mulan* (Tony Bancroft and Barry Cook, 1998) and Incan in *The Emperor's New Groove* (Mark Dindal, 2000).[2] More recently, Alaskan Inuit culture has been represented in *Brother Bear* (Aaron Blaise and Robert Walker, 2003).

The two films featuring North American indigenous peoples are strikingly different. While *Pocahontas* has some historical basis, *Brother Bear* was created anew by a team of Disney writers. *Pocahontas* focuses on a specific place, time and set of circumstances surrounding a particular cultural interaction. *Brother Bear*, in contrast, has a rather ambiguous setting that is neither explicitly identified in the film nor immediately obvious to viewers. Indeed, the setting varies throughout the film with rather incongruous imagery, such as the juxtaposition of glaciers with a geyser field. The time period is best defined as 'long ago' and is not indicated until woolly mammoths are depicted roaming through the wilderness. Finally, it is not particularly obvious which indigenous group is being presented in the film. The audience, then, is left to pull together fragments of information to complete the picture and make sense of the visual and sonic elements presented.

This chapter first provides a brief overview of the representation of indigenous peoples in film. With this background, I turn to the animated film *Brother Bear* and demonstrate that the scripted motifs have antecedents in the folklore of several indigenous cultures. Having traced the narrative that forms the basis of this animation, I focus on the musical representation of indigenous peoples in Disney's *Brother Bear* and consider the decisions the composers made while "scoring the Indian" (see Gorbman,

2000b). Examination of bonus material included in the two-disc Special Edition (released in 2004) illuminates the process of creating *Brother Bear*. Finally, comments from participants who viewed the film in focus groups (discussed below) suggest how particular audiences respond to the musical gestures used throughout and make sense of ambiguous elements in the film, as well as how exposure to bonus material may influence their overall appreciation of the film.

Indigenous peoples in animation film

Since the advent of moving-picture technology, indigenous peoples and their cultures have served as source material for films. For almost as long, the misrepresentation of indigenous peoples has been criticized in trade journals, with perhaps the earliest instance being published around 1910. [3] Attention to historical and cultural accuracy has rarely been the concern of production companies or directors. O'Connor noted that:

> designers of Indian movie costumes have generally given little attention to the actual dress of the tribes in question. Language elements, cultural beliefs and religious rituals of one tribe have been attributed to others or, more often, invented. (1980: 10)

Stripes further explains this style of representation, noting "the tendency, long the focus of Hollywood, to imagine a Plains-inspired Pan-Indian pastiche as the representation of diverse Native cultures" (1999: 98).

Many scholars, including Deloria, who recently published *Indians in Unexpected Places* (2004), and Moses, who wrote *Wild West Shows and the Images of American Indians, 1883–1933* (1996), have traced the representations of indigenous peoples in early films and Wild West shows. There has also been interest in examining audience responses to such films, as exemplified in the work of Seixas (1994, 1993) and Shively (1992).[4] Little scholarly analysis, however, has been done on the representation of First Nations people and culture in animated films. Most notable is the work of Strong (1996), who wrote about the commodification of children's culture, focusing specifically on *The Indian in the Cupboard* (Frank Oz) and *Pocahontas*, both released in 1995.

This seeming lacuna is interesting, given the fact that US cartoon animation is considered to be similar in some ways to live-action film: "By definition, the American cartoon is grounded in drawing, and this allows it great flexibility so that, through scale and perspective, it can imitate the camera's movements and angles" (O'Pray, 2000: 51). As for live-action film, there are differences between early 'silent' animation and animation created after the advent of synchronized sound technology. 'Silent' cartoons made use of strong graphics and the movement of the film camera was not imitated; however, "the introduction of [synchronized] sound established a tendency in cartoons away from a modernist anti-realism, with its stress on the picture plane, and towards a deep-space naturalism-cum-realism" (*ibid.*). With synchronized sound came specific developments in storylines and characterization, and music was incorporated into animation in much the same way that film scores were added to non-animated films. With so many parallels between live-action film and US animation, it seems likely that animation would have followed a similar developmental course with regards to the means by which indigenous peoples are represented. Extending analysis of the representation of different cultures in animation, in both silent animations and those with sound, as well as the musical representation of cultures, highlights the techniques and underlying assumptions of indigenous representation in an animation film such as *Brother Bear*.

"Scoring the Indian"

Over time, musical means of representing Native Americans emerged and became standardized, with the proliferation of "stock Indian music" in the cinema by the 1910s (Gorbman, 2000b: 237).[5] Central to this standardization were collections of music used for silent films, which provided musical motifs to represent a variety of ethnicities, work, events and emotions (Deloria, 2004: 221). John Zemecnik's collection from 1913, like many others available to theatres, featured "pounding tom-tom beats on the interval of the open fifth and a minor-key melody" to represent the American Indian (*ibid.*). With the advent of talkies, such motifs continued to be employed, often to announce the arrival of Indians (Kilpatrick, 1999: 38). Thus, Deloria notes that sound representing Native Americans, "as it crops up in the folklore of non-Indian Americans, has a melancholy, vaguely threatening, minor-key melody and a repetitive pounding drumbeat, accented in a 'tom-tom' fashion: 'DUM dum dum dum DUM dum dum dum'" (2004: 183). Indeed, these means of representing Native Americans have been identified by Michael Pisani (1998) and Claudia Gorbman (2000b), who additionally note the use of parallel fourths and fifths in harmonizing Native melodies, as well as the use of pentatonic scales and two-note motifs.[6] What is particularly significant with regards to such means of representing Native Americans is the fact that one need only supply a brief excerpt of such stereotyped gestures to "conjure up" the image of the Indian, as well as the expectations connected to them (Deloria, 2004: 183). These associations are many and varied, including ideas about primitive Native cultures, violent Native Americans, romanticized noble savages, and "haunted landscapes" (as opposed to landscapes that are imbued with spiritual or cultural meaning) (*ibid.*: 184).

Deloria notes that musical gestures for representing the primitive were already well established in the western art-music tradition and were used to represent *any* primitive, not only Native Americans. Pisani calls this the "ready-made toolbox of exotica" (1998: 230). It includes:

1. Sustained fifths that create the sound of a drone – the rural
2. The 'peasant' rhythmic motif of long–short–short – the pastoral
3. Static harmony; hammering duple metre; harmonization at the interval of the fourth and fifth; and passing chromatic colourings – the Gypsy-Turkish
4. Non-standard scales, such as pentatonic, and folk melodies – the folk

5. Chromatic motion, percussion with a 'buzzing' element, tremolos, repetition – the sultry or lurid
6. Doubling of melodies at fourth, fifth or octave; pedal points – the oriental
7. Three-note descending motifs in short–short–long rhythm – the Native American. (adapted from Pisani, 1998: 230)

These different means of representing Others, however, became conflated and have been used interchangeably to represent any Other as necessary for conveying the narrative or creating the mood and atmosphere. Because some of these motifs, already imbued with meaning and expectations, appeared to be present in some Native American musics, Deloria notes that the collection and transcription of such musics served to reinforce the stereotype of primitivism (2004: 194). This had a great impact on the proliferation of this representational style.

The music heard in movies produced by Disney "originated in the decades between 1890 and 1930 – the founding years and the boom years for the sound of Indian", for it was during this time that "the composers and performers of Indianist music ... [attached] concrete and specific images to sounds" (*ibid.*: 219). The influence of silent film is significant in this development. Early films relied on strong imagery and a musical score (often played on the piano) to convey the story to an audience, as they did not contain spoken synchronized dialogue to carry meaning. When synch-sound was introduced to film, the overexaggerated, shorthand means of musical representation used for silent film was carried over to the accompanying film scores (*ibid.*: 221). This led to the continuation and codification of stereotyped musical gestures to represent indigenous peoples in film, many of which continue to be employed in more recent film productions. With this overview of the means of musical representation employed in film, I now turn to the story of *Brother Bear* and the musical representation of indigenous culture in animated features.

The *Brother Bear* narrative

Brother Bear opens with three brothers, Sitka, Denahi and Kenai, catching fish for a feast that will take place after a ceremony in which the youngest brother, Kenai (voiced by Joaquin Phoenix), will receive his totem. Upon returning home, Kenai is charged with securing the fish in a tree so that bears will not eat it. He does so but the knot releases and the fish fall to the ground. Not wanting to wait another second to receive his totem, Kenai leaves the fish on the ground and runs to greet the shaman and grandmother figure in the story, Tenana (Joan Copeland). Kenai receives the totem that will guide him as he becomes a man – love, as represented by the bear. When they return to collect the fish for the feast, a bear has eaten them. Kenai promises his brother Denahi (Jason Raize) that he will retrieve the fish basket and sets out in search of the bear. His brothers follow him in an effort to prevent him from doing something foolish. When the bear corners Kenai, his brother Sitka (D. B. Sweeney) deliberately causes a large portion of the glacier they are standing on to cave in, and Sitka and the bear fall into the water below. Sitka dies protecting his brothers, but the bear survives the fall. Kenai vows revenge and sets out after the bear once again. This time he kills the bear and immediately afterwards Sitka's spirit transforms Kenai into a bear.

Kenai then 'walks a mile in another's footsteps', making a journey to the "mountain where the lights touch the earth" to ask that his brother transform him back into a man. On his journey, he meets a grizzly bear cub named Koda (Jeremy Suarez). Later, it is revealed that this is the cub of the bear he had earlier killed. Kenai is also accompanied by two Canadian moose, Rutt (Rick Moranis) and Tuke (Dave Thomas), who provide comic relief and are recognizable to North American audiences as the characters Bob and Doug McKenzie from "The Great White North", as featured on the television show *SCTV*.[7] Throughout this journey the group is chased by Kenai's brother Denahi, who is driven by anger to kill the bear, not realizing that it is his own brother. The audience witnesses Kenai's character development from a man who sees the bear as a monster to a man who learns to see things from the bear's perspective.[8] As his anger fades, he befriends the bear cub Koda and they refer to each other as brothers. With Koda's help, Kenai locates the "mountain where the lights touch the earth" and he calls on Sitka to change him back to a man. Kenai realizes that, because he killed Koda's mother, he is now responsible for Koda's care, so he chooses to return to being a bear and lives the rest of his life taking care of Koda. Denahi summarizes this story as one in which "a boy learns to become a man by becoming a bear."

After watching the bonus material that accompanies this movie, particularly *Paths of Discovery: The Making of Brother Bear* (director uncredited, 2004), it becomes clear that the film employed an original story, written by Disney specifically for the purpose of making this animated feature.[9] It appears the story was being written (and rewritten) while also being animated and scored. Indeed, the challenges of scoring are highlighted in the bonus material; Phil Collins and Mark Mancina, who composed original music for the animation, would change or substitute songs along the way as the concept of the story changed. While *Brother Bear* is asserted to be an original story, it is important to note that by consulting the Stith Thompson *Motif-Index of Folk-Literature* (1955) it is possible to locate many analogues in other folk tales, myths and legends.[10] The most striking motif of this story is the transformation of a man to a bear. Narrative forms including this motif have been collected from Icelanders, the Sami, and from Eskimo in Greenland, West Greenland, West Hudson Bay, and the Bering Strait [D113.2].[11] Related to this is the brief transformation from bear back to person, which has also been collected from the Eskimo in Greenland, as well as other cultures such as Korean [D313.3]. Most striking, perhaps, is motif Q584.2, the transformation of a man to animal as fitting punishment. This motif has been collected from Lithuania and from the Tupi in Brazil. In *Brother Bear*, Sitka transformed Kenai into a bear as punishment for killing a bear, forcing him to develop an appreciation for this animal and to learn to follow his totem.

Lesser motifs that are featured in the story of *Brother Bear* are also found in the *Motif-Index*. For example, the motif of the friendly return of a dead brother has been collected from the Eskimo of Greenland, as well as Irish culture [E326]. The motif of a mountain reaching to the sky [F55], collected from South American Indians, and the related motif of the otherworld atop a lofty mountain [F132] appear analogous to the home of the spirits atop a mountain featured in *Brother Bear*. Particularly significant to the story of *Brother Bear* are the actions of Sitka, who leads the bear to the edge of a glacier, which he then causes to cave under them, in an effort to save his brothers' lives by killing the bear. This has some similarity to motif K893.1 – man leads pursuers to edge of thin ice. Kenai's sidekick Koda, who helps him out of a beartrap and takes him to the "mountain where the lights touch the earth", is found to be somewhat of a stock character with the motif of the helpful bear, found in Italian, Jewish and Indian stories [B435.4]. Finally, rage and the frenzied pursuit of the bears exhibited by Denahi after he loses both his brothers finds a parallel in Icelandic lore with the motif madness (rage) from hearing about his brother's death [F1041.8.10].

It is relevant to note a specific Mi'kmaw[12] legend called 'Brother to the Bears' that was published in a collection by Alden Nowlan (1983: 48–52).[13] It tells the story of an orphaned boy who goes to live with the bears, who take care of him, providing him with fish when his abilities fail. In the end, however, the orphaned boy has to return to his human family. In *Brother Bear*, the bears in the salmon-run scene constitute a large, extended family that gathers annually for celebration. Kenai, in this situation, may be read as an orphan in that he does not have a bear family and is estranged from his human family. Kenai is a particularly poor catcher of fish and the other bears, especially Koda, help him. During the song 'Welcome', he is initiated into the family of bears. Not unlike the orphaned boy in the Mi'kmaw legend 'Brother to the Bears', Kenai eventually returns to his human family (though in the form of a bear, rather than that of a human).

Elliot Oring, in discussing annotation, concluded, "Annotation promotes awareness that expressions recorded in specific face-to-face encounters can often be related to broader streams of culture, history, and literature" (1989: 373). While this brief survey of some of the motifs in *Brother Bear* is not comprehensive, it certainly identifies some of the story's parallels with other narratives. These parallels are found in other cultures in some cases, while other analogues are located specifically in Inuit cultures. This said, there is no exact story that matches *Brother Bear*. However, the parallels between it and other pieces of folk-literature might suggest that the process of writing this story was more a process of compilation. Elements and motifs that relate to Inuit culture or are otherwise steeped in a folk-narrative tradition are synthesized in *Brother Bear*, and the storyline of *Brother Bear* is related to them, even though it is an original story. A similar, 'compilation', approach is seen in the musical representation of an Inuit culture group in this film. The composers did not select and maintain a single musical style or tradition throughout *Brother Bear*. Rather, they incorporated a wide variety of styles,

including pop, soul, and Motown, to tell Kenai's story musically. As such, the composers are employing recognizable musical gestures that, like the narrative elements and
motifs, relate to "broader streams of culture, history and literature" (*ibid.*).

Musical representation in *Brother Bear*

The indigenous people represented in *Brother Bear* are not easily identified, for the
relationship between the narrative, the imagery and the musical score is not immediately
recognizable to the viewer. *Brother Bear* is set in a time roughly indicated as the end
of the last Ice Age, a time when mammoths still walked the Earth. The culture represented in this narrative is closest to the Yup'ik or Cup'ik Eskimo in Alaska, but also bears
a similarity to the Inupiaq and St Lawrence Island Yup'ik culture groups there.[14] The
choice to translate one song into an Inuit language (discussed below), combined with
the background research trips to Alaska (especially Denali National Park) to paint
landscapes for the animation, suggests that the film-makers were consciously representing an Eskimo or Inuit culture group; however, there is no evidence that they were
consciously representing a more specific group (such as Yup'ik or Cup'ik).[15] The
narrative is situated primarily in Alaska, though its landscapes and the inspiration for
them are taken from many different parts of the United States, including Yellowstone
National Park. Indeed, Chuck Williams (the producer) explains, "The film is trying to
capture the idealized best of North America."[16]

The musical representation of this culture is curious. There are only a few scenes
of diegetic music in *Brother Bear*. The first scene of a celebration, which returns in
almost identical form at the end of the film, provides only a brief glimpse of the music
and dancing that is taking place. An early sequence depicts a few men dancing with
feathers in their hands and masks on their faces, followed by a scene showing drumming.
The only musical instruments that appear throughout the film are two Alaskan Inuit frame
drums and a barrel-shaped drum that resembles a grandfather drum, an instrument not
found in Inuit culture. What is actually heard, however, is a Japanese taiko drum. What
sense do viewers make of such incongruity?

I held two focus-group sessions during which six participants watched this film and
responded to it through conversations,[17] providing feedback on both the *Brother Bear*
film and the bonus materials.[18] Participants were asked whether what they heard sounded
'native'. Kaitlyn noted the use of rattles and heavy drum as contributing to a somewhat
"native sound" but said that it appeared to be more "flavour music" (28 March
2005).[19] Sean also indicated that the presence of drums made the music sound
indigenous (28 March 2005), while Jennifer pointed out the world-beat associations,
describing a particular sound that she associates with that genre – an emphasis on
percussion and a strong choral sound that is somehow far off in the distance (28 March
2005). She referred to this as "sonic wash". The music was also compared to that of
The Lion King (Kaitlyn, 28 March 2005). While *The Lion King* did not sound particularly
African, it had a similar emphasis on heavy drumbeats. This style of scoring exploits

advances in surround-sound technology, in both cinemas and home theatres, which enhance rhythmic emphases in the soundtrack.

A comparison to *The Lion King* was also made by Kathryn during the second focus group. When I asked this group about the music they heard, Tonya noted that the background music is more likely to be "strange or foreign or mysterious", but the actual songs reiterate the narrative from the past few scenes (31 March 2005). The in-between (underscore, segue) music sounds like something more "cultural", or at least this is what Tonya believes Disney's production team was trying to convey. Karen noted that the only 'native' thing she heard was the emphasis on drums. She continued, "But I didn't hear anything that I would think was Inuit music" (31 March 2005). She noted that the use of what she interpreted to be vocables (actually lyrics in an Inuit language) and excessive reverb assisted the score to sound "mystical" or "Othery" (*ibid.*). Kathryn pointed out that when she heard some flute-playing at one point in the score, it almost had a Celtic "flare" (31 March 2005). She further explained that tossing in little Native flavours here and there gave the film a feel of "pseudo authenticity" (*ibid.*). That is, passing sonic gestures of 'Indianness' or Otherness may reinforce the (perhaps non-existent) relationship between the music heard and the culture that is being presented visually. Interrelated sound and visual elements in film often reinforce meanings; aural cues may reinforce the visuals depicted, or vice versa. Further, brief gestures of (perceived) culture-specific sound or visuals may cause the audience to interpret the presentation as a true or valid expression of that culture.

When I asked about the instruments viewed during the opening scene, Kaitlyn observed:

> They ... didn't go together at all ... the hand drums they were using were
> Inuit hand drums ... and then they had people all sitting around like a big
> grandfather drum. [But] they never, ever, ever go together. (28 March 2005)

Kaitlyn's focus on the drums in the opening sequence was echoed by Karen, who said the film was representing "Inuit peoples, I think, just 'cause of the drum" (31 March 2005). When I asked her to clarify whether it was one or both of the drums that indicated the culture for her, she replied, "Just the frame drum" (*ibid.*). For Kaitlyn and Karen, this was glaringly obvious; however, this is perhaps specialized knowledge. The general public watching this film might not recognize or question the problematic inclusion of a grandfather drum. As Sean noted:

> Disney, I'm sure, isn't making this movie for people who can tell the
> difference between the different cultures. And I just assumed that it was
> nothing in particular but just very token representations. Token, kind of, "this
> will be recognisable to people who've never been on a reservation or to a
> powwow, and this [other] will be recognizable, and we'll just mash them all
> together and that will be the ceremonial thing". (28 March 2005)

These token representations, then, allow a viewer to consider the culture being represented as indigenous and, to those with some level of cultural knowledge, may even allow the viewer to identify the cultural group as Inuit.

Similar ambiguities of place and culture group occur in Disney's *The Emperor's New Groove*. Silverman notes that while Disney does not explicitly identify the society in which the story is placed, "archaeologists will readily recognize it as set in Inca Peru" (2002: 299). In an effort to simplify the film and ensure "legibility" for its audience, Silverman argues that Disney employs visuals that are "generically pre-Columbian or, for the truly uneducated viewer, merely exotic" (*ibid.*: 308). Acknowledging that Disney does not claim the representation to be authentic, nor is it promoted as a historical film, Silverman points out that there is, nevertheless, "a 'real' behind Disney's representations" (*ibid.*: 310). Consequently, issues of cultural appropriation and de-authoring, essentialism, and exoticism emerge, regardless of the film's moral or artistic merit (*ibid.*: 304–10).

If it ain't Inuit, it must be ... Bulgarian?

While there is a 'real' behind *Brother Bear*, as suggested by Silverman's (2002) study of *The Emperor's New Groove*, it does not emerge in the score for the film. In *Brother Bear*, there is no culture-specific music heard, no traditional songs sung, whether diegetic or non-diegetic. The opening theme is sung by Tina Turner in a popular rhythm-and-blues vocal style, much like the opening sequence of *The Lion King*. Likewise, when Koda sings 'On My Way', it is in the popular style and voice of Phil Collins, who wrote the music for the film. Perhaps the most striking feature of the musical score is the music heard throughout the transformation scene at the top of a mountain during which Kenai is transformed into a bear by his brother's spirit (and later, from a bear back into a human). This scene, which may be read to represent a cultural or spiritual belief in the spirits of ancestors and/or in shape-shifting, is accompanied by the 'mysterious' sound cultivated by the Bulgarian Women's Choir.[20] Indeed, their voices suggest spirits and the spirit world throughout the movie. This is not without parallel – Diamond (2005), for example, observed a similar use of the Bulgarian Women's Choir to represent spirits in the film *Atanarjuat* (Zacharias Kunuk, 2001).[21]

Why would the composers of *Brother Bear* make use of the Bulgarian Women's Choir for this purpose? Mark Mancina, who co-wrote the film score with Phil Collins, says simply that he was a fan of the choir and felt that it was a wonderful opportunity to bring them into the film.[22] The song 'Transformation' was initially written in English by Phil Collins. The bonus material, *Paths of Discovery*, indicates that the production team brought a professor from Alaska, a "Native speaker who also spoke very good English", to their studio and had this person translate the song into Eskimo language. Further bonus material titled 'Transformation Song' bears an opening credit noting the English was "translated into Innuit [sic]". While the DVD bonus material curiously does not name the translator, the liner notes for the *Brother Bear* CD (2003) identify her as

Lorena Williams. Regarding the translation of the song into an Inuit language, Chris Montan (President, Walt Disney Music) notes that people viewing the movie likely will not know the language, "but it'll feel real to them at least, and they won't even probably know why". The presence of the Bulgarian Women's Choir during the transformation scene, along with striking images of animals and spirits, effectively works to conjure up the supernatural.

Another curious musical gesture is in the Motown-style song sung by the bears at the salmon run. Here the Blind Boys of Alabama[23] provide the voices for the bears on the track 'Welcome'. This, combined with the opening track sung by Tina Turner, allowed for what Aaron Blaise (director) called a "musically diverse, rich film". This emphasis on African American-derived music cannot be ignored. Almost all of the musicians heard on the soundtrack (other than the Bulgarian Women's Choir) are African American. Sean immediately made this connection while watching the film, without having any knowledge of who was singing. It is his opinion that this film is not really about indigenous culture, but rather that it is about black people in America (focus group, 28 March 2005). Perhaps it is about the reduction of 'race' to a black–white binary.[24] He noted that most bears other than Kenai have darker fur and demonstrate accents that would indicate they are black (there are exceptions, such as the Croatian bear) (ibid.). Karen, in a different focus group, also noted that the voices used throughout were 'black' and that even the title of the film itself sounded African American (31 March 2005). The "ready-made toolbox of exotica", then, does not appear to have been employed in this movie. Rather, black culture has been embedded in this film in association with indigenous culture, and different audiences recognize these allusions on some level. Is this removal of "the sound of Indian" a means of acknowledging the fact that Inuit culture is significantly different from that of Native American? Or is it an outright denial of their musical culture? Does the fact that the film is set in a time outside of modern history explain the ambiguity of place and sound throughout the film?

Without white colonizers or European contact in the plot of this movie, a community of bears provides the contrast to the human characters. Indeed, the bear community and not the Native community is idealized in this film; the purpose of Kenai's entire journey is to become more like a bear. In fact, the first song composed for the salmon-run scene was replaced with the song 'Welcome' because the sentiment was more appropriate. Although the group of bears had initially been conceived of as "frat boys", Producer Williams noted that "the bears [weren't] noble enough" and were therefore recast as a brotherhood. This is undoubtedly a telling choice of words considering the stereotype of romanticized noble savages in early North American film and literature.

In the bonus material on the DVD, there is a section on the scoring process for *Brother Bear* titled "Designing the Score" that is meant to inform the audience about the music heard in the film. Indeed, it may help to clarify the issues raised thus far. In explaining the lack of culture-specific music in the film, Phil Collins noted, "It's impossible to be completely true to the Native American Indian at the end of the ice age, well, because the instruments just don't sound that good."[25] Chris Montan further clarified, "Our reluctance to go all the way there was [because] that is a very limited palette of music. They didn't really have almost any melody instruments. It was primarily drums." Collins continued, "They're kind of pretty low-fi, you know, so you've got to open up a little bit to take in world instruments." Instead of cultural or historical accuracy or authenticity, then, the goal was to create 'hybrid sounds' by layering a variety of drums. In so doing, they were able to create an 'ethnic' sound. An orchestra of typical instrumentation (strings, brass, woodwinds and percussion) was combined with hybrid "flavours" of non-western instruments to create a richness of sound. In discussing the inclusion of indigenous instrumentation, Mark Mancina pointed to their use of Hopi instruments in the score, unproblematically allowing the instruments of one specific culture to stand for another, distinct culture.

Reacting to this, participants in both focus groups were quick to condemn the composers for such an approach to the representation of a culture group – greater cultural sensitivity and more attention to historic and culture-specific detail would have been appreciated by these culturally informed viewers. Participants, however, also felt compelled to argue for the film's merit, seen primarily in the themes and values embedded in the story, such as respect for nature. Artistically, all agreed that the film can be appreciated because it is visually striking, with many layers and much depth captured in the landscape. However, sonic misrepresentation of an indigenous group was seen to reduce a vibrant culture to a lesser version of itself and Disney was seen to have missed an opportunity to introduce its audiences to the sounds of indigenous cultures and foster intercultural understanding.

The risks of Disney's approach to the representation of different cultures seem to be significant for both children and adults. Williams has identified one such problem in her research into cinema reception: "We draw much of what we 'learn' as adults from the popular films and television programs we view" (1980: ix). Such representations may reinforce stereotypes of Native and other cultures. This same concern is echoed in the work of Rollins and O'Connor, who note the misinformation that may accumulate via film and television media and affect attitudes (2003: 10).[26] These critics agree that "contemporary ignorance and stereotypes in popular culture certainly deserve condemnation" (*ibid.*: 2). Specifically referencing film, in 1977 Harrington argued, "Intellectual etiquette requires damning the way Hollywood has treated every group and nationality" (1977: 76). While he noted many scholarly works that did just that, he was also careful to make a distinction between fiction and documentary and to offer a defence for filmmakers:

> The purpose of fiction is to tell us about ourselves, though, not about the facts of ancestors. In telling us about ourselves, a filmmaker needs room to simplify and recreate actuality into his unique vision. His [sic] first concern cannot be for historical accuracy, but rather for articulating and presenting

his perception of a contemporary problem – his own problem or that of someone else. (ibid.: 83)

This need to critique cultural representation in a film, while at the same time defending artistry and creativity, echoes the reactions of members of my focus groups and is indicative of an understanding of the film genre as a creative art form and the film production team as artists.

Indeed, there is more to this issue of representation than authenticity or historical and cultural accuracy. In considering musical representations in Disney's *Pocahontas*, I concluded that musical representations are meant to enhance and reflect that which is occurring visually, while creating emotional ties between the audience and characters. Therefore, musical gestures need not be 'authentic' representations if they achieve the desired effect.[27] I believe this is largely the case in *Brother Bear* and it helps to explain the different ways that participants in my focus groups reacted to the film. Initially, most of them enjoyed it; they laughed at the jokes, rolled their eyes at the 'cornier' parts, expressed distress at Kenai's initially cruel treatment of Koda, and reacted with total silence when Kenai confessed to Koda that he had killed the bear's mother. All of this would suggest to me that they became emotionally invested in the story on some level. The musical score certainly factored into this emotional connection in that it added to the overall mood of the film.

After viewing the bonus material, however, it would be difficult for any of these viewers to admit that they 'liked' a Disney movie. It was the actual bonus material outlining the decision-making process, rather than the film itself,[28] that was most offensive to the participants in my culturally informed focus groups. They felt that Disney had some responsibility to represent indigenous cultures in more culturally sensitive ways, but had failed at this task. It is worth speculating as to whether the production team's presentation of the decision-making process was a defensive strategy on their part, meant to pre-empt anticipated criticism. If so, it appears that it had very much the opposite effect on members of my focus groups. Indeed, it may be the most controversial part of *Brother Bear* and leaves little ambiguity as to whether the production team chose to represent Inuit culture in such a manner or were simply ignorant of it.

Conclusion: an aesthetic of ambiguity

At first glance, the musical representation in *Brother Bear* suggests that the stereotyped sounds used to represent Native Americans noted by Deloria (2004), Pisani (1998), and Gorbman (2000a, 2000b) are breaking down. However, if the representation is merely replaced with one described as employing "world instruments" and is generically 'ethnic' without specific referents, have we transcended stereotypes or changed "the sound of Indian"? Or have we merely expanded the tool-box of exoticism? Gorbman has noted that, after 1960, "new scoring solutions arose" (2000a: 106) in addition to the well-established musical stereotypes already used to represent First Nations in Westerns and that the 1990s saw composers moving towards eclectic combinations of different ethnic musics (*ibid.*: 12–13). This tool-box of exoticism appears to have been expanded to include additional categories of musical stereotypes in *Brother Bear*: smooth, Motown-styled rhythm-and-blues vocals, and complex, often syncopated, rhythms representing the black Other, while the music of the Bulgarian Women's Choir has become a stereotyped musical gesture referencing the supernatural or spiritual.

The Bulgarian Women's Choir illustrates an important aesthetic choice woven throughout *Brother Bear*, namely, ambiguity. Their sound cannot be placed when heard in the context of the film, especially since they are singing in the style they cultivate but in an Inuit language[29] that is foreign to them. The inability to locate interrelated elements in *Brother Bear* is displayed throughout the film. As described, the setting in which the story takes place is ambiguous, with incongruous imagery and animals with 'foreign' accents. Conjecture is required to determine the time period of the story setting, the culture presented is not clearly identified, and the music does not provide anything concrete to clarify these ambiguities. Indeed, this film may actually be more about African American culture than Inuit culture. In this context, then, attention to authenticity or historical and cultural accuracy in the musical representation of Inuit culture would prove inconsistent with the general aesthetic of ambiguity employed throughout *Brother Bear* and would necessitate the use of similarly ambiguous musical gestures in the film. The aesthetic of ambiguity employed in *Brother Bear*, then, is a narrative device that lifts the audience out of space and time, and into the "magical world of Disney".[30]

In a film form that employs anthropomorphized central protagonists, talking creatures voiced by ethnically accented actors, an abstracted visual aesthetic, and other conventions now familiar to animation film – including a complex music track of songs and music backgrounds – perhaps the film's universal themes do not need to be specific to culture or ethnicity. Localized audiences 'own' stories to a greater or lesser degree depending on their attitude to authentic representation and awareness of issues of cultural (mis)appropriation. However, the Disney 'magic' may be intended as an address not to such audiences but to a generalized, transnational Euro-centric western one. Viewed from this perspective, the contradictory responses by focus groups to *Brother Bear* can be reconciled. Ultimately, the 'magic of Disney' evident in films such as *Brother Bear* holds power *because* it is an ambiguous representation; it emotionally addresses feel-good morals, enables escapism through an act of storytelling, and compels audiences through visual artistry, instead of presenting a practical travelogue or ethnographically informed representation of actual communities. Thus, the 'magic of Disney' is in fact the charm of ambiguity.

Notes

1. African people and culture are not directly referenced in this film; however, African elements are strongly present in the setting, narrative and musical presentation, in a style consistent with anthropomorphism in animation.

2. Critical analysis of these and other Disney animated films has focused on gender studies and feminist approaches (Addison, 1993; Bonham, 2000; Henke *et al.*, 1996; Hoerrner, 1996; Lajewski, 2000), thematic content, moral lessons and story types (Gavin, 1996; Wong, 1999), neocolonialist narratives (Buescher and Ono, 1996), race (Kilpatrick, 1995), and orientalism or exoticism (Addison, 1993; Silverman, 2002).

3. O'Connor cites 1909 as the date for the first critique (1980: 3), while Harrington (1977: 77) cites 1911.

4. Adare (2005) illuminates First Nations' responses to stereotypes portrayed in science-fiction television shows.

5. For discussion of the development of such musical gestures in Euro-American music prior to the advent of film, see Deloria (2004), Gorbman (2000b) and Pisani (1998).

6. For more on the manner by which two- and three-note motifs have represented the Other, see J. E. Tulk (2002), 'Multivalent Musical Gestures, Ethnic Representations, and Commodified Culture: Exoticism in Disney's *Pocahontas*', unpublished term paper (Music 616), University of Alberta, pp. 10–11.

7. "The Great White North" was a comedy sketch focused on Canadian culture and stereotypes; it was featured on the television show *SCTV*, which aired on the Global and Canadian Broadcasting Corporation (CBC) networks in Canada from 1976 to 1981. The show's title, *SCTV*, stands for Second City Television and is a reference to the Toronto-based comedy troupe The Second City. "The Great White North" sketch was later turned into a feature-length film titled *The Adventures of Bob and Doug McKenzie: Strange Brew* (Rick Moranis and Dave Thomas, 1983).

8. This point is emphasized in the use of two screen-aspect ratios. The first 25 minutes of the movie, during which Kenai is in human form, are in a smaller than normal aspect ratio, with black strips on all sides of the picture. When he wakes up as a bear, the aspect ratio has changed to a standard wide screen, and the colours seem a little bit brighter.

9. Silverman in her study of *The Emperor's New Groove* suggests that, following harsh criticism of *Pocahontas* as "being romanticized, fictionalized, sanitized and nationalized for popular consumption", Disney has turned away from the presentation of historical events, preferring to "play it safe" when choosing source material for its films (2002: 308).

10. Two participants in the focus groups, Kaitlyn and Kathryn, noted that there are similar stories in Native culture, but that the story does not appear to have an exact analogue. Kaitlyn pointed out that Inuit stories often teach a lesson or demonstrate what humans learn from animals (28 March 2005).

11. These alpha-numeric references are motif designations in the Stith Thompson index.

12. The Mi'kmaq are an indigenous group whose traditional territory encompasses Nova Scotia, New Brunswick, Prince Edward Island, and parts of Quebec and Newfoundland in Canada, as well as parts of Maine in the USA. Mi'kmaq is the plural noun, while Mi'kmaw is the singular noun and adjective.

13. This legend has recently served as the source for an animated short produced by Mi'kmaw film-maker Catherine Martin titled *The Boy Who Visited Muin'sku* (2005, animated by Alan Syliboy).

14. My thanks to Amber Ridington for pointing out the possibility that Disney may be representing the latter groups.

15. 'Mirror to the World: Inspirations', in *Paths of Discovery: The Making of Brother Bear*, 2-disc Special Edition of *Brother Bear*, 2004. Silverman notes that similar research trips to Peru were made in the preparations for animating *The Emperor's New Groove* (2002: 305–6).

16. 'Mirror to the World: Inspirations.'

17. The first group included Sean, Jennifer, and Kaitlyn (28 March 2005), while the second group included Karen, Kathryn, and Tonya (31 March 2005). Every effort was made to include participants with a wide variety of interests and backgrounds; however, due to uncontrollable circumstances, Sean was the only participant not pursuing a graduate degree in Folklore. Further, the imbalance of the male-to-female ratio was not intended. Other males were invited to attend the sessions, but for various reasons were unable to participate. Finally, an effort was made to include two representatives of First Nations culture. Due to prior commitments, both declined the invitation to participate in my research. The analysis of and response to *Brother Bear* that follows, then, should be read with this in mind.

18. All the following quotes are taken from these focus groups unless otherwise indicated. They have been delineated by date.

19. This is an interesting choice of words since she made this comment before watching the bonus material. In the bonus material those working on the film use "flavours" to describe the style of music they wanted.

20. Buchanan (1997) discusses the magical and mystical sounds of the Bulgarian Women's Choir.

21. *Atanarjuat (The Fast Runner)* was directed by Zacharias Kunuk and relates an Inuit legend in Inuktitut.

22. All the following quotes and attributions from personnel involved in the production of *Brother Bear* are taken from the DVD bonus material, unless otherwise indicated.

23. The Blind Boys of Alabama, a soul-gospel group, was formed in 1939 at the Alabama Institute for the Blind. Their biography can be found at http://www.blindboys.com/main.html (accessed 1 July 2007).

24. Although the dialogue also features Italian American accents, and, together with Collins's pseudo-chanting included in the music tracks, suggests a generalized approach to 'ethnic' Americans or multiculturalism.

25. While watching this bonus material, Tonya questioned what is the "Native American Indian at the end of the ice age ... What does that mean?" (31 March 2005).

26. The work of Seixas (1993, 1994) attempts to identify the way in which this acquisition of 'knowledge' plays out among school-age children and whether they can distinguish between stereotypes in film.

27. J. E. Tulk (2002), 'Multivalent Musical Gestures, Ethnic Representations, and Commodified Culture: Exoticism in Disney's *Pocahontas*', unpublished term paper (Music 616), University of Alberta, pp. 17–18.

28. If I suspend my disbelief and watch this film without the use of an analytical lens, I very much enjoy it. Indeed, the landscapes are perhaps some of the best in the history of Disney and the two Canadian moose are two of my favourite Disney characters ever. However, the comments made during the bonus features have coloured my enjoyment of the film and it is increasingly difficult to view it without concerns about cultural (mis)appropriation lurking in the background.

29. As the exact culture group represented in this film is not identified, nor is the language pinpointed more specifically than Eskimo or Inuit, it is not possible to know which language or dialect is employed. It may be Inupiaq, Inuktitut, or another variant of this language group.

30. "*The Magical World of Disney*" was the title of a 1988 television special. This title and variations on it have been used by the general public and critics to refer to various "*Disney On Ice*" productions, as well as stage shows.

References

Adare, S. S. (2005), *"Indian" Stereotypes in TV Science Fiction: First Nations' Voices Speak Out*, Austin: University of Texas Press.

Addison, E. (1993), 'Saving Other Women from Other Men: Disney's *Aladdin*', *Camera Obscura*, no.31, 4–25.

Bonham, M. D. (2000), 'Doing Gender in Disneyland: How Does *Mulan* Affect the Future of Female Protagonists in Disney Movies?', *Michigan Academician*, 32(2), 93.

Buchanan, D. A. (1997), 'Review Essay: Bulgaria's Magical Mystère Tour: Postmodernism, World Music Marketing, and Political Change in Eastern Europe', *Ethnomusicology*, 41(1), 131–57.

Buescher, D. T., and Ono, K. A. (1996), 'Civilized Colonialism: *Pocahontas* as Neo-colonial Rhetoric', *Women's Studies in Communication*, 19, 127–53.

Deloria, P. J. (2004), *Indians in Unexpected Places*, Lawrence, KA: University Press of Kansas.

Diamond, B. (2005), 'The Soundtracks of Indigenous Film', in M. Lovelace, P. Narvaez and D. Tye (eds), *Bean Blossom to Bannerman, Odyssey of a Folklorist: A Festschrift for Neil V. Rosenberg*, St John's: Folklore and Language Publications, Memorial University of Newfoundland, pp. 125–54.

Gavin, R. (1996), '*The Lion King* and *Hamlet*: A Homecoming for the Exiled Child', *The English Journal*, 85(3), 55–7.

Gorbman, C. (2000a), 'Drums Along the LA River: Scoring the Indian', in P. Brophy (ed.), *Cinesonic: Cinema and the Sound of Music*. Sydney: Australian Film, Television, & Radio School, pp. 97–115.

Gorbman, C. (2000b), 'Scoring the Indian: Music in the Liberal Western', in G. Born and D. Hesmondhalgh (eds), *Western Music and Its Others: Difference,*

Representation, and Appropriation in Music, Berkeley: University of California Press, pp. 234–53.

Harrington, J. (1977), 'Understanding Hollywood's Indian Rhetoric', *Canadian Review of American Studies*, 8(1), 77–88.

Henke, J., Umble, B., Zimmerman, D., and Smith, N. J. (1996), 'Construction of the Female Self: Feminist Readings of the Disney Heroine', *Women's Studies in Communication*, 19, 229–49.

Hoerrner, K. L. (1996), 'Gender Roles in Disney Films: Analyzing Behaviors from Snow White to Simba', *Women's Studies in Communication*, 19, 213–28.

Kilpatrick, J. (1995), 'Disney's "Politically Correct" *Pocahontas*', *Cineaste*, 21(4), 36–7.

Kilpatrick, J. (1999), *Celluloid Indians: Native Americans and Film*, Lincoln: University of Nebraska Press.

Lajewski, J. A. (2000), 'Fa Mulan or How I Went to War in Drag and Saved China' *Michigan Academician*, 32(2), 146.

Moses, L. G. (1996), *Wild West Shows and the Images of American Indians, 1883–1933*, Albuquerque: University of New Mexico Press.

Nowlan, A. (1983), *Nine Micmac Legends*, Hantsport, NS: Lancelot Press.

O'Connor, J. E. (1980), *The Hollywood Indian: Stereotypes of Native Americans in Films*, Trenton: New Jersey State Museum.

O'Pray, M. (2000), 'The Animated Film', in J. Hill and P. C. Gibson (eds), *World Cinema: Critical Approaches*, Oxford: Oxford University Press, pp. 50–5.

Oring, E. (1989), 'Documenting Folklore: The Annotation', in *Folk Groups and Folklore Genres: A Reader*, Logan: Utah State University Press, pp. 358–73.

Pisani, M. V. (1998), '"I'm an Indian Too": Creating Native American Identities in Nineteenth- and Early Twentieth-century Music', in J. Bellman (ed.), *The Exotic in Western Music*, Boston: Northeastern University Press, pp. 218–57.

Rollins, P. C., and O'Connor, J. E. (2003), 'Introduction: The Study of Hollywood's Indian: Still on a Scholarly Frontier?', in P. C. Rollins and J. E. O'Connor (eds), *Hollywood's Indian: The Portrayal of the Native American in Film*, Lexington: University Press of Kentucky, pp. 1–11.

Seixas, P. (1993), 'Popular Film and Young People's Understanding of the History of Native American-White Relations', *History Teacher*, 26(3), 351–70.

Seixas, P. (1994), 'Confronting the Moral Frames of Popular Film: Young People Respond to Historical Revisionism', *American Journal of Education*, 102(3), 261–85.

Shively, J. (1992), 'Cowboys and Indians: Perceptions of Western Films among American Indians and Anglos', *American Sociological Review*, 57(6), 725–34.

Silverman, H. (2002), 'Groovin' to Ancient Peru: A Critical Analysis of Disney's *The Emperor's New Groove*', *Journal of Social Archaeology*, 2(3), 298–322.

Stripes, J. (1999), 'A Strategy of Resistance: The "Actorvism" of Russell Means from Plymouth Rock to the Disney Studios', *Wicazo Sa Review*, 14(1), 87–101.

Strong, P. (1996), 'Animated Indians: Critique and Contradiction in Commodified Children's Culture', *Cultural Anthropology*, 11(3), 405–24.

Thompson, S. (1955), *Motif-Index of Folk-Literature: A Classification of Narrative Elements in Folktales, Ballads, Myths, Fables, Mediaeval Romances, Exempla, Fabliaux, Jest-Books and Local Legends*, Bloomington: Indiana University Press.

Williams, L. E. (1980), 'Foreword', in P. C. Rollins and J. E. O'Connor (eds), *The Hollywood Indian: Stereotypes of Native Americans in Films*, Trenton: New Jersey State Museum, pp. ix–xvi.

Wong, V. (1999), 'Deconstructing the Walt Disney Animation *The Lion King*: Its Ideology and the Perspective of Hong Kong Chinese', *Kinema: A Journal for Film and Audiovisual Media*, no.11, 53–65.

Part III
Music and Sonicity

8 Sonic Nostalgia and *Les Triplettes de Belleville*

Daniel Goldmark

> *Noises are the sounds we have learned to ignore.* (Schafer, 1994: 4)

During his first monologue in *Apocalypse Now* (Francis Ford Coppola, 1979), Martin Sheen establishes the intense, almost irrational, fixation he has with, as he puts it, "getting back to the jungle". Sitting in a Saigon hotel, he describes his obsession, while the sounds of the big city surround him – until, that is, his memories become so powerful as to overtake not just his speech, but the ambient sounds in the room as well. Slowly but surely, the people yelling on the street, the cars driving by, all the sounds of the modern city slowly fade away, shifting to insects chirping, birds squawking and an eerie calm that feels – in the context of Sheen's character, Captain Willard – profoundly tranquil. To establish Willard's distracted state, sound editor Walter Murch displaces one soundscape with another, a subtle transposition that allows his desire to be fulfilled early on, if only on an auditory level. Such sonic exchanges, often taking place beneath the obscuring veil of the visuals and any concurrent dialogue, plant the idea of desire on an almost implicit plane, to be eventually displayed as the action catches up to the hints already dropped in the soundtrack.

Les Triplettes de Belleville (*The Triplets of Belleville*, USA; *Belleville Rendez-Vous* UK; Sylvain Chomet, 2003) is the story of two historical eras – the nostalgic past and the crushing present – that intersect on two continents. Madame Souza, a Portuguese immigrant raising her grandson in France, buys the child a tricycle and encourages his professional cycle-racing expertise as Champion grows up. While riding in the Tour de France, Champion is kidnapped by wine-mafia thugs and is taken to Belleville ('beautiful town'), in North America. His loving and inventive grandmother and his dog Bruno travel there in the hope of freeing him. Once in the big city, Souza and Bruno fall in with the Triplets of Belleville, a singing trio who were famous in the 1930s and now live in happy obscurity. Violette, Blanche and Rose (loosely, the three colours of the French flag) eventually help Madame to free her grandson. The film thrives on nostalgia largely based on a narrative element introduced early in the film with a single line of dialogue: "Is that it, then, hmm? What have you got to say to Grandma, eh? Is it over, do you think?"[1] In fact, the only significant dialogue in the film bookends the action with the very idea of sound as something comforting and, ultimately, something fleeting. Presented as a function of memory, the idea of nostalgia relies heavily on sound design (music and sound effects) to establish connections to the characters' past, to distant history, to other places altogether.

Wordless comedy

We might start by asking why the director, Sylvain Chomet, excluded dialogue altogether. Many US critics attended closely to how well *Triplettes* succeeded in spite of the lack of spoken language. One such reviewer was Charles Solomon (2006), who mentioned *Triplettes* positively in an article for the *New York Times* titled 'Pipe Down, We're Trying to Watch a Cartoon', concerning US animation's recent spell of logorrhoea. As Solomon points out, dialogue largely forms the basis of Hollywood animated-film narratives; much of the comedy in such films arises from ironic turns of phrase and malapropisms. A great deal of the animator's time is therefore spent (if not wasted) drawing vowel shapes on mouths and creating appropriate body language for characters that are talking. Such dialogue can easily become a crutch to support a less-than-stellar story and can even call attention to sub-par character design (which happens when too many mouth movements highlight a poorly constructed face).

Chomet explains that his choice came from his approach to animation:

> For me, when you've worked all day on an animation and that moment when you see the drawings move, that's a really magic moment, and there is no sound to it. I also think that an animation without the constraints of spoken words is stronger. If you have to fit everything to the words, all the gestural movement revolves around the mouth. Without it, you are much freer to create true animation, to talk through animation itself. Animation modeled around the dialogue is like something which has already been set in stone, there's less scope for interpretation. I have always wanted the animators to bring something to it. (Chomet in Moins, 2003)

The idea of letting the animation do the talking is far from new. While sound technology for animated cartoons has evolved over time, so too has people's view of the soundtrack's importance.[2] We need only go back to the beginning of synchronized sound cartoons, in the mid- to late 1920s, when dialogue was not the driving force behind cartoon comedy. These early shorts dealt much more in visually based gags, in part because themes in cartoons derived so directly from live-action comedy films and because the technology had yet to get to a place where dialogue was even possible.[3] Even after dialogue became the norm, some studios deliberately called attention to the music or sound effects. UPA's *Gerald McBoing-Boing* (1949), along with helping to popularize the 'limited' animation style for which the studio became famous, redefined the roles of all three parts of the traditional film soundtrack. Maintaining the format of the original storybook, an off-screen narrator tells the film's story, and yet the characters seamlessly chime in at appropriate times, erasing the line between storyteller and actor. The music, a modernist score by Gail Kubik, draws on neither bouncy pop tunes nor frenetic string passages of descriptive 'mickey-mousing'; instead the largely original score describes actions in the story while also emoting for the characters in a highly novel manner (see Sternfeld, 1950). And, of course, the sound effects – the language for Gerald's utterances – comprise his entire vocabulary, giving prominence to a communicative form that had once gone largely unheard.

Chomet's decision to make his film verbally mute doesn't just free up the animation; he is upsetting the way in which we have been trained to interpret animated films – through the dialogue – and thus forcing the audience to watch (and listen) all the more carefully; as he said, he wants to "talk through animation itself" (quoted in Moins, 2003). His first film, *La Vielle Dame et les pigeons* (1998), gives us a good idea of how Chomet prioritizes sound. The film begins with some home movies of a vacation to Paris narrated by heavily accented tourists from the United States. The tourists' banter seems tangential, but actually sets up the story: an obese father, mother and son from the United States are taking pictures at the Eiffel Tower; a lone, scornful gendarme, monitoring the scene, sneaks a handful of the boy's discarded popcorn from the ground. The concentration on food establishes the film's underlying theme: the policeman's struggle to fill his perpetually empty stomach. As he walks his beat, the cop encounters people stuffing their faces, to his disgust and envy. He eventually encounters a woman feeding oversized pastries and other delicious-looking foods to pigeons in a park. His incessant hunger manifests in a strange dream where he follows the old lady into a park and begins feasting, on all fours, on a giant, glistening ham she throws on the ground for him, only to be harassed and then devoured by a group of man-sized pigeons

Figure 8.1   La Vielle Dame et les pigeons (Chomet, 1998). The gendarme's nightmarish inspiration: pigeon-men

wearing suits (Figure 8.1). Awakening with a gasp, the man hatches an idea to take advantage of the woman, not realizing that she has plans for him as well.

A jaunty accordion-led jazz combo (headed by Jean Corti, one-time accordion accompanist to singer Jacques Brel) gives the film's score a playful tone. The sound effects run the show here, however, particularly the sounds of the pigeons tapping, flapping, cooing, and the evocative sounds of food being torn, chewed and swallowed. Chomet wants us to sympathize with this man, and perhaps even feel as hungry as he is. As the story progresses further, Chomet obviates any need for words. The central musical episode occurs after the man's first meal at the woman's apartment. He is the guest of honour at a dinner for one, and wears a suit topped by a massive pigeon head. Back in his own flat, he observes his full, distended belly with some satisfaction. The pigeons that have been a fixture outside his window throughout the film begin tapping on the glass in a semi-distinct pattern (Figure 8.2). A bass picks up on the soundtrack, and the film's main theme, again on accordion, plays in full as the man dances around his apartment with himself, at one point moving with elbows tucked to his sides as he does his best two-step *à la squab* (Figure 8.3). The music continues as a montage begins, chronicling the man's increasing gluttony as the woman continues to feed him over the coming months. The song matches the giddy, almost goofy mood of the gendarme for *most* of his plan. We shall see later that the characters in *Triplettes* likewise have music that not only underscores their actions, but also gives us insight into their personalities.

The song ends as the Christmas season rolls around; the man has become grossly obese and we see that the hallways and stairwells can no longer accommodate his girth. It is now that the woman's intentions become plain: she has been fattening up this 'pigeon' (in all senses of the term) not because she likes birds, as he mistakenly

Figure 8.2   A sea of pigeons

Figure 8.3 The gendarme shuffles while the birds wave their behinds

believed, but because she loves cats and plans on feeding him to the giant cat that lives next door, who is, in reality, an enormous woman wearing a cat outfit. The twist revealed, the benevolent old lady suddenly turns into a maniac, brandishing massive hedge-clippers and setting off a comic chase as the man tries to remove his pigeon head (which he cannot, either from sheer panic or because his own head has grown too big). He runs around the apartment dodging the shears, all the while trying to *show* her he is human by removing a shoe and sock. Why not simply say something? Chomet effectively closed down the one obvious (and least amusing) escape for the greedy gendarme, thus ensuring a much funnier resolution to the film. This sequence – with speeded-up animation of the old lady to make her look even more psychotic – has a new, rapid theme on the accordion, which takes its initial rhythm from the sound of the woman's shears as she gives chase.

The almost complete lack of dialogue in both this film and *Triplettes* in a way enlarges the soundtrack, as it gives more space to the sound design and the score, ultimately compelling us to focus on the visual storytelling. Chomet directs our gaze to the story unfolding before our eyes, rather than assuming our ears will pick up any specific details of the narrative. The point of view is clearly important to Chomet, who shows us the story from multiple perspectives, including those of the man, the man-as-pigeon, the man's dreams, the woman, the pigeons, even the tourists who catch brief, unexplained glimpses of the man on their cameras with no idea of what's going on. His overall attention to visual elements, as well as the depths to which almost all elements of the *mise-en-scène* are made to serve the story in some way, is what gives both films such an effective combination of comedy and pathos.

Chomet has stated in interviews that much of his inspiration comes from character-driven comedy. Referring specifically to *Triplettes* he stated that his style was:

> based on mime and character-acting. I'm more influenced by live camerawork
> than by animation. By Jacques Tati of course, but also by all those silent
> movie stars, Charlie Chaplin, Buster Keaton ... Timing is crucial too. That's
> why I love Louis de Funès and all those British comedies like Absolutely
> Fabulous or Blackadder with Rowan Atkinson. I also like Richard Williams'
> animation and Tex Avery. (quoted in Moins, 2003)

Most, if not all, of the above-mentioned actors, directors and shows, have a propensity
for visual humour in common. Such comic writing can be nuanced but is typically not
understated. And while the director's stated appreciation for Hollywood cartoons can
be seen in much of the visual humour, *Triplettes* comes out of a different tradition from
mainstream Hollywood fare, and therefore draws on a different discourse of both
comedy and sound.

Chomet's avoidance of dialogue-driven stories enables him to make the most of the
rest of the sonic space the film affords him. The most powerful moments in *Triplettes*
have absolutely no music, but instead combine the film's sound design with the many
characters' detailed facial expressions, especially those of Bruno, the dog. In one early
scene, Champion and Madame Souza return home from a training ride through the cold,
sad-looking Parisian suburbs. Champion's energy is channelled into his ride, muscles
straining, and he remains mute. At once happy and exhausted, he sits at the dinner-
table waiting for his food while alongside Bruno waits expectantly for leftovers. Chomet
omits all the background sounds once Madame Souza joins Champion at the table,
working on a bicycle wheel while Champion eats his sardines and mashed potatoes.
Having fewer random sounds, Chomet argues, gives people more time to look around
the room. This scene in particular shows a deft awareness of how the soundtrack can
direct the gaze, and likewise affect the viewer's understanding of the dominant themes
in the film – in this case, the importance of home and family.

The cartoon within the cartoon

Probably the most striking and overt gesture to the past – which establishes the idea
of change from 'then' to 'now' that underpins the film – occurs in the film's first five
minutes with a veritable recreation of a 1930s musical cartoon, combining themes and
tropes, musically, visually and dramatically, into a single meta-performance.[4] Everything
in the opening sequence moves, emphasizing the springy beat of the music. Well-
dressed folk are shown heading into a theatre, a popular plot ploy in cartoons of the
early 1930s, when many cartoons unfolded with an on-screen performance as the central
theme. The overall drawing style reinforces the implied age, as it closely resembles the
fluid feel of the Fleischer Studios cartoons of the 1930s. We see the theatre audience
bobbing along with the music – all the men are small and meek and their wives are
overweight and with placid looks on their faces.[5]

The series of acts in the theatre feature not only the Triplets but also Charles Trenet, Fred Astaire, Django Reinhardt playing in the pit orchestra, and even Josephine Baker (whose topless, banana-clad appearance turns all the men in the audience into screaming monkeys and earned the film a PG-13 rating in the USA). These specific stars further suggest the historical setting, while also placing the Triplets themselves at a level of fame on a par with such stars. Chomet explains their inclusion by saying,

> *major American stars often appear in American cartoons, but French stars of the period never appeared in French cartoons because there was no cartoon industry in France. I wanted my film to be a fake, a film we should have been able to see at the time but never did.* (quoted in Moins, 2003)

Chomet fudges history somewhat by putting all the various stars in one place, but his fanciful re-creation of the past foreshadows the role that nostalgia will have on the entire story.

The Triplets' song establishes them as jazz singers of the 1930s, similar to the Mills Brothers or the Boswell Sisters, although as time passes and fortune moves on, we see how their music clearly evolves into another form. The overall style of the onstage performance in this scene connects the Triplets and the entire film with the classic animation of the early 1930s on which Chomet draws for inspiration. I am thinking here in particular of the early Betty Boop cartoons and the Warner Bros. shorts starring Bosko and Honey. Not only do these cartoons have up-beat tunes sung on screen, but the story often stops while a performance takes place (that is, we watch the performers and do not just hear the music in the background), another characteristic that *Triplettes* has in common with its golden-age forebears.

Longing for the past

Before we get too carried away by the performance, Chomet yanks us into the present when he shows us the main character, young Champion, and his grandmother, Madame Souza, watching the stage show on television. We do not know it at the time, but this sequence provides the dramatic momentum for much of the film. The boy, looking bored, responds with a mute sigh to his grandmother's *spoken* question, "Is that it, then, hmm? What have you got to say to Grandma, eh? Is it over, do you think?" He, in fact, has nothing to say to her. The next time that we hear her speak – or more accurately, the sound of her voice – is in this very room, at the film's close, after many years have passed. Chomet places the first bookend of the story's point of view in this moment. What we ultimately will learn is that all the storylines tie together into the central theme: Champion's memories of happiness connect to his grandmother's desire to make him happy, shown first as they watch a television show featuring sounds and music from years before – a present embedded in a memory of the past.

As Madame Souza begins her quest to cheer up Champion, the Triplets' performance cuts off and switches abruptly to a telecast of Glenn Gould, shown playing (from a recording studio) Bach's C minor prelude from the first book of the *Well-Tempered Clavier* (1722) – the initial appearance of a theme that will recur throughout the film. Seeing the boy transfixed by the music, Madame Souza uncovers an ancient upright piano in the house and bangs away on it, effectively ending the boy's interest in music-making. A puppy and a train set meet with equally nonplussed responses.

Once she gets him a tricycle, everything changes. The tricycle begins the boy's journey to the Tour de France in earnest. As Champion gleefully rides in circles, Chomet pulls the shot back to show the house and surrounding countryside, which shifts through cross-dissolves to progressively more crowded, industry-strewn hills until we reach the cold, modern world in which the remainder of the story unfolds. The passage of time renders Madame Souza's once-quaint country home into a run-down suburban dwelling, simultaneously dwarfed and engulfed by the apparatus of modern transportation. Technology rolls over and changes the house, lying in the path of progress, with each successive moment.

Four shots of the house and its environs appear (Figure 8.4), with the first and last marking the extremes (simplicity and nostalgia at one end, stifling modernity at the other). The intervening (in-between) shots include the addition of construction cranes and smokestacks to the landscape, and planes flying overhead. The sounds of industry discreetly mark the changes time has wrought. The sequence goes by so quickly, eased along by the music, that we might not even notice such a subtle touch in the sound editing: the second shot has a single large plane, complete with the sound of the propellers turning, while the third shot has two jet airplanes. The aural transition from prop motor to jet engine indicates not only progress, but also the profound sense of loss that pervades this film. As the buzzing of the propeller fades into the past, a symbol of outdated technology, the jet-engine roar signifies an unwelcome present, where time passes too quickly. Time for these people is for treasuring, not quantifying. Schafer's prediction (of a "universal deafness" [1994: 3] with ongoing noise pollution) finds a reapplication here as Chomet opts for universal *muteness* for his characters. By these means he compels the audience to hear (by virtue of omitting dialogue) the noise pollution and its effect on the soundscape, showing how it changes over time as well as in the various geographical settings (country versus city, mountains versus ocean, Europe versus North America).

This montage, and this entire sequence, is striking because the noises of the countryside are not only familiar but comforting. Alain Corbin's work examines the drastic changes in the sound of the French countryside at the turn of the nineteenth century:

> In less than three years, the auditory environment, the systems for transmitting information, the signals used to summon the populace, and the methods of expressing collective sentiments changed radically. (Corbin, 1998: 21)

Figure 8.4 Les Triplettes de Belleville. The montage: warm to cold colour tonings, rural to urban, serenity to ruin

While the bulk of the film ostensibly unfolds in the late 1950s, the expansion of Paris to swallow up the surrounding landscape (and, with it, the ripple-like growth and eventual absorption of the surrounding areas into the city's soundscape) echoes a similar growth during an earlier industrial revolution in France in the eighteenth and nineteenth centuries, the period Corbin discusses. Technology and industry ultimately bring about the contemporary shift in the ambient sound of this Parisian suburb, which does not lose but instead gains sounds: the roar of jet engines and locomotives. Chomet is not just pining for the way things were in a figurative sense – innocence, simplicity – he is actually yearning for an aural landscape that has been lost, a kind of sonic nostalgia.

Chomet's nuanced use of colour also helps discern emotional overtones between locations and entire scenes in the film. (Even Bruno's dreams lead to a palette shift, as we shall see shortly.) Champion's childhood days are shot largely in warm earth tones: browns, reds, yellows. When the urban landscape encroaches on Madame Souza's home, things become cold, with blues and greys dominating. The return to the country – riding through the mountains during the Tour – brings back the warm tones, but during the long, grey journey across the Atlantic to Belleville, the cold hues of the modern city return. Once Madame Souza meets up with the Triplets, she is back in a comfortable space: the inside of their apartment is very similar in layout and colouring to her own home, imparting a sense of familiarity and comfort. Finally, when the Triplets, Madame, Champion and Bruno all slowly make their way out of Belleville at the film's close, the countryside around Belleville looks very much like the French countryside where Madame's house used to be (before it became a suburb). By leaving Belleville, then, Madame and Champion suggest a return to home and to the way things were – not just through the similarities in the landscape but also through the music. Here the music is reminiscent of the accordion-driven score heard when we saw Madame's and Champion's simple, comfortable life just before his abduction.

The bicycle as a driving force in the narrative is another manifestation of Chomet's nostalgic bent. We could say that Champion's decision to embrace cycling lets him recapture the joy of his first tricycle, which in turn connects him to his absent parents, whom we see in the film only as blurred images, standing by a bicycle, in an old snapshot (Figure 8.5). Chomet depicts France's cyclemania both lovingly (Champion is a romantic hero of sorts) and cynically (the cyclists' grotesquely exaggerated features).[6] His inclusion of the Tour de France (and the hullabaloo that surrounds it) adds another layer to the collection of ongoing stories that get pulled into the orbit of influence that surrounds the Triplets, Champion and his grandmother, including the place of popular music, the growth of modern cities, corruption in the wine industry, and the gluttony of modern western societies.

One such theme that runs throughout *Triplettes* is a crisis of technology, and yet Champion's *raison d'être* is, in the context of the setting, pre-industrial. Chomet reminds us that the bicycle, a once-revolutionary form of machinery, is now a beloved symbol of an earlier, simpler time. The bicycle is shown as the most understated form of transportation, especially if we compare the sound it produces to the sounds of the considerably louder and more menacing trains that constantly interrupt their lives and so frustrate Bruno. After a training ride with Champion, Madame Souza sets to work

Figure 8.5 Champion's missing parents

adjusting the spokes on Champion's wheels with a tuning fork, a subtle nod to the restrained nature of the bicycle and its pre-technological quality. The train reminds them of what the rest of the world does to get around; throughout the film, our heroes never set foot on a train – although all of Bruno's dreams involve trains in some way. Richard Neupert observes in a review of *Triplettes* that "Chomet's story is in part about transportation; every mode is used, but mechanical means are usually sinister. The best people move on their own power" (2005: 39). We could apply this same idea of pre-technological purity (or, even better, authenticity) to the nature of musical performance in the Triplets' world as a *craft* that has been replaced with something altogether less personal and more modern. Granted, the few snippets of 'current' music that we hear in the film play briefly over radios (at a pedalo rental shack, in a diner filled with fat Bellevillians, in a barber's shop), implying that music has mostly left people's lives. (The woman playing the accordion who forms part of the retinue that travels with the *peloton* of the Tour is clearly an anachronism, having played the same music for ages.) When the Triplets sing in the Cabaret Baroque (discussed below), they not only bring new life to their images as singers from another era, they are bringing a rare and perhaps unacceptable sound – live music – to a place where it is no longer acceptable. The club they sing in is not unlike the Harlem clubs that featured African American jazz musicians in the 1920s, providing the white-only clientele with a chance to hear music that skirted the boundaries between innovative and scandalous in white society.

Hearing through a dog's eyes

Bruno is not immune to the changes that technology brings. Witness Champion's train set, a microcosm of the soundscape that will soon define their lives. As the young Champion plays with his toy train, it runs over Bruno's tail when he sits on the track. Bruno learns in his first experience with a train how disruptive and destructive modern conveyances can be, planting in his mind a permanent fear of trains of all sizes. His frustrated barks at the train's miniature whistle are the seeds of an unending conflict not just with trains, but with the violence they seem to do him, as the full-size version will, in just a few years, end up disrupting his day repeatedly. Bruno first ties the sound of the train to his own mutilation, to the pain it causes him, and barks as the vehicle goes by. Its regular appearance by the house ultimately becomes part of his routine. With the coming of modern contraptions in the country, a commuter train now runs by Madame Souza's house (see Figure 8.4), a noisy reminder to which the human occupants seem to have become accustomed. Not only has the city invaded the rural home, but the train expands the incursion of the modern world to the point of absurdity by invading their personal sonic space: every fifteen minutes a deafening roar reminds them of the silence they used to take for granted. When the clock chimes on the quarter-hour, Bruno runs upstairs to bark at the passing train. In performing this ritual, he is starring in a recurring, miniature sound opera, as his barking plays in counterpoint to the deep rumbling and high-pitched screeching of the train rushing by the house. Just as church bells once regulated pre-modern towns and cities in France, so does an equally disruptive sound now organize all the characters' lives (see Schafer, 1994: 56).

For Bruno, the train becomes an *idée fixe* (besides his meals, that is), something that he not only reacts against but even anticipates. Continuous noise (motors, engines, amplifiers) was unknown in a pre-industrial society (in practice, at least; the theory had existed for some time in the notion of the music of the spheres[7]). Corbin shows that the occasional and temporary deafening by cannon, firework or bell was actually part of public rejoicing:

> The charivari, or 'rough music' we tend to regard as unwelcome disturbance, was all the more appreciated for its breaching of a habitual silence and for its links with the structure of the auditory landscape. (Corbin, 1998: 97)

We might then consider the train as not just an annoying reminder of one painful incident for Bruno, but an almost reassuring alternative to the otherwise sedate life he lives.

This leads to one of the most charming points in the film — Bruno's dreams. We have already seen that Chomet has an interest in dreams; in *La Vielle Dame et les pigeons* the cop's fantasy shows his anxieties and also provides a bit of foreshadowing. In his dream, giant pigeons try to eat the gendarme, and eventually his identity as a human is consumed by his avian alter ego. Bruno's dreams reveal different anxieties — all of which seem rooted in food and transportation, the two recurring elements of his life that depend on both sonic and chronometric signals.

Shot entirely in black and white (a thoughtful detail about a dog's colour-blindness that could easily go unnoticed), the dreams typically consist of day residue, relating somehow to the current story at hand but with other details or neuroses present as well, all combined into mostly inscrutable images. All of his dreams involve trains in one way or another; in the first, he imagines himself moving by the house on an antique locomotive, while the commuter train passengers that usually stare at him as they speed along are stuck in the house watching him go by. This dream has no music and features only the sounds of the slow train and a barking dog — one of the passengers, who looks like an anthropomorphized Bruno. The soundtrack in the next dream consists solely of the rapid, rhythmic sounds of a speeding train as Bruno imagines himself travelling through the countryside. When he falls asleep during a cabaret performance later in the film, the music seeps into his dream and becomes a soundtrack for his revelation — that he somehow, inexplicably, can smell his master's presence in the nightclub (it is attached to the clothes of the gangsters sitting next to him). His memory of Champion relies on the latter as the provider of food — which is how the memory ultimately manifests, as the track that Champion walks on in his dream is revealed to circle Bruno's massive food dish (Figure 8.6). Bruno's olfactory memory is ultimately the key to the mystery of Champion's disappearance.

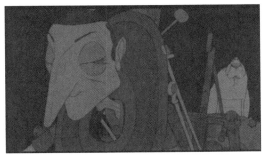

Figure 8.6   Images from Bruno's dream during the cabaret performance

Sounds of civilization

One of the themes of this film is the characters' love or thoughts of past pleasures —
riding a bicycle, making music — as the world changes around them. For the transition
between Champion's childhood and adult life, Chomet stated that the scene was meant
to look especially nostalgic, which makes sense as it is Champion's first cycle (bi or tri);
the entire sequence has a sepia tone meant to imply a certain aged feeling.[8] The sense
of an idealized time slipping away is enhanced by the music (scored by Benoît Charest)
that leads us out of this scene. At first it seems like a slow, orchestral version of the
Bach heard earlier in the film, but it is actually a different piece, although related to
the Bach: the opening measures of Mozart's grand C minor Mass (Große Messe,
1782–3). The Mass was written at a time when Mozart, under the influence of Baron
von Swieten, was studying Bach's *Well-Tempered Clavier* ; a number of Mozart's works

from this time take inspiration from the Bach collection, including several sections of the Mass. The opening of the Kyrie seems clearly modelled on the C minor prelude, not just in the choice of key but also in similarities in the melodic motive, harmonic progression and overall mood. The Mass creeps in just as autumn is poised to arrive in the area; but this is no seasonal transition – the world around them is changing as well.

Chomet times the transition from then to now to coincide with the instrumental opening of the Kyrie. We see just enough of each new phase of the landscape for it to register before it dissolves to the next stage. The music meanwhile builds in intensity, especially when the horns enter and thicken the orchestral texture. It all comes to an abrupt halt when the visuals reach the present (run-down) state of the house. At this point the music reaches a significant cadence, where we would expect the voices to enter. Instead, the music suddenly stops, as if shut down when faced with the ugliness of what the house has become, and a wistful theme on accordion takes over.

The Bach Prelude recognizably returns several times. As Champion and dozens of other riders make a back-breaking climb during the Tour, Charest underscores the painfully slow and deliberate Alpine ascent with the Prelude's main theme. New, extra-musical meanings begin to associate with the Bach: the repetitive nature of the melodic pattern the Prelude is based on takes on a mechanistic contour, as each biker wills himself to the top of the hill by pedalling at a constant rhythm.

This kind of musical urging is not unlike Madame Souza's way of urging Champion along on his training rides with short, urgent blasts from her whistle – practically her only form of audible communication in the film. After Champion is abducted onto a steamer, Souza and Bruno give chase in a rented pedal boat. The long and treacherous journey that Champion's protectors make to cross the Atlantic is, in Chomet's words,

> one of my favorites. We filmed the storyboard to get an animatic assembly, lasting about three minutes. At around the same time I bought a prize-winning record, Mozart's C-Minor Mass conducted by [John] Elliott Gardiner. As soon as I heard the overture, I realized it would make a perfect accompaniment to this sequence. When I laid the music over the pictures, all the effects seemed perfectly synchronized to fit. It was an incredible piece of luck. (quoted in Moins, 2003)

Important to note here is the phrase "over the picture": this is one of very few scenes without *any* sound effects (save the spraying of a whale that swims up under Madame Souza's borrowed pedalo to lift it momentarily out of the water, and Bruno's frantic barking in response). This transition from the old world to the new – one of the key elements of the plot to find Champion – is scored with a piece of choral writing almost operatic in its power. The visuals here guide the music. Our understanding of how the music works is the key to our notion of the weight and drama of the scene. For the raging storm that follows the ships on their transatlantic journey, Chomet relies entirely on the drama in Mozart's music and Gardiner's performance to convey the sounds of the crashing waves and torrential rains.

The text of the Kyrie – which is heard in this sequence, fulfilling the promise made by the opening of the movement heard early in the film – is not insignificant. As one of the most recognizable and succinct pieces of the Catholic liturgy, "Kyrie eleison" (God have mercy) is heard early in the Mass, marking the beginning of an elaborate transformative process. In *Triplettes* the words signify the beginning of Madame Souza's journey to a new and strange land. It might even be heard as her plea – "God, have mercy!" – as she ventures to the godless land that is Belleville. Chomet gives voice to her fears through one of the most well-known two-word phrases ever set to music. As a text likely to be familiar to audiences, we might expect religious overtones created by the scene: the hand of God moving over the waters, the parting of the seas, or something like that. At the very least we can read the crossing as a figurative Mass, for the addition of words, particularly words of the liturgy, signifies the ultimate move – or transformation – from innocence to knowledge. Not including the gangsters' fireworks in the final chase sequence, this move across stormy seas is the most violent episode of the film, marking this shift in the story in a very emotional manner, emotions that (like words) Chomet seldom gives to the characters themselves.

Dramatically, this montage and the Bach montage from earlier on move the story along and connect the various themes across time (the countryside) and space (the ocean crossing). In each case the montages allow the music to extend out in both directions: in both montages the music creeps in, creating a parallel to how the viewer might interpret the sequences. And as the Bach is explicitly tied to Champion's youth, we might hear the Mozart as the music of his adulthood. Just as the move from Bach to Mozart is a move from one period to another, the earlier montage begins with the simplicity and goodness of rural antiquity and moves to the complexity of the urban landscape.

Music in the new world

Two important musical moments occur when Madame Souza first meets the Triplets under a bridge in Belleville: we see and hear for the first time the Triplets' modern performance style (sans instruments), and we hear the first conscious merging of the Triplets' theme with that of the Bach Prelude. The Triplets emerge from the shadows, snapping their fingers, and launch into their theme song with an improvised accompaniment provided by Madame Souza on the spokes of an old bicycle wheel, not unlike the way she used to 'tune' Champion's wheels. The song is rhythmically complex, with finger snaps, handclaps, foot stomps, and the sound of shoe soles rubbing on cement all creating an intricate structure for the Triplets' performance. Perhaps the waning popularity of vocal jazz led the Triplets to hard times so that they could not afford to perform with a band. Whatever conclusion we might draw about their fortunes since we last saw them (pictured in the 1930s opening sequence), the trio's music has definitely shifted in focus, while our attention as viewers has shifted as well.

Chomet offers one explanation for the group's shift, claiming to have been inspired by the show *Stomp*, which features an ensemble of musicians and dancers creating a variety of instruments by using non-traditional objects as idiophones. Chomet also apparently "saw a musician make music out of a refrigerator shelf placed on a sound-box".[8] We can also refer back to *La Vielle Dame et les pigeons*, in which the two main musical cues (neither of which is an on-screen performance but rather they underscore the action) rise out of rhythmic sound effects repeated quickly enough to create a dancelike beat. (Recall that the gendarme's pigeon dance begins with the sound of the pigeons tapping their beaks on his window, while the old lady's snapping shears set up the rhythm for the music of the final chase.)

If for no other reason than to confirm the Triplets' atypical approach to music, we see an impromptu performance in the sisters' apartment, where they are serving Madame Souza and Bruno a meal consisting entirely of one ingredient: frogs. After finishing their frog-kebabs, Souza is tapping her skewer on a plate while two of the sisters 'musick' with their hands, breath, voices, and various table pieces at hand (as in Christopher Small's idea of "musicking" [1988] with any form of musical interaction being fulfilling, from performers to spectators). These on-the-spot performances foreshadow a gig at the Cabaret Baroque, where we see that the Triplets still have a following, even with this new performance style. Their first song at the club neatly explains many (although not nearly all) of the sisters' apparent idiosyncrasies in their apartment: their shooing Madame Souza away from their vacuum cleaner, preventing her from putting food in the icebox, and taking an old newspaper from her hands. All three of these objects are instruments in the Triplets' show, the most expressive of which is the vacuum, nick-named 'Mouf-Mouf' by the film's composer (and apparent vacuum virtuoso) Charest, who calls the piece a "vacuum cabaret".[10] The club performance begins with a back-ground cue comprising a jazz piano version of the Bach Prelude, bringing to full circle the evolution of a piece that we first heard as Bach intended it (that is, on a keyboard), then transformed by Mozart, then merged with the Triplets' song, and finally appropri-ated into a jazz solo. The Bach/Mozart is not just a reference to old music; it actually ties together almost the entire score, making the scenes that take place in Belleville relate back to France and, particularly, to the earliest experience of Champion's youth.

Conclusion: past becomes present

Once Champion is rescued and the gangsters defeated, we return to his grandmother's living room one last time. It takes us practically the whole film to get back to this point, a scene from just a few minutes into the film, and to realize that *this* space – his grandmother's house, at the table where they ate, where Bruno grew fat, where young Champion no doubt watched the Tour on television – was a place of comfort, and was formative for the boy (Figure 8.7). In the last lines of the film we hear Madame Souza's voice-over, "Is that it, then? Is it over, do you think? What have you got to say to Grandma?" and Champion as an old man watching TV responds, "Yes, I think that's probably it. It's over, Grandma."

As things return to normal, Neupert writes, "The past is recovered, the new world is evaded, and the visual nostalgia is reinforced" (2005: 41). Aural nostalgia plays as strong a role here as does the visual. Charest scores the final sequence – with Champion sitting alone in his grandmother's house, a picture of her and Bruno overlooking the scene – with the same music heard as the film opened when Champion and Souza sat together at the table watching the Triplets and Glenn Gould on television. The music

Figure 8.7 Madame Souza's living room, then and now

brings us back to the earlier, happier times, and now we have also got "Grandma's" voice added to the mix, another echo of past happiness.

The notion of making connections flows through *Les Triplettes de Belleville*. The musical themes of the film – the Bach, the Mozart, the Triplets' theme song – tie in to one another, either historically or by design. Visually, the film unites images of not two, but four, different time periods: the Triplets' heyday, Champion's youth, his adulthood (where most of the exposition occurs), and a brief glimpse into his old age. That he is the driving force of the film's plot is clear, but Champion spends little time on screen and never speaks. The music certainly helps to draw together these scenes from his life, but if we think about the interaction of the various soundscapes, the polyvalence of the soundtrack becomes much more rich and complex, as it organizes historical eras, several plotlines, and reminds us that we are still searching for something that has been lost, all without the aid of dialogue. To this end, we have the sounds of motors, signifying modernity in all its violence, challenged by the anti-industrial tones of bicycles. The music, moving from 1930s pop song to Bach to Mozart to jazz, creates its own chronology for the events in the film, yet the continual return to the Bach suggests a musical notion of the craving for past contentment and order that underscores the entire film, back to that epiphanic moment in the courtyard when Champion first rode his tricycle. Ultimately, then, it is the sound design – the music, the added sounds and the few spoken words – that combines all of these elements and gives the narrative and film a continuity, simplifying an onslaught of visual and aural information into an expression of yearning for one's happiest moment of childhood.

Acknowledgements

Thanks to Neil Lerner, Mary Davis, Dana Gooley, Georgia Cowart, Paul Cox and Cyleste Collins for their comments and suggestions on this paper.

Notes

1. Floquet (2006) has written on how cross-cultural nostalgia (France and the United States) can have been so effectively generated in *Triplettes*.
2. See Goldmark, 2007.
3. For more on sound in early animation, see Curtis, 1992.
4. Chomet has said that they intentionally "aged" the film to look old through CGI, adding scratches and other typical types of "film damage" to the finished animation, in order to give the establishing sequence a feeling of something from the past being rediscovered (quoted in Moins, 2003).
5. Floquet (2006) points out that these figures are a tribute to the illustration style of French graphic artist Albert Dubout.
6. For more on the role of the Tour in *Triplettes*, see Floquet, 2006.
7. Neil Lerner, email to the author, 19 February 2007.

8. Sylvain Chomet, commentary track, *The Triplettes of Belleville*, Sony Pictures Classics DVD, 2003.
9. Interview with Benoit Charest. Online press kit for *The Triplettes of Belleville* (2003), online at http://www.sonyclassics.com/triplets/triplets_presskit.pdf (accessed 27 March 2007).
10. As novel as the device may seem, this is not the first piece written for Hoover or Eureka; in 1999 I actually had the pleasure of taking part in a performance in England of Sir Malcolm Arnold's 'Grand, Grand Overture', Opus 57, written in 1956, for orchestra, four rifles, three vacuum cleaners and one floor buffer although, in this case, the instruments were present more for timbral effect than as melodic performers.

References

Corbin, A. (1998), *Village Bells: Sound and Meaning in the 19th-Century French Countryside*, trans. M. Thom, New York: Columbia University Press.

Curtis, S. (1992), 'The Sound of the Early Warner Bros. Cartoons', in R. Altman (ed.), *Sound Theory, Sound Practice*, New York: Routledge, pp. 191–202.

Floquet, P. (2006), 'What is (not) so French in Les Triplettes de Belleville', *Animation Studies* 1, online at http://journal.animationstudies.org/category/volume-1/pierre-floquet-what-is-not-so-french-in-les-triplettes-de-belleville/ (accessed 28 March 2007).

Goldmark, D. (2007), 'Before Willie: Reconsidering Music and the Animated Cartoon of the 1920s', in D. Goldmark, L. Kramer and R. Leppert (eds), *Beyond the Soundtrack: Representing Music in Cinema*, Berkeley: University of California Press, pp. 225–45.

Moins, P. (2003), 'Sylvain Chomet's *The Triplets of Belleville*', *Animation World Magazine*, 20 November, online at http://mag.awn.com/index.php?article_no=1923# (accessed 16 July 2006).

Neupert, R. (2005), 'The Triplets of Belleville (Les Triplettes de Belleville)', *Film Quarterly*, 58(3), Reviews, 38–42.

Schafer, R. (1994), *The Soundscape: Our Sonic Environment and the Tuning of the World*, Rochester, VT: Destiny Books.

Small, C. (1988), *Musicking: The Meanings of Performing and Listening*, Hanover, NH: University Press of New England.

Solomon, C. (2006), 'Pipe Down, We're Trying to Watch a Cartoon', *New York Times*, 19 March, Section 2.

Sternfeld, F. (1950), 'Kubik's Boing Score with Excerpts of Score', *Film Music Notes*, 10(2), 8–16.

9 Resilient Appliances

Sound, Image and Narrative in The Brave Little Toaster

Jon Fitzgerald and Philip Hayward

During the late 1980s to early 1990s US animation cinema experienced a period of (simultaneous and associated) technological transition and generational succession. The main technological development was the move to computer-assisted and/or computer-generated animation, and the main generational shift saw the rise of a new group of animators, many of whom shared common backgrounds and aesthetic sensibilities. Animation features that originated at various moments in this period can be character-ized in terms of their reliance on particular technologies and approaches to production and by their relationship to traditional or more contemporary aesthetics. However, like any period of transition, the shift between animation 'epochs' that occurred in the 1980s and 1990s was both turbulent and complex. It was marked not so much by an incremental shift from one phase to another but rather by a mix of surges, swirls and eddies in the stream of genre history. This phenomenon is clearly apparent in both the production history and the text of *The Brave Little Toaster* (Jerry Rees, 1987). This chapter analyses the film's uses of sound and music, locates these within the interrelated threads of its narrative themes and references to animation history and, thereby, offers a perspective on its production moment and the changing character of the late-twentieth-century animation industry.

Source and context

The Brave Little Toaster is an adaptation of a novella with the same title written by US science-fiction writer Thomas Disch and first published in the *Magazine of Fantasy and Science Fiction* in 1980. Atypically for Disch, who had previously written adult-themed SF novels such as *Camp Concentration* (1968), the story took the form of a children's parable in which loyalty, persistence and idealism are validated and technological obso-lescence is rejected. Disch's narrative involves a group of household appliances that seek out their teenage owner after they are left (apparently abandoned) in a family summer holiday house. After various trials and tribulations they are successfully reunited with their owner, who continues to use and value them.

Disch's story was well received on initial publication, subsequently republished as an individual novella and nominated for the Hugo and Nebula Science Fiction awards. Similar plaudits followed the release of the film adaptation in 1987, including a surprising selection for the Sundance Film Festival in 1988 (which had not previously screened animation films). Despite this, disputes between the independent distributor Skouras Pictures and Disney resulted in the film's planned theatrical release being cancelled. The film then aired on the Disney TV channel before being picked up for specialist 'arthouse' distribution by Hyperion Pictures in the USA. Its critical reputation translated into broader success when it was successfully released on Disney Home Video in 1990.

Disch wrote a follow-up to his original story entitled *The Brave Little Toaster Goes to Mars* in 1988. This featured the same appliances battling alien ones intent on invading Earth. Like its predecessor, this novella was also adapted into an animation film (1998), directed by Robert Ramirez on a lower budget back-to-back with a third and (to date) final instalment entitled *The Brave Little Toaster to the Rescue* (1999), which was also unheralded by critics. In terms of their production moments, concepts, themes and, in particular, less-complex approaches to music and sound, the later films are distinctly different from the initial feature (made a decade earlier) and are not subject to analysis in this chapter. Their chief significance for study may well be as examples of lower-budget/invention straight-to-video/DVD follow-ups to more prestigious 'pilot' features, a phenomenon exemplified by *The Land Before Time* series (commencing 1988) or sequels such as *The Little Mermaid 2* (2000). This topic is, however, beyond the scope of this chapter.

Pre-production

During the 1950s and 1960s Disney dominated the US animation film industry. Many of its key personnel were schooled in the Disney corporate mentality and production tradition through attending the company's training centre in California. Walt and Roy Disney established the centre in 1961 but in 1971, five years after Walt's demise, its operation was transferred to the California Institute of the Arts in Valencia (often – and hereafter – referred to as 'Cal Arts') through a $14 million endowment. The most significant aspect of this was that students selected for the programme had not emerged from within the company and, in many cases, had significantly different educational and social backgrounds from established Disney employees. Offering scholarships and employment prospects with Disney upon graduation, the programme attracted considerable interest, particularly in its host state. Some indication of its significance can be ascertained by identifying those members of its initial intakes who have gone on to become key players in the film industry, such as John Lasseter,[1] Tim Burton,[2] Brad Bird,[3] and John Musker.[4]

Although he was not involved in *Brave Little Toaster*'s actual production, Lasseter is a significant figure in its pre-production history. After completing the Cal Arts programme he began work with Disney at a time when the company was in a transitional period, maintaining an essentially conservative approach to animation aesthetics and production methods while beginning to explore the potential of digital animation. Inspired by the production of the experimental feature *Tron* (Steve Lisberger, 1982), which mixed live characters and digital animation, Lasseter attempted to interest studio executives in exploring a combination of traditional hand-drawn characters and digitally generated backgrounds. With the encouragement of live-action production executive Tom Wilhite, Lasseter worked on a 30-second test animation and developed a proposal for a feature production. As he later recalled:

> I was so excited about the test, and I wanted to find a story that we could apply this technique to in a full-blown movie. A friend of mine had told me about a 40-page novella called "The Brave Little Toaster", by Thomas Disch. I've always loved animating inanimate objects, and this story had a lot of that. Tom Wilhite liked the idea, too, and got us the rights to the story so we could pitch it to the animation studio along with our test clip. When it came time to show the idea, I remember the head of the studio had only one question: "How much is this going to cost?" We said about the same as a regular animated feature. He replied, "I'm only interested in computer animation if it saves money or saves time." ... The studio head had made up his mind before we walked in ... Ten minutes after the studio head left the room I get a call from the superior who didn't like me, and he said, "Well, since it's not going to be made, your project at Disney is now complete. Your position is terminated, and your employment with Disney is now ended" ... The only thing I'd ever wanted to do was work for Disney. I was so excited, and pushing, and I didn't play the political game. I was devastated.[5]

Despite his disappointment, Lasseter's retrenchment turned out to be an opportune one in that it precipitated his next career phase, which took him to Lucasfilm's computer-animation group.[6] Keen to exploit Lasseter's talent, Lucasfilm invited him to work with them, initiating the chain of events that saw Pixar Animation Studios achieve major success (and, paradoxically, Disney backing) for productions such as Lasseter's debut feature *Toy Story* in 1991.

Production

Despite Disney's rejection of Lasseter's pitch, *The Brave Little Toaster* was finally made after Wilhite and Willard Carol (head of Disney's story department) quit Disney to set up their own company, Hyperion. Locating the production firmly within a traditional Disney visual-narrative aesthetic, Wilhite teamed Cal Arts graduates Jerry Rees (director) and Joe Ranft (supervising animator) with veteran animation art director Ken O'Connor (who had worked on Disney classics such as *Fantasia* [1940] and *Pinocchio* [1940]). O'Connor's role involved creating "an emotional palette for the film" by producing "a series of miniature paintings that used color to describe the story's emotional flow from scene to scene", thereby providing the lead animators with a "creative anchor" for their interpretations (Schweiger, 2004: 7). Careful use of this talent pool was necessary given the film's slim budget of $2.2 million, which necessitated the animation being produced offshore. In order to minimize costs the animation was produced at Cuckoo's Nest Studio in Taiwan, a company involved in producing animation to order for US companies such as Hanna-Barbera. So as to raise production standards to ones more comparable with Disney films, key animation staff worked in Taiwan supervising and training local animators.

The film's score was identified as an important element early in the production process. In a somewhat unusual move, four feature songs were commissioned first and the score completed later, developing motifs and arrangements from the song material. The songs were provided by singer/songwriter/arranger Van Dyke Parks. After coming to public attention as a close associate and collaborator with the Beach Boys' Brian Wilson, Parks released a series of eclectic albums as a singer-songwriter (commencing with *Song Cycle* [1968]) and collaborated with performers such as Randy Newman and Little Feat before turning to film-score work in the mid-1980s. Although he provided a memorable arrangement for the song 'The Bare Necessities', featured in *The Jungle Book* (Wolfgang Reitherman, 1967), his first extended score was in collaboration with Harry Nilsson for Robert Altman's live-action version of *Popeye* (1980) and his solo film-composing debut was with *Sesame Street Presents: Follow That Bird* (Ken Kwapis, 1985). He also worked on another relevant project in the early 1980s, recording an album entitled *Jump* (1984) that reinterpreted the Brer Rabbit and Fox folktales for a contemporary audience.[7]

The task of arranging Parks's four songs and completing the overall musical score fell to David Newman, a young composer with direct family connections to classic Hollywood cinema. Newman is the son of noted Hollywood composer/arranger Alfred Newman, who headed the music department of 20th Century Fox in the 1950s and 1960s and composed the scores for films such as *How Green Was My Valley* (John Ford, 1941). David Newman initially trained as a violinist and conductor at the University of Southern California before securing a first composing role in collaboration with Michael Convertino on an experimental Disney short entitled *Frankenweenie*, directed by Cal Arts graduate Tim Burton in 1984. While the film was not released it gave Newman's career momentum and helped him secure composer credits for films such as *Critters* (Stephen Herek, 1986) and for episodes of TV series such as *Amazing Stories* (1985–87). The producers' familiarity with his work secured him the commission for *The Brave Little Toaster*, with the brief to provide a rich orchestral score to complement and enhance the film's images, narrative and characterization. As with the animation, the low budget required the score to be rehearsed and recorded overseas, using non-US musicians. The score was recorded by the New Japan Philharmonic Orchestra, under Newman's own baton, at the Maeda Hall, Senzoka Gakuen, Tokyo, in August 1986 – in an arrangement judged a significant success by both producers and composer.[8]

Voice actors

One of the most distinctive aspects of *The Brave Little Toaster*, particularly when compared to the 1970s and 1980s US animation features that preceded it, was the nature and use of character voicings, which departed from the stock traditions (and vocal personnel) associated with Disney at the time. As Rees has detailed:

> We wanted to have the actors to have something to hang their hats on for each character, so we rounded up the usual suspects who do cartoon voices. And they sounded horrid! ... And the reason was that the people doing the voices were used to affected schtick. (Schweiger, 2004: 6)

In order to address this issue Ranft suggested employing a very different group of performers to develop distinctive voice characterizations, members of Los Angeles's comedy improvisation troupe the Groundling Theatre. The Groundlings (as they were commonly known) were formed in 1974 and had been the launching pad for many actors who went on to appear on TV shows such as *Saturday Night Live*. Notable alumni include Paul Reubens, who achieved fame with his character Pee Wee Herman in the TV series *Pee Wee's Playhouse* (1986–91) and the films *Pee Wee's Big Adventure* (Tim Burton, 1985) and *Big Top Pee Wee* (Randal Kleiser, 1988), and Cassandra Peterson, who attracted cult attention with her vampish character Elvira ('Mistress of the Dark'). As Ranft emphasized, the Groundling troupe comprised "improv actors [who] did comedy for real" and who could readily assume the personae of household appliances without defaulting to stock cartoon voice types (Schweiger, 2004: 6). Additional casting was undertaken for 'Blanky' (an electric blanket), for whom a child actor, Timothy E. Day, was employed. The vocal 'palette' of these actors supplied a key element of the film's characterization and dialogue, with the individual personality of each appliance. The interactions between appliances are a major element of the film's appeal.

The key vocal casting in the film comprised:

- Deanna Oliver: the Toaster. Although this role is voiced by a female actor, her high-pitched, clear and sweet-toned vocal characterization is somewhat androgynous and, in combination with the dialogue she speaks, suggests a childlike innocence and lack of sophistication.
- Timothy Stack: Lampy. Voiced with a high tenor and using fast speaking patterns.
- Jon Lovitz: the Radio. Lovitz provides a dual vocal performance for this role, giving the radio itself a high, edgy, character voice and then extending this voice into a series of vocal impressions of radio broadcasts from the 'golden age' of US radio in the 1920s to 1930s. His switching between announcer voices in a quick-fire succession variously entertains and annoys his fellow appliances through his apparent failure to take adversity (and situations in general) seriously.

- Timothy E. Day: Blanky. Daly's child's voice provides Blanky's principal characteristic as the 'baby' of the group and further emphasizes this by using mannered – and allusive[9] – (mis)pronunciations, such as "that's all wight".
- Thurl Ravenscroft: Kirby (the vacuum cleaner). This appliance provides a counterpoint to both the vocal pitch and the character of his fellow appliances through his slow, deliberate speaking patterns and lower pitched voice, his jaded pessimism and world-weariness suggesting advanced years.
- Phil Hartman: the Air-conditioner. While the air-conditioner doesn't feature in the appliances' adventures outside the house where the narrative begins (due to its immobility as a wall-mounted device), it offers a sour discordant counterpoint to the optimism of the other appliances' initial plans and departure, and a notable dramatic moment as it erupts in fury at its inability to leave. Along with Lovitz's ongoing sonic variety, Hartman provides something of a vocal star turn in the early stages of the film with his deep-voiced vocal parody of Jack Nicholson's laconic (and distinctive) drawl, an 'in-joke' element appreciable by adult audiences.

Providing integration between score and voice recording, these actors (aside from Hartman) also sing (in-role) in the film's four song sequences, adapting their vocal personae to interact musically.

Score and songs

Environmental sounds recur throughout the film and, indeed, provide an introduction to the rural context in which the narrative begins, with insect sounds, water, frogs (etc.) preceding the visual track onto the screen. Music is also unapologetically foregrounded and, while the score is clearly designed to enhance the film's atmosphere, its lushness readily commands attention in its own right. In addition, numerous lengthy, dialogue-free sections allow the viewer ample opportunity to (consciously or unconsciously) savour the musical score along with visual elements. Composer David Newman demonstrates an impressive command of orchestration, employing a wide palette of sounds and sound combinations to enhance the changing scenes and moods within the film.

The opening section is a useful illustration of the ways in which Newman effectively exploits the potential of the large symphonic orchestra. The opening music is minimal and atmospheric, reflecting the dark, mysterious visuals. An evocative solo violin is joined by high string sounds and wind instruments, before low string sounds add a dark, foreboding element. As the visuals move inexorably towards the house where the little toaster and other appliances have been abandoned, the principal four-note melodic motif (used in various manifestations throughout the score) is introduced softly on brass instruments. Colourful and evocative percussion sounds (including piano) add to the mysterious atmosphere as the (apparent) camera pans to the moon, which is seen through a window. Before the main characters are introduced, then, the composer has already effectively exploited every section of the orchestra to enhance the mood of the film – something he does continually throughout. The first appliance to voice its presence is the radio, which clicks on, bids the house "Good morning" and immediately signifies the film's self-reflexivity by announcing "that was A Billion and One Strings playing one of your favourite tunes". The radio's various voices are a continuing – and often anarchic – presence in the film and it also voices the only non-original song featured in the narrative, an extended sequence of Little Richard's 'Tutti Frutti' (1955) that motivates the appliances to clean up the house at the beginning of the film. The appliances listen to the song with familiarity, moving delightedly to a vintage track that suggests a more carefree innocent era and, perhaps, the past of the house and their interaction with the youthful owner who has now left them.

As the central protagonists are introduced, Newman demonstrates his sensitivity to the association of sound and character (examples include the use of low brass for sulky Kirby the vacuum cleaner, and sweet oboe sounds for the good-natured, innocent toaster). He also demonstrates his ability to create effective musical motifs – introducing a new rhythmical brass motif to underscore an argument (and subsequent chase scene) involving the Radio and Lampy characters. Newman is not only an accomplished orchestrator; he also cleverly constructs the main orchestral motif (and its many variants) from material by song composer Van Dyke Parks, thereby creating a seamless integration between the orchestral score and the songs. The four-note verse motif from 'City Of Light' (see Figure 9.1) provides the basic material for the four-note themes that pervade the orchestral soundtrack. In addition, the intervals contained in Van Dyke Parks's motif (tone and minor third) provide material for many of the prominent two-note and three-note themes.

Figure 9.1   Four-note verse motif from 'City Of Light' (authors' transcription)

Figure 9.2 illustrates some of the orchestral variants of the four-note 'City Of Light' motif. Newman regularly includes exact copies of the motif but also alters it by changing the order of intervals, inverting intervals, and changing their quality (for example, tone becomes semitone, minor third becomes major third). Four-note motifs are presented both as prominent melodic motifs and less-prominent accompanying motifs (for example, in the piano ostinato of the junkyard montage).

Figure 9.2   Some variants of the four-note motif (authors' transcription)

The tone interval is also used extensively throughout the score as a prominent element in its own right. A number of sections (for example, the main title sequence, when Blanky looks for a place to sleep and when the Blender's motor is sold) involve the alternation of two notes a tone apart (sometimes a semitone apart as a variant). As noted below, the minor-third interval is used in the verse melody of 'City Of Light', but it also features as a prominent element in the main hooks of 'Cutting Edge' and 'Worthless'. It is not surprising, then, that Newman should also use the minor third as a recurring element in the orchestral score (for example, the pond scene; the happy travel scene) and he also incorporates many other recurring elements (such as whole-tone passages, fourth-based harmonies) to bind the score into a convincing, integrated musical whole.

The 'City Of Light' song

The film's first original song, 'City Of Light', is important for establishing a narrative theme, the characters' goal of reaching the city where the owner is believed to be, and for a set of musical motifs that recur throughout the film. The song's lyrics signal recognition of the need for change and the disruption of the appliances' cosy domestic environment, embracing the prospect of travel to metropolitan modernity. The composition is a musical theatre-style ensemble piece with pop-song influences in its arrangement (most notably the use of electric bass and [less prominent] drums). It begins with the sound of sweet, high-set, descending string triplets over an electric bass pedal point followed by a rising string passage that leads to the establishment of the seductive, gently paced song groove. A solo voice enters with a four-note, major pentatonic motif that appears in many guises throughout the film and then the slow string triplets of the introduction reappear as faster eighth-note triplet figures as the song unfolds. The use of a tone step up and back within the verse is a typical music-theatre device. The chorus enters after the second verse, introducing vocal harmony parts and a new melodic-rhythmic hook and key centre. The hook involves musical/lyrical phrases that end with a triplet-eighth rhythm well-suited to the quickly articulated, conversational-style lyric hooks (e.g., "city of light", "fuss and a fight"). Van Dyke Parks extends the use of the triplet rhythm in a playful manner at the end of the chorus, using this with a deliberately contrived rhyme scheme (e.g., "and I'm satisfied/just to be not denied/to reside with some pride/what a ride/to the city, the city of light"). The triplet idea is further extended so that it permeates the orchestral backing for the next verse. This verse also sees a development of the vocal scoring, as the various characters now take short phrases in turn – highlighting the strongly contrasting vocal tones and phrasing. The entry of the second chorus is cleverly designed to overlap with the verse ending, and the song fades to the sound of the pervasive triplets (now delivered by woodwinds). The overall feel of the song, in both its lyrics and arrangement, is optimistic, even triumphal; its resolve and buoyancy serve to counter the air-conditioner's negativity and anger and to carry the vacuum cleaner along with its camaraderie.

Occurring shortly before the appliances depart on the first stage of their adventure outdoors, 'City Of Light' also provides a sonic link to one of their first notable experiences. On entering a swamp area the travellers are greeted with a recontextualized performance of what previously appeared as their departure song. This is one performed by musical instruments, wordless vocal parts (humming) and sound effects, as if 'voiced' by the creatures and environment of the swamp they stray into. In its musical representation, its choreography of elements as an extended dance routine and its gleeful whimsy the sequence clearly evokes the classic Disney *Silly Symphony* series of the 1920s and 1930s. Visually and choreographically the scene also invites comparison to the set pieces featured in Busby Berkeley's work for 1930s and 1940s musicals such as *42nd Street* (Lloyd Bacon, 1933) and *Million Dollar Mermaid* (Mervyn Leroy, 1952).[10] In terms of narrative, the sheer audio-visual spectacle of the scene also invites comparison to Berkeley films in that it mainly serves as a divertissement within the wider narrative – rather than an overt progression – and is an opportunity for the composer and animators to have cinematic fun in the film.

'It's a B-Movie' Song

The second featured song sequence is the antithesis of 'City Of Light' in terms of style, topic and representation of narrative predicament. In a manner that suggests the 'road trip gone wrong' scenario of many horror films, the appliances find themselves imprisoned within an electrical parts shop and realize the threat that they may be cannibalized for spare parts at any time. This prospect is reinforced by the overhead light, whose amused malevolence is communicated in a character voice that is as clearly based on B-movie-style acting by Peter Lorre as the air-conditioner unit's Jack Nicholson shtick. Adding further allusion, the song is titled (after its chorus line) 'It's a B-Movie'. The song opens quasi-diegetically. As the overhead light mocks the appliances' desire to escape, an old gramophone drops its needle down onto its acetate 10-inch disc and a clichéd, horror-film organ sequence, featuring large, loud chords with low pedal notes, diminished intervals and a chromatic descending passage, immediately sets the mood. Vocal parts enter in a dramatic, half-spoken, staccato fashion, name-checking a range of horror-movie references – including Frankenstein and actor Vincent Price. The dramatic impact (and sonic interest) is enhanced by the use of a wide range of male and female voices with distinctive accents and tonal qualities. The song then moves into a section with funky bass and disco-style beat, together with string lines, brass stabs and synth drum accents. The vocal parts become more sustained, and incorporate multi-part harmonies. Vocal unisons and harmonies continue through the subsequent verse, contrasting with the solo voices of the opening verses, and providing further interest and variety within the repetitive song framework. As the song moves into the chorus ("It's like a movie/It's like a B-movie show"), the rhythm straightens out into an eighth-note feel driven by a relentless pedal line on the electric bass, with more brass stabs and heavy synth drum accents. The vocal hook is a simple, singalong idea performed in dramatic, multi-part harmony and, when combined with the rock feel of the rhythm parts, provides an effect reminiscent of modern musicals such as *The Rocky Horror Picture Show* (Jim Sharman, 1975). The horror-style organ returns in a musical interlude that features dramatic ascending chromatic lines augmented by rattling xylophone sounds. After a repeat of the powerful chorus, the music ascends chromatically to a dramatic climax. Once again Newman's sophisticated arranging skills are in evidence, as he heightens the drama of the rising phrases by adding a new element in the form of high-set female voices.

The visuals of this sequence also utilize, parody and play with vintage conventions of horror cinema including dramatic uses of light and shadow and visual angularity, while its hooks and instruments of dismemberment suggest the contemporary charnel-houses of films such as *The Texas Chain Saw Massacre* (Tobe Hooper, 1973). The appliances finally make their escape after turning the horror conventions back on the parts shop owner. Using scary voices and visual disguises (emphasized by noticeable strings), they frighten him before leading a general escape, with the four appliances finally glimpsing the city of light as the score's main musical motif rises on the soundtrack.

'Cutting Edge' Song

Once in the city the appliances find their way to their owner's apartment, arriving just after he leaves to return to the country house to pick them up and take them away to college with him. In his city home, they encounter a group of more modern counterparts – all of which have their own highly charactered voices. The song is sung by these appliances to emphasize their technological superiority to the 'country cousins'. The number starts with two quirky, angular, electronic-sounding riffs that emanate from the computer before morphing into relentless sixteenth-note patterns as the musical number begins. The riffs are joined by a bluesy melody, harmonized by a voice at a perfect fourth interval, before drum sounds are added to the texture. A funk groove is then established – combining a syncopated sixteenth guitar part, heavy bass drum, slap bass and electronic brass stabs. A distinctive male lead vocal effectively evokes the seductive, yet impersonal, world of modern electronic devices, as characterized by low range, smooth tone (emphasizing bass and mid-range frequencies) and a slow, deliberate style of vocal delivery. The male voice is joined by an equally smooth female voice, before the song moves to the catchy, syncopated main hook to the lyrics "More, more, more!" The arrangement playfully moves the simple hook idea through shifting key centres, and adds various electronic sounds, slap bass and drum hits to complete the musical texture, before leading the arrangement into a humorous electronica-style 'Latin' section replete with multiple percussion parts, horn lines, syncopated bass and rapid-fire vocal lines. As in 'It's a B-Movie', rising phrases are regularly used to create excitement and drama (a typical music-theatre technique). In a style reminiscent of 1980s music videos, the song is accompanied by sequences of choreography, special effects and inserts that also – in the context of the film's original 1987 release date – further signal modernity (especially in contrast to the radio's permanent retro setting and audio style). The appliances' redundancy is emphasized by a sequence that cuts between the owner's item-by-item search for the appliances in the summer house and these same items being thrown, one by one, out of the apartment window into a skip in the street below.

'Worthless' song

The film's final song sequence occurs at the narrative climax. The skip in which the appliances find themselves is transported to a large scrapyard where old cars (and other devices) await their fate of being crushed into metal cubes ready for melting down. Visually, the scrapyard is dominated by huge tottering piles of grey metal and dark shadows. The acoustic space is marked by a repetitive bright metallic thudding riff from the crushing machine, which overlaps a brief, enigmatic piano introduction (using a motif previously featured in the orchestral score) before the song's verses commence. Sung with resigned bitterness by a series of cars as they head towards the crusher, the song's title – 'Worthless' – is reiterated in its chorus. The song proceeds with a straight-ahead, eighth-feel rock groove and the first voice enters with a catchy melody consisting of a bluesy, rising minor third followed by a descending phrase. The melody is harmonized in an unusual manner (i iii VII VI III) with the minor iii chord accentuating the upward minor-third movement in the melody and providing an element of surprise. In fact, the arrangement appears to delight in 'playing around' with key centres and phrase lengths, with the result that the very repetitive melody becomes somewhat unpredictable: the listener is never entirely sure when, and in what key, it will start. The two-note 'worthless' hook also moves through a variety of pitch areas. Parks's lyrics also offer playful phrases, for example, the first female voice entry contains an obvious internal joke ("I just can't, I just can't, I just can't seem to get started"). Further evidence of playfulness is provided by several 'false endings' based around the enigmatic piano riff idea of the introduction.

Of all the songs in Rees's film, this is the most heavily rock-influenced. In addition to the bluesy melodic and harmonic ideas, the song uses a repetitive rock bass line, a number of raw, rock-style voices and a featured sax solo. This musical context allows its vocal characters to express their predicament with passion. Parks's lyrics complement this in condensed narrative cameos that recall his accomplished work on solo albums such as *Tokyo Rose* (1989).[11] As Benshoff (1992) has also recognized, the penultimate verse, voiced by a 'First Nations' truck, is particularly expressive of redundancy, in lines such as:

> Who would believe they would love me and leave me
> On a bus back to old Santa Fe?

After witnessing the procession of cars heading into the crusher, the owner arrives in time to try and rescue his favourite appliances from the conveyor belt, only to slide towards the crusher himself, until the toaster intervenes by jumping into and jamming the crusher mechanism. In the film's final sequence the appliances sit quietly while the owner repairs the toaster and then drives off to college accompanied by a triumphal orchestral crescendo.

Conclusion

In the only sustained analysis of the film to be published to date, Benshoff (1992) reads the film against a history of US animation and, most specifically, Disney, and considers the film's position within a spectrum of 'low' to 'high' culture. Drawing on this, he considers the film's counter-hegemonic potential as (what he characterizes) a postmodern text capable of endorsing "a formerly subaltern ideology within their encoding and subsequent dominant decodings" (1996: 5). His analysis of the film crystallizes this aspect by offering a reading available to audiences aware of genre history and able to read analogy:

> The classical cel animation of The Brave Little Toaster *may indeed be making a last ditch stand against the increasingly computerized technology of contemporary animation art, much in the way that the toaster and his pals bravely fight off the demands and rigors of a system that finds them increasingly outmoded.* (ibid.: 83)

Whereas Walter Benjamin's 'angel of history'[12] was famously powerless to do any more than watch the rubble of history accumulate as he was blown away from paradise, the boy saviour of *Brave Little Toaster* is credited with more agency. He snatches his appliances from the scrapyard and restores them to wholeness and functionality in a present where newer technologies are competing in increasingly shorter cycles of obsolescence. (The latter point is all the more apparent to contemporary spectators since the computers featured in the penultimate sequence now appear hopelessly outdated, while the toaster at least is engagingly familiar, even 'retro chic'.) While Benshoff's identification of the film's use of traditional cel animation as a deliberate embrace of (what the industry might perceive as) an outmoded technology is tenable, *listening* to the film in the early twenty-first century also gives another perspective. The film's use of analogue instruments (an orchestra), foley and vocable effects, along with its voice actors and music-theatre/film-musical-derived songs, appears to be prepared from a markedly different recipe book from contemporary animation cinema (with its reliance on digital composition and – often – inserted song types derived from mainstream popular music genres). Indeed, some twenty years after its genesis, while *The Brave Little Toaster*'s traditional cel animation may seem somewhat anachronistic in a more digital environment, the 'charm' – in both senses of the word[13] – of its sonic text has, if anything, been enhanced by the passing of the years. Its sonic complexity and integration offer a richer realm of engagement than the simpler sonic texts produced by mainstream animation industries in the USA and Japan alike.

The seamless, quasi-organic integration of sonic elements in *The Brave Little Toaster* arguably offers a more humanely anthropomorphized environment than the more technically 'advanced' features that emerged from Pixar and the like in the years that followed. While features such as Lasseter's *Toy Story* and a slew of more recent feature films have used known lead vocal actors to lend depth of characterization and identification (and saleability) to the projects, *The Brave Little Toaster*'s cast of (then) unknown voice actors worked as an ensemble, their dialogue suggesting the live improvised context from which they emerged. In this regard *Brave Little Toaster*'s sonic animation set a benchmark that few subsequent productions have approached.

Notes

1. Director of the first fully digital animation feature *Toy Story* (1995).
2. Director of various live-action and animation feature films such as *The Corpse Bride* (2006). See Janet Halfyard's chapter elsewhere in this volume.
3. Director of *The Incredibles* (2004).
4. Director of *Aladdin* (1992).
5. Brent Schlender (2006), 'The future of Hollywood: Pixar's magic man', *Fortune* (online at http://money.cnn.com/2006/05/15/magazines/fortune/pixar_futureof_fortune_052906/index.htm; accessed 15 April 2007; paragraphing condensed from original).
6. Lasseter recalls:

   > As I put together my pitch for 'The Brave Little Toaster', I had started looking for people who could do computer animation. That led me to Lucasfilm, because they had this computer division that had some of the world's best computer scientists. I even went up to San Rafael and visited Ed Catmull and Alvy Ray Smith, the two guys who started the group. Ed and Alvy had approached Disney Studios to try to get them interested in computer animation, without much success ... Soon after I was fired, I went down to a computer graphics conference at the Queen Mary in Long Beach. I'll never forget it. I saw Ed give his talk, and when he saw me he came up all excited and asked, "How's Toaster?" All I could say was, "It got shelved." I didn't have the guts to tell him I got fired. So he asked what I was doing next, and I told him I wasn't sure. (in Schlender article, see note 6)

7. Three associated illustrated children's books followed (in 1986, 1987 and 1988).
8. As Newman has characterized: "My experience in Japan with *Brave Little Toaster* was fantastic ... We went there because it was cheap but the hall was gorgeous and I had a great engineer and the orchestra was terrific. I still think that recording sounds beautiful" (Kremer, 2002: np).
9. Evoking Elmer in the classic *Road Runner* series, who routinely refers to his adversary as a "wabbit".
10. Indeed, the soundtrack CD identifies this musical sequence as 'The Swamp/Busby Berkeley/The Meadow'.

11. See Fitzgerald and Hayward (1999) for further discussion.
12. Discussed in 'Über den Begriff der Geschichte' (On the Concept of History/ Theses on the Philosophy of History), 1939, published posthumously (see Benjamin, 1969).
13. That is, its appeal and 'magic'.

References

Benshoff, H. M. (1992), 'Heigh-Ho, Heigh-Ho, Is Disney High or Low? From Silly Cartoons to Postmodern Politics', *Animation Journal*, 1(1), 62–85 (online at www.chapman.edu/animation/harryb.html).

Benjamin, W. (1969), 'Theses on the Philosophy of History', in *Illuminations: Essays and Reflections*, New York: Schocken Books, pp. 253–64.

Fitzgerald, J., and Hayward, P. (1999), 'Musical Transport: Van Dyke Parks, Americana and the Applied Orientalism of *Tokyo Rose*', in P. Hayward (ed.), *Widening the Horizon: Exoticism in Post-War Popular Music*, Eastleigh, Hampshire: John Libbey Publishing/Perfect Beat Publications, pp. 145–67.

Kremer, J. (2002), 'David Newman Interview (1999)', *Film Score Monthly* (online at http://www.filmscoremonthly.com/articles/2002/30_Jan—Lost_Issue_David_Newman_Interview_Conclusion.asp, accessed Nov 2006).

Schweiger, D. (2004), 'The Brave Little Cartoon', CD booklet essay for *The Brave Little Toaster (Original Motion Picture Soundtrack)*, Perception Records.

10 Lupin III and the *Gekiban* Approach
Western-styled Music in a Japanese Format

Kentaro Imada[1]

Lupin III (*Rupan sansei*) comprises several television anime series and theatrically re-leased films that were screened in Japan over a twenty-five-year period. The first series, of 23 episodes, was televised in Japan in 1971, and the second series ran for a massive 155 episodes, broadcast from 1977 to 1980. This was followed by a third series of 50 episodes that were screened in the mid-1980s (see Table 10.1). Repeated broad-casts of these television series (particularly the first two) provided a solid popular following for the programme both in Japan and later internationally, and enabled the production of six theatrical feature films featuring Lupin III, the last of which was released in 1996. The original Japanese manga series, which first appeared in 1967, was written and illustrated by Kazuhiko Kato (under the nom de plume 'Monkey Punch') around the character of Arsène Lupin III, who was the grandson of the gentleman-burglar described in Maurice Leblanc's novels from the early twentieth century. In the animation products, Lupin III leads a gang of thieves who travel the world accumulating treasures and evading the law. While originally targeted to a teenage demographic, Lupin III has maintained a following across several age groups.

Of the six theatrical films featuring Lupin III, three films – *Rupan sansei: Mamo karano chousen* [*Lupin III: Lupin vs. The Clone*[2]] (Yasuo Ôtsuka and Soji Yoshikawa, 1978), *Rupan sansei: Kariosutoro no shiro* [*Lupin III: Castle of Cagliostro*] (Hayao Miyazaki, 1979), and *Rupan sansei: Babiron no Ogon densetsu* [*Lupin III: The Golden Legend of Babylon*] (Seijun Suzuki and Shigetsugu Yoshida, 1985)[3] – were produced while the TV series were still being broadcast (see Table 10.2). The releases were undoubtedly part of a well-timed strategy to take advantage of the series' popularity (see Figure 10.1). As about half of all theatrically released animated films in Japan are currently produced in this way,[4] the Lupin III films can be analysed as typical examples of a common strategy used in the Japanese animation industry.

This integrated box-office strategy also informs several aspects of the productions, including the film music. For example, much of the music for the TV series can be heard in the first three Lupin III films (listed above) and the music duration for the films is relatively short compared to western counterparts, particularly animation feature films. In the second film, *The Castle of Cagliostro*, which was directed by one of Japan's most highly regarded and internationally famous animators, Hayao Miyazaki, about one-third of all the inserted music is appropriated from the TV series. This suggests that musical decisions were dictated by the need to economize on time and labour, although, as I will discuss below, other factors have impacted on this process.

Table 10.1 Lupin III TV series data

	First TV series	*Second TV series*	*Third TV series*
TV series title	*Lupin the 3rd*	*Lupin the 3rd (new)*	*Lupin the 3rd PART III*
Number of episodes	23	155	50
Telecast period (original broadcasts)	24 October 1971– 26 March 1972	3 October 1977– 6 October 1980	3 March 1984– 25 December 1985
Telecast time (original broadcasts)	Sunday 19:30– 20:00	Monday 19:00– 19:30	Saturday 19:00– 19:30
Composer	Takeo Yamashita	Yuji Ohno	Yuji Ohno
Production	Yomiuri Telecasting Corporation, Tokyo Movie	Tokyo Movie Shinsha	Yomiuri Telecasting Corporation, Tokyo Movie Shinsha
Key station of broadcasting network	Yomiuri Telecasting Corporation	Nippon Television Network Corporation	Yomiuri Telecasting Corporation
Network	Currently TMS Entertainment Ltd	Currently TMS Entertainment Ltd	

Source: Studio Hard, 1999.

In this chapter, I analyse *gekiban* (dramatic accompaniment), the music used in Japanese animated films, by examining the Lupin III film products. Regardless of whether a production is animated or live action, the musical accompaniment for a theatrical or dramatic production is called *gekiban* in Japanese. The word combines two Chinese characters that can be translated as 'music that accompanies drama', and the term is frequently used derogatively in reference to such music and those who make it. I argue that there is a fundamental difference between Japan and the West in terms of the conceptualization and uses of music in theatrical film releases due to the influence of the history of music, dance and acting largely derived from *kabuki* theatre. Music in Japanese animated features can be characterized as a point of confluence between the traditional sound production styles employed in Japanese theatre and silent cinema, and the system, conception and aesthetics of western musical accompaniment.

Table 10.2 Lupin III theatrical releases

	Title					
	Lupin vs. the Clone (The Secret of Mamo)	The Castle of Cagliostro	The Legend of the Gold of Babylon	The Plot of the Fuma Clan	Farewell to Nostradamus (To Hell with Nostradamus)	Dead or Alive
Release date in Japan	16 December 1978	15 December 1979	13 July 1985	26 December 1987	22 April 1995	20 April 1996
Director	Souji Yoshikawa	Hayao Miyazaki	Seijun Suzuki and Shigetsugu Yoshida	Yasuo Ohtsuka	Shunya Ito	Monkey Punch
Music	Yuji Ohno	Yuji Ohno	Yuji Ohno	Kiyoshi Miyaura	Yuji Ohno	Takayuki Negishi
Senkyokuka[a]	Seiji Suzuki	Seiji Suzuki	Seiji Suzuki (as Musical Director)	None	Seiji Suzuki (as Musical Director)	Seiji Suzuki (as Musical Director)
Production	Tokyo Movie Shinsha	Tokyo Movie Shinsha	Toho Co., Ltd, Nippon Television Network Corporation, Yomiuri Telecasting Corporation, Tokyo Movie Shinsha	Toho Co., Ltd, Tokyo Movie Shinsha	Lupin III Production Committee	Lupin III Production Committee
Notes	Currently TMS Entertainment Ltd					

Source: Studio Hard, 1999.
a. A full description of this position occurs on page 184.

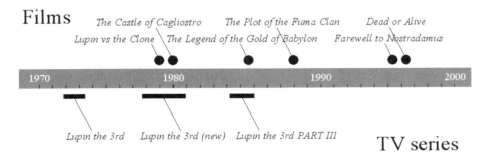

Figure 10.1 Relation of TV and film releases

In his seminal film-theory work from the 1930s and 1940s, and particularly his *Manga Eiga Ron* (1992), Taihei Imamura (1911–86) suggests that there is an indelible link in Japanese animation between the traditional storytelling format and its music. Imamura's contention, however, is not based on a thorough examination of animated films, is overly general, and offers many examples which cannot be applied in a consideration of the contemporary situation. In addition, given that Imamura was writing in the (still) early period of synchronized sound film in Japan, his thesis lacks a significant address to specifically filmic deployments of music and sound. Nevertheless, inasmuch as it identifies current animation as an extension of traditional performing arts, Imamura's work is relevant to this study and informs my argument here. The first part of this chapter introduces the Lupin III characters and discusses how a historical model of dramatic music enabled the development of animation productions like Lupin III in the contemporary era. This provides a context for the second part of the chapter, which analyses the music in specific Lupin III films.

The Lupin III characters and creators

In the picaresque action drama depicting the antics of Lupin III and his cohorts, Lupin III (sometimes called 'The Wolf') is a shrewd master-thief who always gets what he wants and has an eye for attractive women. Despite being the world's most wanted thief, he sometimes uses incompetence as a ruse, and likes gadgets. In addition to Lupin himself, there are four main characters: his friends Jigen Daisuke and Ishikawa Goemon (the thirteenth representative of the Ishikawa samurai family, whose namesake was also a famous bandit), a mysterious woman named Fujiko Mine, who essentially functions as Lupin's arch-enemy as well as 'love interest', and Inspector Koichi Zenigata, whose mission in life is to arrest Lupin. While the first series sometimes represents antagonism between the characters and is more overtly violent, the second series is lighter in approach, featuring simpler action and tongue-in-cheek asides.

Whether on TV or in the movies, each episode or film narrative consists of a discrete story that does not require knowledge of previous instalments. The TV episodes run for 30 minutes and each story is resolved by the programme's conclusion. Similarly, the films have a running time of about 100 minutes and the plot is resolved by the end of the film. This enables production by several different animators – including the aforementioned Hayao Miyazaki[5] – using the main characters and independently producing each episode. While the sketches of character and the settings are subtly different, the same five characters appeared throughout the animated series and this ensemble formed the core of Lupin III.

Another consistent aspect of the Lupin III oeuvre was the significant musical contribution made by Yuji Ohno (b.1941). A composer and arranger of film and TV music, Ohno started out as a jazz pianist and based much of his later work on jazz and fusion. He was directly involved in the second and third TV series, and four of the Lupin III films. The band that performed all of this music, You & the Explosion Band (which consciously adopted an English name), was a group of musicians that Ohno himself had assembled. The members were not fixed, however, and Ohno chose them according to their availability for each recording session.

In this chapter, I concentrate primarily on Ohno's work in the films *Lupin vs. The Clone*, *Castle of Cagliostro* and *The Golden Legend of Babylon* (henceforth referred to in a group as 'Lupin III films', unless otherwise differentiated) because they were released during the airing and production of the TV series. These films offer a useful model for discussion of the musical production and recycling that was employed by Ohno. With the exception of the third TV series, the music production company was virtually the same and some common melodic elements are found throughout the TV series and the films. As such, the Lupin III works suggest a type of musical auteurism on the part of Ohno but a pragmatic auteurism that operated in the context of practices common in the Japanese animation industry and, as I will show in the next section, was significantly informed by *gekiban* practices.

Gekiban's derivation

It has only been about 130 years since the western musical system – that is, an acoustic system structured on particular tones, scales and harmony – and the Japanese word for any music, *ongaku*, were adopted in Japan. Prior to that time, acoustic accompaniment using percussive, blown and plucked instruments was used in Japanese stage productions. Known as *hayashi*, this accompaniment was heard in staged performances of *noh*, *kabuki*[6] and various folk arts. Given this history, it is inevitable that, since *gekiban* merely adopted the function of *hayashi* and then replaced the original sound with western music, the western aesthetic approach would not integrate smoothly with established aesthetic practices. Over the last 130 years, however, the word *ongaku* has come to include not only western but also traditional Japanese music. At the same time, the approach and sounds of *hayashi*, which was once the essence of *gekiban*, have been marginalized and western aesthetics have come to define the direction of much musical enterprise in Japan. Thus, the low value and exaggerated expectations placed on *gekiban* are a reflection of this socio-historical background.

Hayashi became an essential part of Japanese stage productions and ceremonies in the Middle Ages and encompasses a variety of acoustic genres. In most Japanese–English dictionaries (see, for example, Watanabe *et al.*, 2003), *hayashi* ensembles are said to consist of drums and flutes (specifically *shinobue, shime-daiko, oh-daiko*, etc.). But the roots of the word *hayashi* can be traced to the noun form of the intransitive verb 'to favour' or 'to praise'. In other words, rather than the actual performance, at the core of the word lies the implication that the festive mood associated with an instrumental ensemble was created in praise of something else. *Hayashi* refers to a variety of genres and sounds, but its significance as a form of praise is consistent. What distinguishes *hayashi* from the western concept of music is that, rather than regulating sound, it suggests sound's function.

This is evident in the way *hayashi* is used in *kabuki*. There are several different types of sound-related performances in *kabuki* but *kage-bayashi* is the comprehensive term used for all of them.[7] The basic *kage-bayashi* ensemble consists of various percussion instruments, flutes and *shamisen* (a stringed instrument). Miyamaru notes that the performers have a stockpile of over 800 rhythm patterns, ensemble parts and melodies:

> The instrumental passages in kabuki *are intended to express the nature of the principal characters and the situations in which they find themselves. Some of these are newly created for each production, but many are reused and their significance is well known to the audience.* (1993: 222)

The scenes that require *kage-bayashi* are generally already decided, as Miyamaru continues:

> Kage-bayashi *is generally used to advance the production when the curtain rises or falls, in transition sequences (setting changes including revolving stages and traps) ... and with people's movements and gestures as well as certain lines (including recollections).* (ibid.)

In rehearsals the leader of the *kage-bayashi* ensemble selects appropriate pieces from the group's repertoire based on these principles. Then s/he creates a cue sheet (known as either a *tsukecho* or *kikkakecho*) that the ensemble refers to during the performance. Miyamaru describes the effect created by *kage-bayashi* as follows:

> In terms of function, kage-bayashi *presents aspects of character, scenery, and situation ... For example, the* hayashi *used as the curtain is raised sets the scene, while the nature of the main character emerges through the entrance music, and climatic situations like rain and wind are expressed through the sound of* oh-daiko *(large drums). In addition, the* hayashi *has the function of making certain lines and gestures resonate by emphasizing the content and movements. For instance, by effectively colouring passages of reminiscence*

with bamboo flutes or kokyu *(Chinese fiddle), stressing formulaic movements
in dramatic or silent scenes, and adding beautiful songs to* koroshiba *(murder
scenes), it asserts the unique world of beauty in* kabuki. *(ibid.)*

Seen in this light, the basic routine and objectives of *kage-bayashi* seem very similar to
the character and scene themes used in Lupin III. In both productions, each acoustic
piece represents a single element, is only performed intermittently, and, with the
exception of the bridges, it never continues across scenes. In addition, the conventional
nature of *gekiban*, to which Ohno objected, seems based on the concepts of *hayashi*.

Of particular interest is the fact that, among the rhythm patterns in *hayashi*, there are
sounds like *amaoto* (rain) and *kazaoto* (snow), indicating that sound effects are also a
part of *hayashi*. Thus, though the recording of *gekiban* and sound effects are now seen
as two separate things, in *hayashi* these elements were seen as part of one whole and
developed as part of an overall sound design. This proved particularly potent in relation
to ghostly elements, as James Wierzbicki (2008) observes in his analysis of sounds
associated with 'J-horror' cinema.

The similarities between *gekiban* and *hayashi* are not limited to the way in which they
were performed; *gekiban* was also the successor to *hayashi* in its role as musical
accompaniment for silent films. In the 1910s, *kabuki*, which had until that point been
one of the main forms of entertainment, suffered massive cutbacks with the sudden rise
of the motion picture. The *hayashi* performers who found themselves out of work formed
private brass bands that introduced western music to Japan during the period and
accompanied silent movies. The musicians are thought to have performed *hayashi* using
brass instruments and to have composed original western-styled tunes. Analysing the few
cue sheets that are extant from the period reveals that the music was structured like
hayashi and that, even when accompanying films, the performers relied on their knowledge of these traditional practices (Imada, 2000, 2004).

The accompaniment for silent movies was therefore an amalgam of *hayashi* and
western-styled brass band music. While using *hayashi* as a model, the performers
adopted music derived from the West to create the archetype for *gekiban*. This situation
changed with the introduction of synchronized sound to film production in Japan in the
1930s. From 1933, many *gekiban* performers were once again out of work. Some
managed to begin a new career as a composer or performer of music for the 'talkies'
or radio broadcasts. Most of this music was either western or an imitation of it, and
the performers no longer had an opportunity to play the *hayashi* repertoire as part of
a stage production and, at the same time, were unable to share these sounds with other
people. Also in this period, a performer emerged who was specifically in charge of
sound effects.[8] The literal association of on-stage activity with 'onomatopoeic' sounds
is analogous to animation-cinema sound, where the sound assists in 'animating' the on-
screen activity.

The stage productions that this music was used for were not as developed as western
opera or musicals, so the western-style acoustics were actually invoked using *hayashi*

methods. The basic working methods of *gekiban* and sound production were defined by pre-war mass media and these media forms were also instrumental in the development of entertainment formats[9] and the introduction of western musical genres like classical, jazz and rock. Nevertheless, the elements of *hayashi* were still present in these formats. With the emergence of a new mass medium – synchronized-sound cinema – and the subsequent evolution of an appropriate musical genre, the approach and operations of *gekiban* were subtly altered by the form's unique aesthetic objectives and limitations. In terms of the music used for Lupin III, it is clear that the basic working methods retained elements of the *hayashi* practices on which they were modelled.

Lupin III themes and musical support

The Lupin III music takes the form of opening and closing themes, segues that support scene changes, character themes and music accompanying action. Among the melodies that are used as musical accompaniment in Lupin III are themes that reflect the appearance, activities and development of a particular character. Inevitably, the most common of these is Lupin III's own theme. This tune was composed by Ohno as the main theme for the second TV series and, as the composition was used in the show's opening for each episode, it is extremely well known. The lively theme is performed by a brass ensemble featuring a lead saxophone part (Figure 10.2) with unison brass riffing on instrumental choruses. In its up-tempo, funky style, the theme invites comparison with US television programmes such as the 1970s cop show *Hawaii Five-O*. Its prominent rhythm section is supported by Latin-styled syncopation on conga, and the theme includes gunshot-like sound effects.

Figure 10.2   Author's notation of main melody for Lupin III theme.

The music for both the TV series and the films was often rearranged and recycled. For example, the main theme appears three times in *Lupin vs. the Clone*: in the opening, the car chase, and the last scene; twice in *The Castle of Cagliostro*: in the opening car chase and the scene in which Lupin III rescues the heroine; and once in *The Legend of the Gold of Babylon*, when Lupin III makes off with the treasure. As Lupin III is at the heart of the action in all of these scenes, the theme emphasizes his actions and personal style as central to the narrative.

Short melodies and specific tone-colours are also used for the other characters. For example, appearances by Inspector Zenigata are accompanied by an *enka* (traditional-style Japanese popular song) known as the 'Zenigata March'. This theme appears once in each of the three movies in association with Zenigata's actions. Other themes signal specific actions, for example, when Goemon whips out his sword the action is always accompanied by the sound of a *shakuhachi* (a five-holed bamboo flute). These regular themes were devised for the second TV series and were reused in the films.

Additional themes were created for the individual characters who featured in specific films. For example, Clarisse makes her only appearance as the heroine in *The Castle of Cagliostro* but is given a theme of her own called 'Fire Treasure', a composition that was also released as a single and served as the main theme of the film. Similarly, Rosetta, the heroine in *The Legend of the Gold of Babylon*, is accompanied by a composition called 'Song Of Babylon'. These themes are played when the characters appear on the screen and function to emphasize their presence.

By using each of the themes repeatedly, Ohno creates and reinforces an effective identification with the characters and their contributions to the storylines. Despite this, he tried to avoid overusing the character themes, as he notes:

> *Actually, I don't really like creating specific themes for each of the characters but, in the Japanese movie industry, there's this strange hang-up about having to have music that matches a person's feeling when the scene deals with a certain character's perspective. A lot of people seem to think of* gekiban *in these terms; people used to say this kind of thing to me all the time.* (Ohno, cited in Fuwa, 2003b)

At the time, it was commonly believed that the use of *gekiban* should include set character themes. However, rather than being Ohno's own working style, this was a practice commonly required of composers. In fact, by the beginning of the second TV series, Ohno still had not decided on all of the character themes and they were completed about two years after the show began, in 1979.

Following this experience, Ohno planned to employ the themes from the second TV series in the third one. However, this series was scheduled for broadcast by a different television station that did not own the rights to the original music. Ohno reflected that, "When I was told I couldn't use the same 'Lupin III Theme', I wasn't sure what to do ... because it had already been written and was already very well known" (Ohno, quoted in Fuwa, 2004). Rather than writing a completely new score as the musical accompaniment for a new series, Ohno wished to exploit the existing popular support by reusing established themes; his solution was to generate themes that were new while also reminiscent of the originals.

Beyond character themes, throughout the Lupin III products, action scenes are invariably accompanied by music that supports and explains the events on screen. Additional musical cues portray the situation in a scene but tend not to be synchronized to the action. As such, they are differentiated from the opening and ending themes, the bridges that express a change from one scene to another, and the character themes.

In *The Castle of Cagliostro*, closely synched music is used only in the opening car chase and the scene in which Lupin III jumps from roof to roof and, even then, the track was created not by composing music specifically for the scenes but by editing an already recorded passage. The production process for these films avoided the use of 'bar sheets', charts of the type used in Disney films to synchronize the music with the screen image. Ohno's work only began after a detailed editing plan had been made by the director and producer, as he recalls: "After it was determined which sections required music in the film, I would create something that lasted a certain number of seconds to go with an image or scene" (Ohno cited in Fuwa, 2003a).

Ohno's only reference point between the image and the sound was his impression of a scene provided by early sketches, and the cues were not composed as tightly synchronized elements. The necessity for a specific piece of music in a certain scene was fairly low, and it was possible to substitute another melody as long as the atmosphere was not greatly altered. In fact, the job of placing the music with specific scenes was delegated to someone other than the composer (as detailed below).

The music in the Lupin III works can be broadly categorized into two groups, each of which has its own characteristics. One type of music was used to symbolize on-screen elements – a character, action or event – and, fundamentally, this was limited to a single melody for each element. The melody might also appear in a different arrangement to create a different impression. For example, as Inspector Zenigata fluctuated between hope and despair in his pursuit of Lupin III, 'The Zenigata March' was changed to create a variety of impressions while representing a single character. These themes were included intermittently, and only one theme was used per scene. Once the music had served its function, it quickly faded out. There are almost no instances of the music continuing on from one scene to the next and rarely a smooth connection of melodies or juxtaposition of two or more melodies as counterpoint. Whether the theme stands for a character or scene, the music is meant to express something that is already visible on the screen. Once a character in a particular scene and development of the story is visually recognized, the music becomes unnecessary and even excessive.

The second type of music was used to assist the flow of the scenes. Rather than organically connecting and developing the story, the music suggests the content of the images on the screen and does little more than acoustically lead the listener. In this scenario, the need for the composition, selection and position of a certain melody cannot be shown to derive from its relationship to a specific visual scene. Instead, its use is a reflection of particular customs and historical circumstances.

The composer's role

The Lupin III films employed a production process for the music that began with the composing of the music and ended with the dubbing of the tunes in the film. Melodies are used at various points in the films:

> One approach is to create a new tune according to the length of the parts in the film where music is deemed necessary. In other cases, tunes for a record that are created without any special consideration for the scene are recorded to be sold on the day [that the film is released] as a soundtrack album. And other times, music that has already been created for the TV series is reused – there are really a variety of approaches. It's a combination of all of these elements. (Ohno, cited in Fuwa, 2003a)

In cases where new material was written for a film, it was generally recorded over a couple of days using a group of musicians assembled by Ohno.[10]

However, the music was not simply combined with the animation as it was recorded. By referring to the duration and master tapes of the music, it is clear that the melodies were cut and edited during the dubbing stage of the film. In *The Castle of Cagliostro*, for example:

> There were almost no scenes in which the music was used in its original form … In the finishing stages, detailed edits would be made according to the ideas of the Senkyokuka, *Suzuki Seiji*, and [the music] would be added to complete the film. (Ohno, cited in Fuwa, 2003a)

In the animation industry in Japan, the *senkyokuka* (literally, 'music selector' but functionally a sound and/or musical director/producer) selects the music for each scene in the film and edits the melodies in the most appropriate manner. Even when the composer records a new melody for the film, the *senkyokuka* may find something more appropriate in other material, and this will be inserted instead. The *senkyokuka* also edits the music for the required duration and connects it with the other recordings while maintaining the music continuity. Ultimately, then, in terms of the dubbing and overall sound design of the film, it is the *senkyokuka* and the director who, by supervising the overall project, wield considerable authority over the music, well beyond that of the composer.

The practices described above contrast to classic auteurist perceptions of western art-music composers. In the world of Japanese animation, rather than creating one-of-a-kind melodies to fit particular image sequences, the job of the composer is largely to develop a stockpile of material that can be used as necessary.[11] This is not just a matter of economic expediency, but also reflects the roots of *gekiban* as a practice in Japanese stage and media productions.

Conclusion

The ways of creating music and sound for the Lupin III movies are similar to the working methods used in TV series and other animated films. They are also common in live-action film series[12] and TV dramas. However, Lupin III's music demonstrates several issues about the role of *gekiban* in the production of this kind of animation. The music is decidedly subordinate to the visual aspect of the work and, since the music cues tend to be interchangeable, the music is considered to be of equal value to the sound effects. The placement of music in relation to the image track is ultimately entrusted to the judgement of non-composers and this suggests that *gekiban* is a less-than-essential part of Japanese films and TV dramas.

However, on closer inspection, it is evident that certain contributions are expected of the composer. Unlike the sound effects, the music performs the necessary role of connecting the images and helps determine the overall design of the film. As such, the expectations for *gekiban* can be seen as akin to the aesthetic objectives of stage music in a western opera, given the way the music operates in relation to staging and sung text. In addition, nearly everything related to *gekiban* is derived from the western concept of 'music'. In this sense, it is not surprising that *gekiban* is expected to function according to western aesthetics. With Ohno's own fundamental reliance on musical genres such as jazz and fusion, the music of Lupin III abides by this expectation.

Studies of music in Japanese animation have been limited in scope and in their address to histories of popular music forms in Japan. The tendency in analysing Japanese animation music has been to compare it to a model provided by tightly synchronized western (especially USA) feature films. As such, Japanese animation is deemed inferior, particularly in respect of its music. Although it is impossible to ignore the influence of western animation, this may be irrelevant to most contemporary Japanese mainstream productions in terms of music production. While Japanese animation employs western musical elements, it does so with a specific socio-historical approach and this determines a sound and style that is notably different from US and other western mainstream productions.

Analysis of Japanese animation-film music must be conducted within the context of histories of popular musical forms and their deployment in Japanese media forms. This chapter offers a preliminary address to this project. In addition, the industrial production practices used for Japan's animation feature films significantly inform the musical elements. Yuji Ohno's experience as composer for Lupin III products demonstrates how the role of *gekiban* composer in the animation context reflects a certain ambivalence between the art of the composer and the pragmatism required by the industry. Ultimately, the Lupin III film products show how music is a vital but historically complex element in Japanese animation cinema.

Notes

1. All names in this chapter follow the English convention of given name first, then family name.
2. Originally released as simply *Lupin III*. Japanese promotional material subtitled the film *Lupin vs. The Clone(s)* (*Rupan tai Kuroon*), and it was subsequently titled *Mystery of Mamo*, and later *The Secret of Mamo*.
3. The first three films were followed by: *Rupan sansei: Fûma ichizoku no inbô* [*Lupin III: The Fuma Conspiracy*] (Masayuki Ozeki, 1987), *Rupan sansei: Kutabare! Nastradamus* [*Lupin III: Die, Nostradamus*] (Shunya Ito and Takeshi Shiado, 1995), and *Rupan sansei: Dead or Alive* [*Lupin III: Dead or Alive*] (Monkey Punch, 1996).
4. See Aki Yamasaki, elsewhere in this volume.
5. In addition to directing *The Castle of Cagliostro*, Miyazaki directed several episodes of the first two TV series (Studio Hard, 1999).
6. While *noh* is generally considered a more refined art form, *kabuki* is deemed popular entertainment.
7. The word *kage*, or 'shadow', in *kage-bayashi* refers to the fact that the creators of these sounds are positioned at stage right, out of the audience's view.
8. One of the pioneers in this area was Nakamura Heizo, who, in 1930, was employed in this capacity by NHK Radio's Tokyo station. See also Iwabuchi (1981).
9. From the 1930s to post-war Japan, a new form of *enka* (popular song) flourished that incorporated Japanese pentatonic scale with western harmonies. In the melodramatic performance style and themes of love, loss and endurance, the form may have influenced cinematic *gekiban*, and is worth exploration elsewhere.
10. According to information from the recording sessions, the music for *Lupin vs. the Clone* and *The Castle of Cagliostro* was completed in one day each, while *The Legend of the Gold of Babylon* took a mere two days (Fuwa, 2003a, 2003c and Takahashi, 2003).
11. Sound effects such as footsteps, murmuring voices and car engines that were referenced on the screen were sourced through libraries or on location. Consistent with the process used for the music, the sound effects were added to the soundtrack during the dubbing process and according to a director's instructions. In the Lupin III TV series, they were frequently used to mark a transition in a literal fashion, for example, birds twittering to indicate morning.
12. See Koizumi's analysis of Tôru Takemitsu's music for *Kwaidan* (Masaki Kobayashi, 1964) in which she argues that the composer "transcended conventional distinctions between underscore and sound effects in an attempt to produce tone colours appropriate for *Kwaidan*'s eerie scenes." (2009: 74).

References

Fuwa, R. (2003a), 'Special interview with Ohno Yuji', liner notes for *Lupin the Third, 'The Castle of Cagliostro'*, Columbia Music Entertainment.

Fuwa, R. (2003b), 'Special interview with Ohno Yuji', liner notes for *Lupin the Third 1977*, Columbia Music Entertainment.

Fuwa, R. (2003c), 'Special interview with Ohno Yuji' and recording data, liner notes for *Lupin the Third 1978*, Columbia Music Entertainment.

Fuwa, R. (2004), 'Special interview with Ohno Yuji' and recording data, liner notes for *Lupin the Third, 'The Legend of the Gold of Babylon'*, Columbia Music Entertainment.

Imada, K. (2004), 'Aspects of Audiovisual Experience by the Exhibition of Silent Film: The Relationship between Sounds and Images in the First Decade of the 20th Century in Japan', *Philokalia* [*Journal of the Science of Arts*], 21, 15–34.

Imada, K. (2000), 'Sounds of Silent Movies', *Toyo Ongaku Kenkyu* [*Journal of the Society for Research in Asiatic Music*], 65, 33–53.

Imamura, T. (1992), *Manga Eiga Ron* [*Comic Animation Film Theory*], Tokyo: Iwanami Shoten (first published in 1948).

Iwabuchi, T. (1981), *Watashi no Onkyoushi: Koukaman no Kiroku* [*My Personal History as a Craftsman of Sound Effect*], Tokyo: Shakai Shisou Sha.

Koizumi, K. (2009), 'Creative Soundtrack Expression: Tôru Takemitsu's Score for *Kwaidan*', in P. Hayward (ed.), *Terror Tracks: Music, Sound and Horror Cinema*, London: Equinox, pp. 74–87.

Miyamaru, N. (1993), 'Japan – 3. Court and theatrical music, 4. Kabuki', in *New Grove Sekai ongaku daijiten* [*New Grove Dictionary of Music and Musicians*], vol. 13, Tokyo: Kodansha.

Ohno, Y. (2004), *Lupin the Third, Jazz Note* (with accompanying performance DVD), Tokyo: Kodansha.

Studio Hard (1999), *Lupin III Kenkyu Houkokusho* [*Research Report on Lupin III*], Tokyo: Futabasha.

Takahashi, M. (2003), 'Overview of the Music of *The Castle of Cagliostro* and This CD', liner note for *Lupin the Third: The Castle of Cagliostro*.

Watanabe, T., Skrzypczak, E. and Snowden, P. (eds) (2003), *New Japanese–English Dictionary*, Tokyo: Kenkyu Sha.

Wierzbicki, J. (2009), 'The Ghostly Noise of J-Horror: Roots and Ramifications', in Hayward, P. (ed), *Terror Tracks: Music, Sound and Horror Cinema*, London: Equinox, pp. 249–67.

Part IV
Music and Industrial Contexts

11 DreamWorking Wallace & Gromit

Musical Thematics in The Curse of the Were-Rabbit

Rebecca Coyle and Peter Morris

70% of the composer's job in this sort of scale of filmmaking is politics and personalities ... So it isn't just how the music evolves but how the music evolves within the context of ... many nervous executives with plenty of money to spend. (Julian Nott[1])

Wallace and Gromit are the claymation characters devised by British animation director Nick Park.[2] The pair first appeared in three half-hour films: *A Grand Day Out* (1989), *The Wrong Trousers* (1993) and *A Close Shave* (1995), the last two of which were produced by Aardman Animation Ltd, a British animation studio[3] known for their stop-motion productions.[4] After winning an Academy and other awards for the shorts,[5] in 2000 Aardman released their first feature film, *Chicken Run* (Nick Park and Peter Lord). Following the box-office success of the film, Aardman signed a multi-picture deal with DreamWorks Animation SKG, a major Hollywood producer of animation feature films. In 2005, *Wallace & Gromit: The Curse of the Were-Rabbit* (Nick Park and Steve Box) was released and subsequently won an Academy Award for Best Animated Feature.[6] The film represents a transnational product, as well as a negotiated process in which creative and aesthetic concerns and personnel operate within a profit-oriented cultural industry. In his observation quoted above, composer Julian Nott reflects on art versus commerce debates in relation to his adaptation to a Hollywood film production context.

This chapter charts an aspect of Aardman's transition to feature-film productions in Hollywood through an exploration of the music approach employed in *Wallace & Gromit: The Curse of the Were-Rabbit* (henceforth *Were-Rabbit*). We discuss the structured thematic approach adopted by composer Julian Nott, working with Hans Zimmer and a team of composers. Drawing on production study interviews with Nott alongside analysis of the filmic text, we examine the role of the music in crafting the naturalism of the comedy, presenting secondary characters introduced for the feature film and intertextually referring to horror-film conventions. We argue that music is integral to establishing familiarity with Wallace and Gromit as the central protagonists, as well as holding the narrative together, and ensuring the movie created some 'laughing out loud' moments despite the 'horror' implicit in the creation of a were-rabbit.

Were-Rabbit storyline

Centred on the symbiotic duo Wallace and Gromit, *Were-Rabbit* both draws on inter-actions and locations previously established in the shorts and extends these for the longer format by using secondary characters, elaborate sets, and horror-cinema parody. Wallace, a North of England, cheese-loving inventor (voiced by Peter Sallis in a broad Lancashire accent), and Gromit, his mute but expressive and smart canine assistant, run a vegetable-security and humane pest-control business named Anti-Pesto in a village preparing for its annual Giant Vegetable Competition. This event is hosted by local noblewoman, Lady Campanula Tottington ('Totty', voiced by Helena Bonham Carter), who has a passion for vegetable growing and 'fluffy creatures'. She employs the Anti-Pesto team to deal with the excessive rabbit population on her estate, against the wishes of her suitor Lord Victor Quartermaine (Ralph Fiennes), who is obsessed with hunting and lusts after Totty's fortune.

In the course of trying to solve the rabbit problem using his Mind-O-Matic 'mind-manipulation' invention, Wallace accidentally transforms himself into the monstrous were-rabbit, who, in scenes drawing on horror-film conventions, appears on moonlit nights to ravage the village's vegetable gardens. The storyline develops with Gromit attempting to restore the 'human' Wallace, Victor pursuing and trying to destroy both Wallace and the were-rabbit, the townsfolk expressing dissatisfaction with Anti-Pesto's strategies to rid the village of the monster, and, ultimately, Totty rejecting both Victor and Wallace in favour of her furry friends. The film culminates in an elaborate showdown that parodies *King Kong* (Merian C. Cooper and Ernest B. Schoedsack, 1933), in which the were-rabbit kidnaps Totty, there is a mid-air toy aeroplane 'dogfight' between Victor's dog and Gromit, and Victor attempts to shoot the were-rabbit with golden bullets. After falling to the ground as if dead, the were-rabbit morphs back into Wallace, who is revived by Gromit with some 'Stinking Bishop' cheese. Victor is run out of town, Gromit is awarded the competition trophy and Totty turns her Tottington Hall into a wildlife refuge for the rabbits. The visual jokes and parodic moments in *Were-Rabbit* are highlighted and enhanced by sound, character voicing and an energetic score that draws on a variety of musical styles.[7]

As detailed below, *Were-Rabbit* employs various styles of music and approaches to thematic material, using them to unify scenes, support characterizations and suggest generic references. These operate in conjunction with adaptations of the established Wallace & Gromit brass band-styled signature theme. The score required the services of the original Wallace & Gromit composer Julian Nott working with Hollywood's Media Ventures team under Hans Zimmer and within the DreamWorks production approach.

Nott and Zimmer

Julian Nott is a British film composer who is best known for his work on the Wallace & Gromit films. He studied music at Oxford University[8] before specializing in film-music scoring at the National Film and Television School (1986–90), where he met Park and worked on *A Grand Day Out*. Between producing music for documentary films, Nott continued to work with Park on subsequent Wallace & Gromit films. After the success of *The Wrong Trousers*, Nott scored other films and television programmes, and his partnership with Park was interrupted with the director's first feature film, *Chicken Run*, which was co-produced with DreamWorks. After pitching for the film and scoring the promotional trailer, Nott was not contracted to score the film, as DreamWorks opted to contract Hans Zimmer's Media Ventures composers to produce the score.[9] With Park exercising more creative control over *Were-Rabbit*, Nott returned to work with Aardman as part of a music team. As this chapter analyses, Nott's experience of creating music for *Were-Rabbit* was profoundly different from his other Wallace & Gromit work in terms of production approach, musical composition and thematic style.

Were-Rabbit commenced pre-production in 2000, and Nott's involvement with the film spanned two years, contributing to the massive 72 minutes of music originated for the 80-minute film release. His first engagement was to produce a temporary ('temp') track to accompany dialogue recordings on which the animation could be modelled. However, the storyline for the film continued to evolve until very close to the film's completion[10] and this impacted on the music track. Hans Zimmer and a team of Media Ventures composers were engaged to work on the film after the temp track was completed. This required a change of approach for Nott, as the score was produced by a creative ensemble. In an interview he noted the transition from Wallace & Gromit shorts to *Were-Rabbit*:

> The shorts had only really been supported by a small niche audience before. The feature had to appeal to the mass market. Obviously my Wallace & Gromit style for the shorts is not a conventional sound for a Hollywood movie. That sort of thing makes Hollywood studio executives nervous. They prefer to stick with what they know and what people have done before. I don't think they would have allowed their big movie to be scored like the shorts.[11]

Hans Zimmer is an established and highly acclaimed film-score composer, who came to prominence with the Academy Award nomination for his score for *Rain Man* (Barry Levinson) in 1988. He has subsequently composed music for many blockbuster Hollywood films, including several animations. In 1995 he was awarded the Academy's Best Original Score for *The Lion King* (Roger Allers and Rob Minkoff, 1994). Despite having commenced his musical career playing keyboard and synthesizer with bands like Ultravox and the Buggles (best known for their 1979 'Video Killed The Radio Star' track), Zimmer's approach is commonly associated with large orchestras and highly produced arrangements. In the 2000s he has mostly worked with the Media Ventures (now

Remote Control Productions) operation that he co-founded with Jay Rifkin. This company employs several composers, technical staff and performers, who have worked as teams on Hollywood movies such as the *Pirates of the Caribbean* trilogy (Gore Verbinski, 2003, 2006, 2007), *Gladiator* (Ridley Scott, 2000) in collaboration with Lisa Gerrard, *Mission: Impossible II* (John Woo, 2000) and the anime series *Blood+* (Junichi Fujisaku, 2005).[12] Over the last decade, Zimmer has established a production method and musical approach that is recognizable and accepted by the industry as a reliable and effective – if predictable – resource (see Black, 1998, and Beek[13]). Nott characterizes the operation in the following description:

> *Although most Hollywood composers use teams (additional composers, orchestrators and technical people) they keep very quiet about it. Zimmer is different in that he is totally open and honest about this process. He openly credits the additional composers, talks about them in interviews and on his website, promotes their careers and very generously looks after their interests. Once you have been accepted into the team, a tiny elite, in return for extraordinary hard work and dedication that must be demonstrated, you become a part of a 'family' in which your longer career path may well be furthered. Hans provides an unparalleled training ground and career launchpad for a very few, very lucky (although invariably highly skilled) musicians.*
> (personal communication to the authors, 23 February 2008)

In addition to its music personnel, the *Were-Rabbit* score was allocated a sizeable music budget, enabling the use of an orchestra with a large brass section and a choir. Nott argues that "very loud, intense sounds" (research seminar, 2006) are expected by Hollywood producers, and describes the significance of large budgets in the music for the Wallace & Gromit shorts and feature film:

> *As a student film,* A Grand Day Out *could afford only a handful of musicians, augmented by nasty, 1980s synths. The third short,* A Close Shave, *on the other hand could afford a 65 [person] orchestra. I would say the style of music is fairly consistent between the shorts, just the sound of it changed with bigger orchestras. The style of music has changed quite a bit for the feature: it is bolder and bigger, more contrapuntal and busier. More Hollywood, in short. Essentially that comes from pressure from DreamWorks to make it like that.*[14]

Themes and adaptations

Unlike his work on the shorts, Nott was brought in at an early point in *Were-Rabbit*'s pre-production, scoring to storyboards. An important element that was retained in the feature film was the Wallace & Gromit theme that is introduced in the opening sequence and adapted for different moods (sad, comedic, patriotic, etc.) throughout the film. The theme tune was originally written for the first Wallace & Gromit short and arose from Park's request for music *that was somehow associated with music from the North of England where Wallace & Gromit come from. That suggested brass band music to both of us, a big tradition in that part of England. However, we couldn't afford a real brass band, so we had to use 7 or 8 brass players for the score generally, using conventional orchestral brass instruments. Anyway, the idea was that the main tune would be something you might hear [performed by] a brass band.*[15]

Brass bands developed in the UK in the nineteenth century alongside the introduction of rotary-valve instruments, standardized tunings and new instruments such as Aldolphe Sax's saxhorn (Myer, 1991). Comprising players of cornets, flugelhorns, tenor and baritone horns, euphoniums, trombones, tubas and percussion, British brass bands often formed around geographic communities and local industries (e.g., mills, factories and mines)[16] and were widespread up to the mid-twentieth century. Their repertoires embraced a wide range of music, including 'art', 'light' and specialist band music. The last incorporated musical idioms that exploited wide dynamic and tempo ranges and demonstrated a virtuosity of specific instrumental techniques such as tonguing and pitch range. From the 1860s on, contests were a vital part of brass-band culture, assisting in the development of a set of conventions. Brass bands have traditionally been associated with the North of England, working-class men, and (disputably) under-accomplished performance, although Herbert (1991) argues that this is a problematic stereotype.[17] Russell notes that humorous media representations of brass bands, reinforced by the use of bands in advertisements for breweries, led to an "oompah-syndrome" (1991: 91) in the UK.

The use of a brass band-styled theme for Wallace & Gromit therefore represents a convergence of conventions associating brass bands with the central protagonists, in addition to comic allusions common in animation film (discussed below) and film-music conventions that draw on audience familiarity with popular music sounds and styles. The musical theme has become like a brand for all products associated with Wallace & Gromit and was deliberately retained in the feature both for its recognizable sound and, for Park, to connect *Were-Rabbit* with his Wallace & Gromit characters: "we were keen to keep the feeling of 'smallness' in the feature film, the feeling that characterizes the shorts. And ... that's why we kept the sound of the North [of] England brass band in the score."[18]

The Wallace & Gromit theme tune exhibits two important traits of filmic scoring: it is simple and it is malleable. For a melody to be simple, it needs to be primarily diatonic and easily sung. Thus, Maurice Jarre's *Lara's Theme* from *Dr. Zhivago* (David Lean, 1965) may be recognizable but does not qualify as simple because of its wide range, awkward intervals and chromaticism, making it, for most people, unsingable. By contrast, Nott's theme is narrow in range, mainly single step (as shown in Figure 11.1, 21 out of 31 intervals are major or minor seconds) and it is primarily diatonic. The second trait, melodic malleability, requires that the music does not rely on elements that might colour its musical transformation. Where a theme relies on chromatic patterns, 'signature' intervals or individual rhythmic patterns, it may not be malleable enough to unify a score. In this respect, the simple chord structure and primarily step-wise movement create a template that can be morphed as required by the diegesis.

Figure 11.1 Main Wallace & Gromit theme (transcribed by Peter Morris)

When used as title music, Nott's theme is generally presented as a celebratory march.[19] Scored with brass instruments and an open-interval tuba bass line, it is given energy by the off-beat quavers and answering phrases, sometimes mini-fanfares, sometimes trill-like passages. By contrast with the earlier shorts, the substantial music budget for *Were-Rabbit* allowed for a full symphony orchestra with choir, and the arrangement (orchestrated by Nic Raine) exhibits the style of the orchestral marches of Johann Strauss and Elgar more than of brass or marching bands.

There are, however, essentially British aspects of the music, such as the use of the brass band, particularly for moments of pathos, the march style[20] and the suggestions of Elgar's music. This last aspect occurs on several occasions, with the earliest example being found at 0:05:30[21] just after Wallace and Gromit capture the first rabbit. The main theme, played at half-tempo, is scored much like the C major second section of Elgar's 'Pomp and Circumstance March No. 4', with repeated crotchet chords underlying the melody played by strings and euphonium. In the context of the film's entire sound design, these musical inflections sit alongside regional accents, varying from Received Pronunciation to working-class Northern dialect,[22] reinforcing the Britishness of the film.

While the theme tune used in the opening sequence is recognizable from earlier Wallace & Gromit products,[23] other adaptations and shortened forms were used at different moments. These uses of thematic material led to debates between Nott and Zimmer that reflected their previous industrial experiences. While Zimmer regularly employs themes as significant structural devices that carry through the entire film, Nott had been familiar with writing 'for the moment', that is, composing in a specific musical style that may vary for each scene. This latter style is commonly associated with cartoon soundtracks in which sound and music often match (although not always literally) the on-screen emotion and events. Brought into the production at a later stage in the score's development, Zimmer enquired as to why the distinctive Wallace & Gromit theme tune was not being used more frequently. Nott believed that its 'oompah melody' meant that it could not be squeezed into other cues requiring different emotions. Zimmer's response was that he could (and did) "turn any theme into any mood, even if it's only the first four notes". While Nott argued that a theme employing only its first four notes, a different rhythm and transposed into a minor key would not be recognizable as the original theme to audiences, Zimmer contended that it is the accrual of brief adapted references to the theme that serve to build up the core theme and give it impact. These 'unity' themes can be seen to offer integrity (and, according to Nott, a certain 'neatness') to the film score as a whole.

This approach was adopted by Nott, and can be seen to have both advantages and disadvantages. The 'system' works well with a team of composers who can be brought in to create a cue based on the agreed theme at short notice and when the film composer is not available. Given that the entire *Were-Rabbit* film was re-edited in the last month and required modified cues, having a team available to make the changes was essential.[24] As a result, authorship for specific cues is difficult to establish:

> The role of the additional composers [was] complex ... The original idea was they used my themes and material, in the manner used at Media Ventures, but in practice things developed forward from that principle. The score is a great melting pot of collaboration. Rupert Gregson-Williams provided one major theme of the film, although Part B of it I wrote. Sometimes the additional composers used material written by another additional composer. (Nott, personal communication to the authors[25])

A further matter of debate in relation to themes is the extent to which their variation can be overdone. Nott devised a 'sad' cue for Wallace's 'death' scene, for instance, believing that the jauntiness of the Wallace & Gromit theme could not be adequately adapted, but this was rejected in favour of another composer's arrangement of the main theme. At this point in the film (1:11:38 but presaged at 0:52:17) the malleability of the main Wallace & Gromit theme is demonstrated by its transformation from celebratory march to *marche triste* (sad march), albeit in a major key (Figure 11.2). Preceded by sustained strings and a slow, falling, brass figure, the main theme is accompanied by chromatic alterations and substantial dissonance in bar 3.

Figure 11.2 Adaptation of Wallace & Gromit theme for death scene (transcribed by Peter Morris)

The mood is enhanced by rescoring for primarily brass instruments that evoke a brass-band sound, together with a melody played on flugelhorn and sustained strings. The segment, while still in 4/4, has little pulse and the timing is keyed to the visuals so that the final sustain disappears as Gromit takes the Stinking Bishop cheese to revive Wallace. From there, via an episodic section, a fragment from the second half of the main theme is worked into a lively section celebrating Wallace's recovery (Figure 11.3).

Figure 11.3   Wallace & Gromit theme adapted for recovery scene (transcribed by Peter Morris)

In the examples thus far, the multiple uses of the main theme have maintained the melodic contour of the original. However, this is by no means the norm within *Were-Rabbit* overall. For example, at 0:48:09, at breakfast, after Gromit has discovered the true identity of the were-rabbit (namely, Wallace who transforms into the were-rabbit by night but does not recall this during the day), the theme is given a new contour (Figure 11.4).

Figure 11.4   Wallace & Gromit theme adapted for Gromit's realization (transcribed by Peter Morris)

Nott argues that adapting themes to flow throughout a film is more difficult than writing 'for the moment', given that the latter does not require a cue to be devised within the same constraints. Nevertheless, the task of theme adaptation – as well as teamwork in a compositional project such as *Were-Rabbit* – was expedited through digital technology used for orchestration, recording, editing and mixing,[26] regular visits by DreamWorks to Aardman's Bristol studio (in the southwest of England), and via detailed instructions.[27]

This approach to thematic-based scores is sometimes (derogatorily) termed formulaic, suggesting that standardized themes and conventions are employed. However, this is a structural approach and process that Nott argues also enables latitude in the musical treatment of the designated themes. Furthermore, in the case of *Were-Rabbit*, Nott recalls that occasionally directors Box and Park or DreamWorks producer Jeffrey Katzenberg requested music scored 'for the moment':

> The trouble is that, when you have this thematic approach, your bosses don't get it … They don't have the same musical skill … Hans [Zimmer] has to go through this process of explaining what he was doing. "Trust me, I'm laying pipe", that would be his phrase … "I'm laying pipe. I need to establish this here"… but it's not quite perfect. Producers don't take such a long-term view as the thematic composer. (Nott, interview with Morris, 2007)

Nott contends, however, that the thematic approach described above is not uniformly the best one, especially in the context of a comedy film.

> Every now and again a bit of scoring for the moment is better for the comedy: that is what Zimmer called "putting kippers on the cake".[28] Zimmer is happy to do it. Sometimes one of your themes, even though intellectually correct, doesn't work as well as sticking a fresh and unrelated bit of music against it. It would be far too dogmatic to insist a theme must always be applied with a character or a place once you have established it. (Nott, personal communication to the authors, 23 February 2008)

This occurred most often for comedy cues such as the big band music used in a scene in which the Anti-Pesto pair drive their Austin A35 van with a huge stuffed rabbit strapped to its roof, in an attempt to lure the were-rabbit to them. The rabbit's limbs (and even eyelids) are operated by strings connected to Gromit, who is in the back of the van puppeteering the rabbit's actions. When Wallace decides that the trap has to be love interest ("Ahh, love, Gromit. That's the biggest trap of all!"), Nott's musical approach is to split the scene into two parts. The first, when Gromit is merely waving his legs up and down (and the huge rabbit's movements appear stilted and unattractive), is understated, with a simple walking bass and swing patterns from reeds and brass. Flattened thirds, fifths and sevenths indicate the bluesy, swing style but this music is deliberately going nowhere. The second part, triggered by Wallace's exhortations to Gromit to make the rabbit appear more alluring, uses the 1962 musical burlesque number 'The Stripper' by David Rose. This piece is already known in its comic context, at least in the UK, from its use on *The Morecambe and Wise Show* in the 1960s and *The Full Monty* (Peter Catteneo, 1997). Using 'The Stripper' immediately carries Gromit into the comedy caricature, emphasized by his step-kicks, hip shakes and the facial appearance (with bright red lips and heavy eye-shadow) for the raunchy female rabbit. Gromit is not meant to be alluring to Wallace and therefore the main Wallace & Gromit theme is not used in this instance, since its use normally binds the two characters. However, at 0:56:14 mins, when Gromit, dressed in the female rabbit costume, is trying to entice the transformed Wallace out of the house, Nott uses a raunchy version of the main theme, complete with brass glissandi, trumpet shakes and plunger mute.

The thematic approach discussed above can be differentiated from the device of character themes commonly used in film scoring. Audiences are alerted to characters and their developments through musical motifs that can change as the character emerges or evolves through the narrative. These character themes must be integrated with the overall compositional style. In *Were-Rabbit*, an appropriate musical signifier was devised for Lady Tottington,[29] which, in its simplest form, is shown in Figure 11.5 (at 0:14:23 mins).

Figure 11.5   Lady Tottington's theme (transcribed by Peter Morris)

Other statements of the theme occur at 0:16:30 (Wallace's first farewell to Totty), 0:38:20 (tea at Tottington Hall) and 0:56:55 (the apparent killing of the were-rabbit), with this last occurrence being a minor-key version, perhaps indicating that Lady Tottington's love for the "the poor thing" is stronger than her love for Wallace.

In common with standard romantic treatments, the orchestration of the statement at 0:14:23 comprises strings, mellow woodwind/brass and choir, with the melody played on violins. The harmony is simple: just tonic and minor subdominant chords, rocking as if yearning. The melody is open, has a regular phrase length and uses the flattened submediant to require harmonic resolution. As with the main Wallace & Gromit theme, this simplicity allows it to be morphed as required.

Although ultimately the relationship between Lady Tottington and Wallace does not thrive,[30] their two themes do come together in several places. The strongest of these occurs at 0:55:07 when Lady Tottington leaves Wallace's house, having admitted that she "recently developed feelings for [him]". The themes are combined (Figure 11.6). The first bar contains the first four notes of Wallace's theme and leads into the notes

Meno mosso

Figure 11.6 Lady Tottington's theme merges with Wallace's theme (transcribed by Peter Morris)

of the second bar of Lady Tottington's in what is the only musical conjunction of this kind in the film.

In the final scene, when the rabbits are released into the sanctuary at Tottington Hall (1:14:46), Lady Tottington's theme is made happier by removing the flattened sixth, with fragments of Wallace's theme punctuating the accompaniment. Wallace says, just before freeing the rabbit imbued with his psyche: "There'll always be a part of me here at Tottington Hall", giving his permission for the two themes to be linked, albeit not in the romantic way he had envisaged. Influenced by Zimmer and the DreamWorks approach to richly saturated soundtracks, the Lady Tottington theme suggests a cartoonish musical idea appropriate to the introduction of an additional comic character who influences the familiar Wallace and Gromit characters and their relationship.

Comedy meets horror

Were-Rabbit extends elements that were first introduced in the Wallace & Gromit shorts and can be characterized as a British style of humour that draws on self-reflexivity, intertextuality and understated social comment, inviting, as French observes, "consistent chuckles, perhaps, rather than belly laughs, but always fun" (2005: np). Much of the humour in *Were-Rabbit* derives from the enactment of filmic conventions by claymation characters and activities, and this technique is also exploited in the music. A sense of the ridiculous is combined with the eccentricities of the main characters, and interspersed with double entendres directed to adults. Intertextual references are used throughout, often to propel the parody. In addition to horror-genre and specific film references,[31] the Wallace & Gromit Anti-Pesto alarm system and call-out routine parodies television superhero series such as Gerry and Sylvia Anderson's British puppet animation television series *Thunderbirds* (1965–66), the music for which (by Barry Gray) also influenced the *Were-Rabbit* score. Several elements refer to other animation conventions, including the British rabbit-tale animation feature *Watership Down* (Martin Rosen, 1978),[32] and are supported by the approach to comedy in the score.

Mera (developing the argument by Morreall, 1983) argues that comedy operates at three levels of humour: superiority, incongruity and relief, which are "set up by creating a sense of anticipation that is then subverted or dislocated" (2002: 91). Whereas concert music humour operates via a series of rules that are broken or manipulated in a highly articulated style, film music, by its very nature, often employs other musical codes to create humour. These include parody, referentialism, instrumentation, and diegetic/nondiegetic ambiguities. Ultimately, film-music humour is contextual rather than "an intrinsically musical feature" (*ibid.*: 94), as Mera argues:

> ... humor does not arise solely through specifically composed musical gestures, but ... it is dependent on the situation and context in which those gestures are heard. In film music, the situation is stronger than in concert music, because of the effect of the film medium on the soundtrack, and vice versa. There is a different, contextual backdrop – that of filmic language and rhetoric. (*ibid.*: 96)

This model of film music and humour is supported by Julian Nott, who argues there is no such thing as intrinsically 'funny' music, in terms of a particular sequence of notes or chord, but rather "what is funny is the connection" to the on-screen events or characters. Nott notes that

> there is a difference between laughing out loud and being amused. Film aims to make people laugh out loud. There is little the composer can do to make people laugh without other parts of the film – but music can prime the audience to laugh. (Nott, quoted in Morris, 2007)

One way in which music may have intrinsically humorous features is through what Mera characterizes as "the purest of music codes: the sound of instruments" (2002: 102). He notes that the tuba, for example, is an instrument generally regarded as a "joker" in part due to the broad expectation that melodies are heard in "a comfortable middle register" (*ibid.*). Given that the tuba operates most successfully at the lower frequencies and within a limited pitch range, it is often relegated to the 'oompah' style of music characteristic of its role in brass bands. Mera opines that "the tuba has no clarity in its lower register, sounding more like an outbreak of flatulence than anything else" (2002: 103), so it suggests taboo bodily functions and breaks the rules of etiquette, thereby providing relief from societal stricture. The use of the tuba in the Wallace & Gromit theme music accords with this characterization and primes the audience for (naughty) comedy.

In addition to the use of 'funny' sounds, *Were-Rabbit* also employs parody to create humour. Prior to the Wallace & Gromit theme, *Were-Rabbit*'s opening sequence commences with music that establishes the parodic horror genre. Co-director Steve Box originally wanted to place Wallace and Gromit into a horror-film scenario, and the first storyboards featured narratively dark and gloomy scenes. The temp music accompanying these scenes included excerpts from the chilling liturgical theme 'Ave Satani' and Carl Orff's dramatic choral *Carmina Burana* used in the score produced by Jerry Goldsmith for *The Omen* (Richard Donner, 1976). This plan was rejected by DreamWorks producer Katzenberg, who argued that it was too scary for a film aimed at children and young people, so the directors created a lighter, non-threatening version of the film's opening with a musical theme to signal the faux-horror moments in the film.

In common with the second and third Wallace & Gromit shorts, Nick Park's choice of a dark opening, with a sting on the main titles, foretells melodrama in a manner reminiscent of the title sequences of many 1950s B-movies. Nott employed generically conventional music (titled 'Celeste Mystery' in the score) to create the menace in the opening scene that introduced the antagonist by way of shadows and distant glimpses. Its first statement is given in Figure 11.7.

Figure 11.7 Opening 'Horror' theme (transcribed by Peter Morris)

The use of celeste (with the melody doubled by middle-register violins) and 3/4 time creates an uneasy feeling of anticipation, further unbalanced by the extra bar inserted after the first, 4-bar phrase. A pseudo-gothic sting with organ and descending wood-wind scales are underscored in the soundtrack CD by a theremin, itself very much a signifier of the unknown in 1950s B-movies and science fiction (see Hayward, 1997). However, the theremin does not appear in the actual film score (presumably because of the tonal conflict with the wolf howling in the film scene). A patrolling village policeman, PC Mackintosh, breaks the mood to some extent by stepping into the puddle that had reflected the full moon on screen and whistling the motif. His jaunty, diegetic statement of the theme is at double speed and in 4/4, above comic discords, low strings and bassoon, all of which conspire to indicate his naivety. When the underscore continues without PC Mackintosh, the 'Celeste Mystery' theme is stated in slow 4/4, as if to say that the threat is still there, despite the bumbling policeman who has missed all the evidence.

The repeated use of this motif elsewhere in the film clearly establishes and reinforces it as a leitmotif of the were-rabbit: it can be found when the were-rabbit runs riot at the harvest festival [0:22:50], when Gromit is in the car outside Harvey's Fruit and Veg shop [0:30:43], when Wallace transforms to the were-rabbit in front of Victor Quartermain [0:43:36] and in other scenes. The theme offers a useful juncture for Wallace in reconciling the familiar character (identified by the Wallace & Gromit theme) with Wallace as were-rabbit. As such, this thematic manipulation may stand for the transition of early shorts to feature film, and the mutation of a British-oriented production within the Hollywood "machine" (Nott, 2006).

Conclusion

In reviews of *Were-Rabbit*, several authors specifically refer to the 'British' sensibility apparent in the film (see, for example, French, 2005; Carlsson, 2005; and Stephen Rowley[33]). It is not the function of this chapter to make claims for British animation per se but rather to identify and specify certain attributes that sonically suggest British characteristics or suggest location in the film. *Were-Rabbit* appears to have maintained a 'British' feel while operating as a DreamWorks production, and the music played a significant role in creating and enhancing this impression.

While Zimmer is associated with Hollywood and major corporations like DreamWorks, he claims to have been driven by a desire to retain integrity for each project, arguing that, "It's my personal responsibility not to ruin all these wonderful projects I get given".[34] In relation to *Were-Rabbit*, prior to the film's release, Zimmer observed:

> I'm a German and for years I've described America back to Americans without knowing what it's about, but at least I spent fifteen years living in England so I know a little bit about it … I'm here to preserve the archetypal Wallace and Gromit-ness of it. It's got to be quintessentially English. (*ibid.*)

Nott has endorsed Zimmer's perception of his role in the score's production and observed that a synthesized score was created out of the collaboration.

> Hans was very respectful of the established Wallace & Gromit style, and he never tried to ditch it. The music for the feature is therefore a very interesting mixture of haut-Hollywood, after all who is more Hollywood than Hans Zimmer and his team, and the eccentric English style we had on the shorts. (Nott, quoted in Carlsson, 2005)

Were-Rabbit was lauded for its animation, winning an Academy Award for Best Animated Feature, several Annies (including, notably, Best Music in an Animated Feature for Julian Nott) and other awards. However, perhaps its major achievements were its transnational production at a time when studio animation was experiencing upheaval[35] and its fruitful realization of a regional and nationally associated product in an international marketplace. It illustrates that cultural 'grey-out' and/or blandness do not necessarily result from international collaborations enabled by Hollywood, particularly if – as in the case of *Were-Rabbit* – careful attention is paid to the blending and synergy of the distinctive production practices of the collaborating creative agencies.

Acknowledgements

Thanks to Julian Nott for invaluable interviews and other input, and to Philip Hayward for additional research assistance.

Notes

1. All quotations from Nott, unless otherwise indicated, are taken from Peter Morris's interview with Julian Nott, conducted in London on 29 June 2007. Additional research information was drawn from Julian Nott's research seminar presentation at the University of Surrey, Guildford, UK, on 17 January 2006. Further input was provided by Nott in several emails to the authors, as indicated.
2. Park originally devised the characters as a student at the National Film School, where he met Nott.
3. Also known as Aardman Studios, founded in 1976 as a small backyard project based in Bristol by Peter Lord and David Sproxton. Nick Park joined Aardman in the mid-1980s.
4. Lord and Sproxton had made shorts using Plasticine puppets animated to actual recorded street conversations, e.g., in the *Conversation Pieces* series made for UK Television Channel 4 (1983). When Park joined the studio, he made *Creature Comforts*, featuring Plasticine animal figures 'speaking' to human observations (see Bendazzi, 1994: 278). More recently, Aardman has moved into CGI productions, for example, *Flushed Away* (David Bowers and Sam Fell, 2006) with a more conventional approach to sound.
5. For example, *The Wrong Trousers* and *A Close Shave* both won the Best Short Film, Animated Oscar and the Best Animated Film BAFTA award, along with others.
6. The film also earned Best Music in an Animated Feature for Julian Nott at the Annie Awards, the animation-specific award ceremony. In fact, the film was nominated for 16 of the 26 awards in this event, and won 10. It also won several BAFTA and other awards.
7. In addition, the verbal and sight gags are accompanied by sound effects such as the car alarm-like bleeping sound used for the activation of the Anti-Pesto greenhouse security system and the sci-fi sound of the Bun-Vac 6000. According to Park, these sound effects are devised at the writing stage; see A. L. Urban (2005), 'Park, Nick – Wallace & Gromit. The Curse of the Were Rabbit', in *Urban Cinefile*, 15 September, online at http://www.urbancinefile.com.au/home/view.asp?a=10823&s=Interviews (accessed 28 September 2007). This is consistent with the 'mickey-mousing' (tight synchronization of sound and image) conventions of animation and in contrast to the music that was devised along general lines with the composer.
8. As well as economics and politics. He subsequently worked in investment banking in the City of London before realizing it was not for him.
9. Zimmer had developed an effective working relationship with producer Katzenberg since their success with *The Lion King* (1994) – as discussed elsewhere in this volume (pp. 235–41).
10. Owing to its use of highly sophisticated claymation together with some CGI, the film took five years to be made, with principal photography alone taking 18 months.
11. Julian Nott, in M. Carlsson, 'Julian Nott: Wallace & Gromit', *Music from the Movies*, 15 November 2005, online at http://www.musicfromthemovies.com/sotw.asp?ID=44 (accessed 28 September 2007).

12. Tracks from Zimmer's scores have also charted as UK and US singles (for example, 'Spider Pig' from *The Simpsons Movie* [David Silverman, 2007] and 'Hoist The Colours' from *Pirates of the Caribbean: At World's End* [Gore Verbinski, 2007]).

13. M. Beek, 'Film Music of Hans Zimmer', *Music from the Movies*, online at http://www.musicfromthemovies.com/review.asp?ID=6860 (accessed 7 February 2008); E. Black (1998), 'Hans Zimmer Interview', *Film Score Monthly*, online at http://www.filmscoremonthly.com/features/zimmer.asp (accessed 7 February 2008).

14. Julian Nott, in M. Carlsson (2005), 'Julian Nott: Wallace & Gromit' (as in note 11).

15. *Ibid.*

16. Herbert identifies early brass-band categories from the mid-nineteenth century as sponsored workplace bands, community subscription bands, and volunteer bands (1991: 23–4). An important instigator and promoter of brass bands was the Salvation Army and its bands continue to perform widely today.

17. Most brass bands are amateur, yet many perform consistently better than several UK amateur orchestras. The top bands (still community- or industry-based) comprise extremely accomplished musicians and attract paying audiences to rival high-rating orchestras.

18. Nick Park, quoted in A. L. Urban (2005); see note 7.

19. Examples of this genre include the Royal Canadian Air Force March Past and the US Air Force song 'Off We Go Into The Wild Blue Yonder'.

20. As distinct from John Williams's heavy-duty 'Imperial March' from *Star Wars* (George Lucas, 1977).

21. All timings taken from the UK DVD release.

22. Received Pronunciation – sometimes known as 'the Queen's English'– is a particular accent associated with an educated class ('Oxbridge') and southern England. The vocal pronunciations (and wordplay) employed in the film are worth considerable discussion and analysis elsewhere (see, for example, Lane and Simpson, 2005) and are not the subject matter of this chapter. Peter Sallis's characterizations for Wallace have been notably consistent across the Wallace & Gromit series, although, in an interview, Nick Park recalled that after screen tests with British and American children, "we made sure the British accents were more even and understandable, and more clear" (quoted in M. Szymanski (2005), 'Helena Bonham Carter shows off her acting choppers for director Nick Park in Wallace & Gromit', *SciFi Weekly* 10 October, online at http://www.scifi.com/sfw/interviews/sfw745.html).

23. Nott recalls the theme tune creating a moment of hilarity during a particularly tense production meeting. During a momentary stony silence, Nott's mobile phone rang with the Wallace & Gromit theme as its ringtone, provoking laughter and dissipation of tension.

24. Nott notes that the orchestra was "virtually on standby for a month at the end" and teams were available for re-recordings and remixing in the recording and dubbing studios.

25. Email from Julian Nott to Peter Morris, 15 October 2007. It is notable that Nott is credited for 'original music', with Zimmer credited as 'music producer' and a considerable list of additional personnel named under 'music department'. In addition, all the basic instrumental tracks (by a family of instruments) were provided separately to the film dubbing mixer so further manipulation of the music tracks occurred at this stage and without input from the composers.

26. Nott employs Gigastudio as a sampling system, Logic for demos, converted to MIDI files that are emailed to the orchestrator, who creates parts using Sibelius. The recordings are synched using Logic to QuickTime on an Apple Mac.

27. Nott recalls how the DreamWorks jet created an impression when it arrived at the small Bristol City airport. He notes how Katzenberg's reactions to cues would be immediate, and instructions arising from these responses would be followed up in an efficient manner (Nott, 2006).

28. Kippers are salted and smoked herrings.

29. Totty's voice (like the music theme) identifies her (and her class background) but a discussion of this goes beyond the focus of this chapter's analysis. See Szymanski (2005), in note 22.

30. Perhaps due to class issues, a discussion that is worth analysis elsewhere. See also the class issues explored in a subsequent DreamWorks/Aardman production, *Flushed Away* (David Bowers and Sam Fell, 2006).

31. The scene in which the were-rabbit stalks the local vicar suggests John Landis's *An American Werewolf in London* (1981); and the scientific-invention-goes-wrong scene suggests *The Fly* (David Cronenberg, 1986). References to puppet animation may suggest the popularity of this form for British TV audiences, extended to US audiences through Aardman's work as well as the transnational marketing of 'Bob the Builder'.

32. In one scene, Gromit tunes the van's radio to a station playing Mike Batt's 'Bright Eyes' sung by Art Garfunkel, the theme song for another 'rabbit-tale' animation, *Watership Down* (Marin Rosen, 1978).

33. Stephen Rowley (2005), '*Wallace and Gromit: Curse of the Were-Rabbit*. Review', http://www.infilm.com.au/wallaceandgromit.htm (accessed 28 September 2007).

34. Quoted in J. Utichi (2005), 'Exclusive: Zimmer talks Wallace and Gromit', *Film Focus*, 3 July, online at http://www.filmfocus.co.uk/newsdetail.asp?NewsID=343 (accessed 8 February 2008).

35. See the Introduction to this volume.

References

Bendazzi, G. (1994), *Cartoons: One Hundred Years of Cinema Animation*, Eastleigh, Hampshire: John Libbey.

French, P. (2005), 'Wallace & Gromit in the Curse of the Were-Rabbit', *Observer*, 16 October, online at http://film.guardian.co.uk/News_Story/Critic_Review/Observer_Film_of_the_week/0,1592985,00.html#article_continue (accessed 28 September 2007).

Hayward, P. (1997), 'DANGER! RETRO-AFFECTIVITY! The Cultural Career of the Theremin', *Convergence: The Journal of Research into New Media Technologies*, 3(4), 28–53.

Herbert, T. (1991), 'Nineteenth-Century Bands: The Making of a Movement', in T. Herbert (ed.), *Bands: The Brass Band Movement in the 19th and 20th Centuries*, Milton Keynes: Open University Press, pp. 7–56.

Lane, A., and Simpson, P. (2005), *The Art of Wallace & Gromit: The Curse of the Were-Rabbit*, London: Titan.

Mera, M. (2002), 'Is Funny Music Funny? Contexts and Case Studies of Film Music Humor', *Journal of Popular Music Studies*, 14, 91–113.

Moreall, J. (1983), *Taking Laughter Seriously*, New York: State University of New York Press.

Myer, A. (1991), 'Appendix 1: Instruments and Instrumentation in Brass Bands', in T. Herbert (ed.), *Bands: The Brass Band Movement in the 19th and 20th Centuries*, Milton Keynes: Open University Press, pp. 169–95.

Russell, D. (1991), '"What's Wrong with Brass Bands?" Cultural Change and the Band Movement, 1918–c.1964', in T. Herbert (ed.), *Bands: The Brass Band Movement in the 19th and 20th Centuries*, Milton Keynes: Open University Press, pp. 57–101.

12 Cowboy Bebop

Corporate Strategies for Animation Music Products in Japan

Aki Yamasaki

In the early twenty-first century, the Japanese domestic animation market is thought to be worth about US$8200 million annually. Animation-related products can often be sold at higher prices than entertainment products in other fields, indicating that, by gross monetary amount alone, there are a considerable number of animation fans in Japan. However, according to a survey into the consumption trends of animation fans conducted by the Nomura Research Institute[1] (Otaku Forecasting Team, 2005), fans of celebrities outnumber fans of animation by more than two to one, although the animation market is close to nine times larger in terms of market size. So it appears that animation is not supported by large numbers of people but rather is strongly supported by a small number of people. This can be regarded as a result of corporate innovation to ensure steady sales.

Japan is one of the leading countries in the world when it comes to music consumption. The International Federation of Phonogram and Videogram Producers (IFPI) ranks Japan second (after the USA) in worldwide music sales.[2] The large record stores supply music from a huge range of countries and genres and sizeable sections are devoted to TV and movie soundtracks. By far the majority of products in the soundtrack sections consist of music from animation films and TV programmes. This popularity is due to the unique structure of Japan's animation industry.

This chapter examines recent trends in animation soundtrack CD sales in Japan in relation to the distinctive character of the animation business. Animation music is well supported in Japan due to industry factors that impact on the sound of animation films. While soundtrack as music was once considered of marginal interest, industry changes in the 1980s initiated new approaches to music genres and marketing of animation CDs. This resulted in a higher profile for animation music generally. This chapter commences with a discussion of the music producer's role and the cooperation between different media industries. This information is applied to animation music in Japan and recent approaches to its production. In Japan, film animation is integrally connected to television animation, given that relatively few feature-film animation productions arise independently of the television *anime* production (and *manga*) context.[3] This chapter offers examples of companies who have introduced new ways of packaging music related to animation programmes and films, and features a case study of the promotion of *Cowboy Bebop* products, including television and film music.

Animation music soundtracks in Japan

Each production process for animation in Japan is outsourced by the animation studio, which agrees to the outline of new programmes and coordinates the contracts of relevant personnel. For each project, different specialist companies are brought together including a recording company to devise the music. At present, three types of music are categorized as animation music in Japan: namely, 'theme song', 'character song', and 'soundtrack'.

In the animation industry, 'theme songs' are deemed the 'face of the programme' and are always provided at the opening and the end. Previously, the theme song was regarded as an opportunity for the composer to show his or her skills, and was the main component of the music production. The songs were used to promote the film, with catchy melodies and distinctive lyrics, and were designed for a general audience rather than devoted fans. In karaoke, a generic category called '*anime* song' arose to reflect this. However, since the 1990s, it has become a general trend for record companies to use the opening and closing slots as opportunities to promote a singer, and today it is not unusual for animations to be used as the debut event for a new singer.

'Character songs' are sung by characters who appear in the story (that is, by the voice actor who performs the character role). The lyrics reflect the story concept and the personality of the character. However, it is unusual for these songs to be heard in the course of the animation programme or film; instead, they are recorded and marketed as character-song CDs and included as tracks on the soundtrack CD.

'Soundtrack music' is background support music used during the animation, as the name suggests, and is almost always instrumental music with no lyrics. It is very unusual for songs (either pre-recorded or original) to be used in the soundtracks of Japanese animation, except in the case of works for small children, or those with storylines dealing with songs or music. Soundtrack music also includes 30- to 60-second musical phrases, cues or leitmotif items used like sound effects for transformations or character action. In many cases the individual tunes are unfinished, insofar as they do not have a musical resolution, but rather fade out. With the increased use of digital recording and editing, and of synthesized sounds, the recording of live performances with many musicians has declined, and it is now common for composers to devise music entirely on digital facilities.

Soundtrack music has generally low status in the production of animation works and the creation of the visuals is prioritized in terms of time and effort. Also, there is basically little potential for selling animation music compared to related products like plastic models. These toys can be devised in association with many items and characters that appear in the animation and are popular with consumers, so they are important promotional products. Music products, on the other hand, lack this appeal and the average unit price per product is higher than other artefacts. Furthermore, sales from music have been regarded as limited due to the difficulty in producing multiple types of music products that also maintain interest in the animation and additional merchandise.

For fans, an animation CD is just one item in their collection. Special bonuses are commonly included with the initial pressings of animation music CDs. These bonuses include special packaging and a wide variety of gifts such as picture books, posters and sticker books.[4] These gifts cannot be obtained elsewhere, so they command high prices in internet auctions. Rather than the quality of the music, fans and collectors debate the visible and tangible features of the artefact, such as a new jacket illustration, the commentary booklet in full colour, or special bonuses that may have been released with the initial version. Record companies noticed this trend and, from the late 1980s into the early 1990s, CD shops were overflowing with products with elaborate packaging and bonuses. In recent years, the trend has been to simplify these marketing products and, in line with the increased use of multimedia, the bonuses have shifted to data products like CD extras, PC wallpaper and screen savers.[5]

In the last twenty years, the focus of interest for the music industry, the animation industry and for fans has become the theme song and character song. These are regarded as a type of character merchandise that enhances the appeal of the singer as well as the animation character. The next section focuses on two companies engaged in distinctive production in the area of theme and character songs.

From theme to character song

Theme songs weave the titles of animation TV programmes into the lyrics and have a catchy melody designed for viewers to sing along to. It has been widely recognized as something completely different from other forms of popular music. Changes in songs used for animation music began in the early 1980s with the sudden increase of works targeted at young viewers and the employment of popular singers to perform theme songs. At first, the animation programme producer commissioned the singer who would be appropriate for the work. However, in the latter half of the 1980s, the industry was influenced by the 'tie-up' that had become popular in the TV commercial industry (where the name recognition of both product and singer is enhanced by using a song by a specific singer in a TV commercial). This led to record companies putting pressure on production companies to use particular singers for their shows (Tada, 2002: 47–50). A programme can raise its profile in the media if a popular song becomes its theme song, and so the tie-up has become common due to the advantages for both sides.

Sony Music Entertainment (SME) is a company that regards the theme song as an opportunity for cross-promotion and is especially eager to use new artists. SME conducts its business relating to animation production – such as video sales, programme production, and voice actor management – through subsidiaries. This is a trend that began in the middle of the 1990s when a slump in CD sales was predicted due to the switch to digital and online distribution of music. It started as one part of a new business expansion by record companies that were moving away from their strict focus on CD production and sales.

Animation production has been regarded as a field that is difficult to break into. This is because its production requires considerable resources, and additional time and effort must be expended to manage a variety of rights after the product has been completed. However, profits from animation can also be recovered for many years after a work's initial release through conversion to DVD and television (re)broadcasts. Furthermore, producing the programme through their own companies does not require payment for intermediaries. It is also possible to determine the directionality of the story, so that the work itself can be incorporated into the artist's promotion, and vice versa. The aim is to boost artist popularity via animation programmes by using new artists in works for animation enthusiasts and high-ranking artists in works for a mass audience, for example, the Japanese rock band L'Arc-en-Ciel was used for the television show *Rurôni Kenshin: Meiji kenkaku roman tan* (*Samurai X*; in USA *Rurouni Kenshin: Wandering Samurai*), produced by Aniplex and Fuji TV for broadcast in 1996–8. From 2004 to 2006, an annual festival called the *Sony Music Animation Festival* was held in Tokyo and Osaka, which brought together musicians from SME who performed theme songs. This festival was well supported by animation fans.[6]

In the latter half of the 1980s, at the same time as singers of popular songs in Japan took charge of theme songs, tracks that were not 'background' music began to be incorporated in soundtrack CDs. Called character songs, they featured voice actors singing as their characters, for example, in a love duet where romance was a narrative theme in the animation, or a song expressing an interior monologue by a suffering solitary hero.

At the beginning of the 1990s, King Records was the first company to produce character songs, creating a new genre of animation music to complement theme songs and soundtracks.[7] For various reasons, including the intense attention that fans pay to characters and the voice actors who play them, character songs have rapidly gained popularity. Initially, they were incorporated into soundtrack CDs as bonus tracks. CD reviews noted if a soundtrack contained a character song and promoted this as a reason to buy the CD product. As a result, reviews of character songs appeared frequently in animation magazines in the first half of the 1990s. For fans, this became an important purchase criterion. After achieving this sort of popularity, some record companies subsequently shifted the focus of production from soundtrack music to character songs. Since various types of song could be produced, the sale of character songs succeeded in overturning the perceived wisdom that there was a limit to the number of animation music products that could be sold.

In recent years, King Records has also used character songs for theme songs in their animations. Generally speaking, the theme song of a television series changes every three to six months.[8] But for 'Happy Material' (Sayo *et al.*, 2006), the theme song of the TV show *Negima! Magister Negi Magi* (Nagisa Miyazaki *et al.*, 2005–2007), King Records changed the theme song to monthly releases as single CDs. Of these singles, according to *Weekly Oricon* (a Japanese music-chart magazine), 45,000 units was recorded as the highest initial sales figure (that is, number of units sold in the week after a CD goes on sale).

Recent trends in animation music

The changed practices associated with theme and character songs outlined above impacted on the quality of soundtrack recordings. Theme and character songs are designed for distribution within Japan, and the language (Japanese) is considered a barrier to expanding export sales.[9] However, in many cases, as animation has gained popular appeal outside Japan, sales of soundtrack CDs have increased.

Music in the soundtrack CD refers to themes and musical ideas from the animation, so it is usually closely tied to the audio-visual form. Since the early 1980s, fans in the readers' columns of animation magazines have criticized the brevity of the musical items included on CDs. When character songs first began to gain popularity, the soundtrack was produced at the lowest possible cost, and this reinforced the trend of shifting resources to character song (Oguro, 2002: 104).

The Victor Entertainment company transformed the animation music scene and shifted the soundtrack production from one of secondary importance. The company earned a reputation for collaboration with directors who were looking for distinctive music via examples such as *Akira* (Katsuhiro Ôtomo, 1988) and *Inosensu: Kôkaku Kidôtai* (*Innocence*;[10] Mamoru Oshii, 2004). Shiro Sasaki, the director of the animation department at Victor Entertainment approached the recording company with the aim to make soundtrack CDs sell as well as other music products (*ibid.*: 106). The soundtrack production was separated from the budget provided by the animation studio and instead composers negotiated a separate budget based on their musical aims for the soundtrack and the CD.

Until the early 1990s, Victor released character songs as actively as other record companies. While recognizing the interest factor of projects based on the concept and characters of the work, Sasaki felt that the animation CDs distributed in the market were just character songs and the quality of soundtracks no longer mattered. Thus, the company decided on a new production approach – namely, to make their animations more distinctive by bringing the soundtrack music out of the shadows, making it as recognizable as the visuals.

The television *anime* series *Kaubôi Bibappu* (*Cowboy Bebop*; Hajime Yatata and various directors) was a typical work from the period immediately after Victor decided on its new approach. Despite the fact that only 12 of the total of 26 episodes were broadcast terrestrially from April to June 1998 (owing to conditions at TV stations[11]), the series became popular. It was re-broadcast from October 1998 to April 1999 via both satellite and terrestrial broadcasting prior to the release of the feature film *Kaubôi Bibappu: Tengoku no tobira* (*Cowboy Bebop: Knockin' on Heaven's Door*, Shinichirô Watanabe) in September 2001.[12] Videos and DVDs were also sold later. Even though all the episodes were not broadcast initially, it is extremely unusual for an animation to be re-broadcast twice in the space of only three years, highlighting the programme's overwhelming popularity.

Even outside Japan, the *Cowboy Bebop* series attracted a devoted following (Yamaguchi, 2004). In the USA, videos and DVDs went on sale in 2000, prior to TV broadcast, and in 2001, the series was broadcast by TV stations devoted to animation. Even though the series was rated as suitable for mature viewers due to its violent action scenes, it had sold approximately one million copies by August 2005.[13] This was quite a feat in terms of nationwide video sales in the USA, where it is unusual for a video to record sales of more than 10,000 copies over five years. The box-office proceeds of the feature film released in 2003 were approximately US$1 million (surveyed by Box Office Mojo[14]). As a comparison, box-office receipts for *Innocence*, which was released the following year and won an award at Cannes, were just over US$1 million. High sales for the *Cowboy Bebop* film were impressive considering that *Innocence* was the sequel to *Kôkaku Kidôtai* (*Ghost in the Shell*, Mamoru Oshii, 1995), a movie that was popular worldwide.

Set in the year 2070, *Cowboy Bebop* tells the story of bounty hunters who crew the spaceship *Bebop*. Sunrise Inc., the production company for the *Cowboy Bebop* programme, specializes in robot animation with classic stories like the *Gundam* series.[15] The company feared that animation fans would support its products only if the works featured robots, and they looked for a method to expand its consumer base. Sunrise set out to design a programme for younger television viewers (in their late teens to early thirties) who did not routinely watch animation, and *Cowboy Bebop* was the first work of this audience-expansion project.

In the *Cowboy Bebop* production, significant resources were directed to the soundtrack, as it was seen as a means of capturing the youth audience as well as a means of recovering production costs. Previously, Sunrise had recovered its production costs through income derived from the merchandising rights for toys based on the robots that appeared in the animations. However, since it was decided that robots would not feature in the new work, the same method could not be used with *Cowboy Bebop*. Instead, the production side looked to CD sales as the major source of income to replace plastic models (Technology Research Division, 2000: 155). This resulted in Victor Entertainment improving the quality of soundtrack music.

The distinguishing aspect of *Cowboy Bebop*'s first soundtrack (*Cowboy Bebop Soundtrack 1*, 1998) was that it was devised as a set of completed tracks, not just a collection of musical phrases. This meant that it was possible to listen to the soundtrack as a collection of interrelated musical numbers. *Cowboy Bebop*'s soundtrack was composed as a mixture of jazz, blues and early rock and, as such, was very unusual for Japanese animation. *Cowboy Bebop*'s composer was Yoko Kanno, who performed and recorded with a band called the Seatbelts that was specifically formed to produce the soundtrack. The Seatbelts comprised twenty-eight Japanese popular musicians who were highly regarded in Japan. Usually, the theme song for animation has Japanese lyrics (with English included only in some parts) and the singer is generally a popular singer in Japan, a voice actor, or a singer who specializes in animation song (although this trend has declined in recent years). In the case of *Cowboy Bebop*, the opening was an instrumental number, and the ending was a song in English by Mai Yamane, who most often worked as a backing vocalist. The music was mainly recorded as live performance and was highly praised in reviews published in *Music Magazine* (Takahashi, 1998: 47), and the online information magazine of Tower Records *bounce*,[16] for its effective and innovative sound.

In three other respects, the *Cowboy Bebop* soundtracks differed from others of the time. First, the CD titles departed from the usual practice in which the title of a soundtrack CD was 'Title + OST' (abbreviated from 'original soundtrack'), such as *Tsubasa Chronicles, Original Soundtrack 1, Composed By Yuki Kajiura*. But for the *Cowboy Bebop* CDs, each of the eight albums apart from the first had its own title[17] credited to the band the Seatbelts. This meant that the CDs could not be immediately recognized as animation soundtrack products. A second departure from usual practice was in the CD jacket design, which targeted consumers who did not normally view animation. Most commonly, the CD jacket was illustrated by the animators but, in the case of *Cowboy Bebop*, jackets featured the animation logo and photographs of the band, and this served to distance the CD from the animation. The third difference in approach was in the CD accompanying booklet. It was usual for such booklets to have comments about each track and the film storyline, but for *Cowboy Bebop* there were no comments in the booklet, only some pictures of the music performers.

Nine CDs were released for *Cowboy Bebop*, with the expectation they would be commercially successful. Of these CDs, four were original soundtracks, and the others were 'best of' compilation albums, maxi-singles or mini-albums. The distinctive element in this strategy was the release of remixed albums. This kind of album requires musical resources beyond those expended on the soundtrack, and this cannot be achieved if the programme has only a short broadcast life. All the *Cowboy Bebop* CDs achieved substantial sales records, indicating that Victor's innovation had succeeded. In particular, in 1999 the first album *Cowboy Bebop* won the Japan Gold Disc Award for 'Animation Film Album of the Year', for the album with the best sales record for the year.[18] Of the works that received awards from the first year (1986) to the twentieth award ceremony (2005), soundtracks from Studio Ghibli and Disney Motion Pictures won four times, vocal compilations won seven times, and compilations of backing music from extremely popular works broadcast on prime-time television won seven times.

Cowboy Bebop was the only TV series with a short broadcast run to receive this award in this period. By winning this award, Kanno (who was known as a composer only within the Japanese animation industry) gained a wider reputation and became known internationally. Last FM, one of the largest internet radio and music sites in the world, is a useful index to the international popularity of Japanese musicians, and it is significant that Kanno was the foremost artist who appeared in the list of favourites there[19].

Music producer, copyright and cross-media production

Prior to *Cowboy Bebop*, animation soundtracks were produced by the sound director and a composer who specialized in soundtrack creation. The work of the music producers was only to assist in communicating the ideas of the sound director and composer, and to conduct the recording. They were not consulted in the music composition or development of musical ideas for each scene (see Yamasaki, 2007). In fact, until the beginning of the 1990s, the music producer was merely part of an assembly line, akin to the producer's role in a record company's strategy, described by Hirsch as a 'system model' (Hirsch, 1972). Even though the record company had bought the right to produce music (music-conversion rights), music producers were unable to insert their opinions into the creation of the music. For a company specializing in music production, this limited the opportunities to develop innovative music for both music producers and other producers in the animation department who had musical expertise. The production of character songs, special bonus products and commentary booklets was an active intervention in the animation industry, designed to optimize the exhibition of music-production skills within the record company.

Until the success of *Cowboy Bebop*, both the animation industry and the music industry had accepted that sales of soundtracks would be very limited. The efforts of Victor Entertainment, the record company that produced the *Cowboy Bebop* soundtrack, changed this perception through a particular strategy. The first element mobilized by Victor was its strength in song production. Music became a distinguishing characteristic of Victor thanks to the company's selection of musicians. The success of this strategy (detailed below) has subsequently been adopted by other companies, particularly in marketing music and animation products to young people.

Victor strategically employed musicians who did not specialize in soundtrack, believing that using 'general' musicians, rather than specialists who were overly familiar with devising soundtracks, made it easier to create unique music. When songs by non-soundtrack artists were set to the visuals, the effects could be unpredictable, which proved both challenging and rewarding for the producer (Takahashi, 1998: 50). Yoko Kanno, for example, had composed music for TV commercials, and was familiar with the need for musical elements to attract the audience's attention within the first few seconds. She applied this compositional technique in her soundtracks, resulting in distinctive screen music that drew attention to the animation as well as to the music itself. This was a departure from the previous tendency in animation soundtracks in which the music was designed merely to complement the content of the visuals.

Victor required composers to create tracks like those on a standard artist's album. These are not soundtrack cues for each scene but rather items that stand on their own as self-sufficient pieces of music. For this reason, composers involved with the company are testimony to the fact that it is possible to devise soundtracks without special training or direct experience of the genre, and this offers an alternative model of music production for the animation industry. Soundtrack CDs devised in this way can be more accessible for consumers who are unfamiliar with soundtrack music, and this can improve album sales.

In this form of artist album-styled soundtrack CD, Victor consults the composer over the budget and timeframe, as well as the recording artists required for the production of music. A diverse range of music was recorded for *Cowboy Bebop* including vocal songs, orchestral tracks and electronic music. In animation soundtracks produced cheaply and quickly, it is rare to use bands of around thirty musicians. However, the Victor company does not place limitations on the procurement of musicians or instruments requested by the composer, even accepting requests for international orchestras such as the Israel Philharmonic or special instruments from abroad. In general, soundtrack recording is finished before production of the moving-image track. However, Victor adopts a flexible approach to recording and allows artists like Kanno time to get deeply involved in the work and create songs for each scene. Once recording extends into the broadcast period, significant costs must be paid to secure studios and staff. Despite this, the company offers an environment where the composer can become absorbed in composing, without severe restraints on personnel and costs. Four CDs have been released for the soundtrack of *Cowboy Bebop*, highlighting the large volume of songs that were produced for just 26 episodes and one movie.

Victor has adopted this approach to the *Cowboy Bebop* music production as company strategy. While encouraging composers to create soundtracks with individuality, according to Victor's music producer Sasaki, they are encouraged to operate with performers as a music group. As a group, they can propose music different from that envisioned by the director, or provide advice on presentation in order to create scenes where music can be used effectively. Sasaki argues that, if music was only being made to match the visuals, it could be "handled with just a composer and director" (Oguro, 2002: 106), but at Victor it is the music producer's job to integrate melodies and songs that provide a surprising, unexpected quality.

It is common knowledge in the Japanese animation industry that producing animation is expensive and rarely profitable. Raising funds is the biggest problem for production and a guarantee system against product failure has not been developed. What has functioned to improve profits is copyright. More specifically, this involves buying and selling the various rights that derive from copyright, for example, merchandising rights when using characters, sales promotion rights and TV broadcasting rights that arise when characters are used for advertising. Rights are applicable not only in Japan but also when programmes are exported overseas. The industry recognizes this as a way to obtain large profits with little additional production effort, and these arrangements can be undertaken by business rather than creative personnel. Among the numerous rights, merchandising rights for characters have been exploited more actively than other rights due to the potential profits involved. Indeed, in Japan, the animation business is often called the 'character business' because merchandising of characters (such as dolls, toys modelled after the weapons used by characters in the work, or confectionery packaging printed with character pictures) has been particularly lucrative.

The cross-media promotion derived from the merchandising of characters has been particularly exploited in Japan as a way of off-setting and supporting production costs (Technology Research Division, 1999). Until recently, internationally, 'cross-media promotion' meant releasing a single work across various screen media, such as TV, movies, and so on. However, the cross-media promotion used in recent years in the Japanese animation business (commencing with the mobile police series *Patlabor* [Kido Keisatsu Patoreiba and Mamoru Oshii] in 1988) carries across a wide variety of media including radio, videogames, comics, trading-card games, and stage productions. By these means, fans are encouraged to collect all the media available. This technique caught on after the mid-1980s, when there was an increase in animation programmes for youth. Historically, compared to the USA, Japan was less conscious of rights associated with animation products, but this changed in the 1980s when Japanese companies realized the earning potential from copyright payments. Where corporations like Disney in the USA applied this knowledge by using characters on various products to increase merchandising sales and indirectly market the animation, in Japan, funds from merchandising rights would become part of the budget that funded the animation production itself. In this case, the licensee has more power than the licensor (who in Japan is mostly the animation production company). Music products are one of these sources of income and include releases that create sales income prior to the feature film or television release.

Due to the establishment of links between different types of business, changes occurred in animation production companies and other firms. In previous animation business strategies, the animation needed first to become popular, and then various companies would make offers for the use of characters. This proved unwieldy and unpredictable. Companies today determine an overall media-deployment and release sequence during the planning stage. A typical scenario might be that first a buzz is created using *manga* (comic books), then wider popularity is achieved with TV animation, supported by soundtrack releases, and then popularity is secured through merchandising. In addition, videogames are sold in anticipation of the bonus-season sales boom, events are held during summer vacation, and a feature-film cinema release may result from a successful season. All of the companies involved become like a team supporting a single work and they coordinate not only in terms of timing, but also in terms of content. As a result, it has reached the point where the different businesses promote each other. The relations between programmes, games, comics, theatrical films and events are almost equal, so that all of the projects are expected to return a certain amount of profit. Music CDs are also included as part of this collaboration between different industries and can be significant players in their own right.

The maintenance of character life, which accompanies the establishment of cooperation between different industries, gives a boost to the conversion to movies of works that have attained popularity as TV series. In recent years, there has been a tendency for the broadcast periods of TV animation to be shortened. Once an animation's popularity has been confirmed on TV, it is converted into a feature film, and it is not unusual for TV broadcasting to have ended by the time the movie premieres. Collaboration between different industries functions effectively in building a buzz in the interval after a planned theatrical movie has been announced, until it is released. Table 12.1 shows *Cowboy Bebop* cross-media products and summarizes the main media- deployment timing for them in Japan, in three-monthly increments. Remix CDs and compilation DVDs are counted as single works.

Table 12.1 Media deployment of *Cowboy Bebop* products

Year	Month	TV/movies	DVDs	C Ds	Videogames	Mangas/novels	Fanbooks
1998	April	@		@	@	@	
1998	July		@				
1998	October	@	@	@		@	@
1999	January		@				@
1999	April		@	@		@	@
1999	July		@				
1999	October					@	
2000	January						
2000	April					@	@
2000	July						
2000	October						
2001	January						
2001	April	@					@
2001	July	@	@	@	@	@	@
2001	October		@				@
2002	January						
2002	April		@	@			
2002	July						
2002	October					@	
2003	January						

Shaded cells with an @ symbol indicate product releases.

It is evident that products have been deployed using all forms of media and notable that the release of CDs, videogames and comics is concentrated around April 1998, when the TV series, the main axis of the project, began. The programme was revitalized around September 2001 when the movie was released. The promotional opportunities are exploited with the simultaneous release of multiple media products. The effects outweigh those of a single promotion and, today, a cross-media approach is well established in Japan for both live-action and animation. Previously, this only applied to planning in Japan but in recent years sales timing for overseas markets has also been incorporated into planning. The time lag between releases in Japan and those outside Japan has been virtually eliminated.

Conclusion

The strengthening of links between different types of businesses related to animation has changed both the hierarchy of production and the consciousness of consumers. In the traditional hierarchy of producing animation, story and picture dominated and the director and sound director determined the music while the music producer, who belonged to the record company, only engaged in recording. When the Japanese recession declined in the early 1990s, music producers began to contribute to story-production meetings because soundtrack CD sales became more significant. This impacted on the actual music soundtracks, because the music producer was making soundtrack music not merely as a way to support and elucidate the image track but as music to be consumed in its own right, without the images. This in turn helped music producers to improve their attitude to music in an audio-visual context and specifically in animation screen products.

Digital information networks, such as official websites for animation productions, have assisted the promotion of all related products. Websites have surpassed animation magazines as the principal promotional tool, and they contain advertising space bought by each company including record, video, toy, game and other companies. As the official websites carry information about all associated products, they have become a convenient forum for fans and collectors.

Alongside other animation products, this cooperative approach to advertising and marketing has benefited sales of animation soundtrack CDs. In the past, animation magazines mainly promoted theme songs, and information about soundtrack CDs was marginalized. But this has changed markedly in the last decade with a revitalized approach to music products combined with marketing approaches that centre on websites. Animation music has increased in popularity in Japan, in part due to media-deployment campaigns. This in turn has served the music well by improving the animation industry's approach to music.

Notes

1. The Normura Research Institute is a think-tank that was one of the first to conduct research on consumption trends among animation fans in Japan.
2. Based on annual reports by the Recording Industry Association of Japan, *The Recording Industry in Japan – Statistics, Analysis, Trends* (in Japanese), 2002 to 2007.
3. Although see Kyoko Koizumi's discussion of the music in Miyazaki's films (Chapter 3 in this volume).
4. Books of sticker sheets.
5. Recently, packaging gifts with CDs has shifted to DVD.
6. 'Event Guide', *Asahi Shinbun* (in Japanese), 1 May 2006, evening, p. 2.
7. Unattributed (1994) ,'The secret of soundtrack' [Gekihan no Himitsu], *Animage (Animêjyu)*, December, Tokyo: Tokuma Shoten, pp. 75–8.
8. This is the minimum number broadcast in Japan. The usual number of episodes is twelve. Most programme broadcasts last for six months (24 stories). It is quite rare to broadcast for a year or more. For *Cowboy Bebop* 26 episodes were broadcast over six months.
9. When broadcast in countries outside Japan, the Japanese theme song is often replaced with a song produced by a local company in the local language.
10. The English title has been used for the rest of this chapter.
11. Two factors affected the broadcasts of *Cowboy Bebop* episodes. First, after a series of murders of Japanese youths at the time, TV programmes that included violence were denounced; this meant that *Cowboy Bebop* broadcasts were cancelled due to their portrayal of violence. Second, in December 1997, an episode of *Pokemon* included visual effects that caused seizures in some viewers. This event (dubbed 'Pokemon Shock') led TV Tokyo, which broadcast both *Pokemon* and *Cowboy Bebop*, to restrict broadcasts of contentious *anime* episodes for at least four months.
12. 'Cowboy Bebop – Knockin' on Heaven's Door' (official website), online at http://www.cowboybebop.org (accessed 12 December 2006).
13. *Anime* news network 'Bandai Entertainment announces over one million units of Cowboy Bebop sold', 25 August 2005, online at: http://www.*anime*newsnetwork.com/press-release/2005-08-25/bandai-entertainment-announces-over-one-million-units-of-cowboy-bebop-sold (accessed 24 June 2007).
14. Box Office Mojo (undated), 'Cowboy Bebop', online at: http://www.boxofficemojo.com/movies/?id=cowboybebop.htm (accessed 28 June 2007). Box Office Mojo is a website that provides film box-office revenues.
15. The *Gundam* series, which originated in the late 1970s, helped steer *anime* into adult stories. Although the animation may have been limited (in line with TV *anime* of the time), the music score by Takeo Watanabe attracted positive feedback, and the *Gundam* concept continued to spawn TV titles, feature-film offshoots and other products well into the 2000s.

16. T. Baba (2004), 'Musical Journey vol. 6' (Myûjikaru Jyanî), online at: http://www.
    bounce.com/article/article.php/1917/ALL?K=%BF%FB%CC%EE%A4%E8%A4%A6%
    BB%D2 (accessed 27 June 2007).
17. The titles are as follows: *Cowboy Bebop*; *No Disk*; *Blue*; *Vitaminless*; *Cowboy
    Bebop Knockin' On Heaven's Door*; *Future Blues – Cowboy Bebop Knockin' On
    Heaven's Door*; *TANK! The! Best!* (Greatest Hits); *Music For Freelance* (remixes);
    Cowboy Bebop (CD-box set). All the soundtrack albums were released under the
    name of Yoko Kanno and the Seatbelts. Shiro Sasaki was music director of
    Cowboy Bebop and these productions comprise his major works in this role.
18. The late-night animation *Initial D* (first and third series directed by Noburu
    Misawa; second series directed by Shin-ichi Masaki) won the same prize in the
    following year, but this was due to collaboration with the dance-music series
    Super Euro Beat, which was about illegal amateur car racing and was popular with
    street racers. Telecasting at 'golden time' (19:00–21:00) is costly and therefore
    this period is occupied by major production companies. Midnight was the only
    option for Avex as a new animation company.
19. Accessed 25 October 2005. Since then, Last FM opened a Japanese chapter that
    does not clearly indicate the popularity of Japanese musicians internationally.

References

Hirch, P. (1972), 'Processing Fads and Fashions: An Organizational Set Analysis of
    Cultural Industry Systems', *American Journal of Sociology*, 77(4), 639–59.
Oguro, Y. (2002), '"Konohito ni Hanashi wo Kikitai" ["Please tell us something about
    you"]', *Animeijyu [Animage]*, 25(12), 104–7.
Otaku Forecasting Team (2005), Nomura Research Institute, *Research on the Otaku
    Market (Otaku Shijyô no Kenkyû)*, Tokyo: Tôyô Keizai.
Tada, M. (2002), *Kore ga Anime Bijinesu da [This Is the Animation Business]*, Tokyo:
    Kôsaidô.
Takahashi, O. (1998), ' "Animeisyon Kara Mirai no Ongaku ga Kikoeru" [We can listen
    to the music of the future from animation]', *Myûjikku Magajin*, June, pp. 46–51.
Technology Research Division (eds) (1999), *Anime Bijinesu ga Kawaru [Changes in the
    Anime Business]*, Tokyo: Nikkei Business Publications, Inc.
Technology Research Division (2000), *(Shinkasuru Anime Bijinesu [The Evolving Anima-
    tion Business]*, Tokyo: Nikkei Business Publications Inc.
The Recording Industry Association of Japan (2002–2007), *RIAJ Year Report (Nihon no
    Recôdo Sangyô)*, online at: http://www.riaj.or.jp/issue/industry/index.html (accessed
    18 May 2008).
Yamaguchi, Y (2004) *Complete History of Animation in Japan [Nihon no Anime Zenshi]*,
    Tôkyô: Ten-Books.
Yamasaki, A. (2007), 'Gekihan Ongaku no Sakuhinka [Selling Sound Track: Research into
    the Cross-media Animation Industry]', *Nenpou Ningen Kagaku [Annals of Human
    Sciences]*, Department of Sociology, Anthropology and Philosophy, Graduate School
    of Human Sciences, Osaka University, 28, 39–54.

13 Disney Does Broadway

Musical Storytelling in The Little Mermaid *and* The Lion King

Rebecca Coyle and Jon Fitzgerald

> *I remember a film composer … I was asking for his advice and he said, "Look, man, nobody takes the score for an animated film seriously … Just take a powder …" You think about how that must have, like, turned on its ear within five years.* (Alan Menken, co-composer for *The Little Mermaid*[1])

The Little Mermaid (Ron Clements and John Musker, 1989) launched a new era for the Disney corporation in the post-Walt period. As a successful animation feature at a time when the genre was in transition, the film enabled Disney to re-establish a prestigious profile in long-form animation production. Integral to the success of *The Little Mermaid* was a fresh approach to music. Generic techniques associated with Broadway stage musicals were incorporated into the animated feature, at a time when successful US movie musicals tended to revolve around the creation of loosely integrated popular 'hit' songs. The success of *The Little Mermaid* paved the way for subsequent Disney animation features – most notably *Beauty and the Beast* (Gary Trousdale and Kirk Wise, 1991) and *The Lion King* (Roger Allers and Rob Minkoff, 1994) – that also drew on aspects of the Broadway stage musical. Completing a neat circle of events, these three films were later adapted for Broadway, and became successful stage musical productions. In a relatively brief period of time, then, Disney was able to confirm its reach across the USA and to revive its reputation as a force in animation and popular music by bringing the studio aesthetic of Hollywood together with the musical-theatre style of Broadway.

This chapter discusses approaches to the place and role of music in *The Little Mermaid*, and analyses some of the specific techniques employed in the songs and orchestral score. It then discusses the ways in which *The Lion King* successfully adapted and extended these approaches, using additional musical elements. The chapter demonstrates that music played a central role in Disney's revitalization of the animated feature film and that this impacted on the prestige associated with composers scoring animated film, as Alan Menken suggests in the quote above. We argue that Disney's successful animated features were able to give new life to both animation feature-film music and music-theatre approaches employed in Broadway.

The extensive history of film productions by Walt and Roy Disney has been chronicled in many and dispersed texts (see, for example, Johnston and Thomas, 1995; Allan, 1999). *The Little Mermaid* production occurred at a particular moment of the corporation's development. Most relevant to this is the post-war period in which the Walt Disney company diversified and grew into an international entity with several branches of cultural production. After a series of classic fairy-tale features, animation features included stories based on contemporary children's novels (such as *One Hundred and One Dalmatians*; Clyde Geronimi, Hamilton S. Luske and Wolfgang Reitherman, 1961). At the same time, Walt Disney was involved in live-action films, television shows and new directions in outdoor entertainment, as well as exploring approaches to combined live action and animation, in films such as *Mary Poppins* (Robert Stevenson, 1964). After Walt's death in 1966, Roy continued several of these projects, including the opening of The Florida Project's Magic Kingdom[2] in 1971 and the development of the California Arts (widely known as CalArts) media arts school. After Roy died in 1971, Ron Miller, Walt's son-in-law, took a creative role in overseeing animation films and was president for several years in the 1980s.

The mid-1970s was a time of transition – with the retirement of many animators who had worked with Disney since the 1930s – but Disney continued to release animation features, including *The Rescuers* (John Lounsbery, Wolfgang Reitherman and Art Stevens, 1977), as well as a musical with live action and animation, *Pete's Dragon* (Don Chaffey, 1977). The 1980s was a period of technological upheaval for animation, and Disney responded to this with the release of the computer animation feature *Tron* (Steven Lisberger, 1982), which had a synthesized score by Wendy Carlos. Most significantly, in 1984 Michael Eisner and Frank Wells were brought in to overhaul the company and set about evaluating all Disney productions including theme parks,[3] live-action TV (including successful shows such as *The Golden Girls* [1985–92]), and animation films currently in process, such as *The Black Cauldron* (Ted Berman and Richard Rich, 1985) and *The Great Mouse Detective* (Ron Clements, Burny Mattinson, David Michener and John Musker, 1986).

Meanwhile, as a further diversification of Disney's operation, Ron Miller launched its Hollywood studio, Touchstone Pictures,[4] to produce live-action adult-oriented movies such as *Splash* (Ron Howard, 1984), starring Darryl Hannah as a mermaid. *Splash* was a box-office hit and provided a significant thematic prelude to *The Little Mermaid*. The latter film, released at the end of the 1980s, represented a return to form, being a fully animated feature based on a fairy-tale with musical highlights, and extended familiar Disney approaches through the music. This element was effectively incorporated into a comprehensive marketing and merchandising campaign that assisted the success of the film. The availability of the film as a Disney Classic for home video just a few months after the theatrical film debut[5] meant that *The Little Mermaid* was positioned as a descendent of the classic canon of full-length animation features, a series of releases originally launched in the 1950s that are considered iconically Disney.

In order to contextualize the music and the working methods employed for the music production in *The Little Mermaid* and *The Lion King*, the chapter commences with an overview of approaches to music in pre-1980s Disney animation films. While Walt Disney demonstrated an interest in making European art music accessible to broad audiences, in productions such as *Fantasia* (1940) (see Taylor, 1940; Culhane, 1983, 1999) and the adaptation of Tchaikovsky's ballet in *Sleeping Beauty* (Clyde Geronimi, 1959), he was also keen to exploit the latest musics and songwriting styles in animation features.

Disney's music for animations

Despite the company's longevity, breadth of film production and diverse range of styles, Disney is often associated with children's (or, at least, family entertainment) films, and narratives and music with middle-American values (Bell *et al.*, 1995; Giroux, 2001). Although the studio's 'sound' evolved over a long history of productions, a significant approach to music and its importance was determined at an early period of synchronized sound. According to Ross Care (2002), the catchy scores associated with the early Mickey Mouse character were integrated with the Carl Stalling orchestral music of the *Silly Symphonies* series (1929–39) to achieve Walt Disney's aim of appealing to broad audiences. In the 1930s composers Frank Churchill and Leigh Harline created Disney animation scores that were melodic, inventively orchestrated and essentially accessible. In 1937 *Snow White and the Seven Dwarfs* (David Hand) incorporated a score (by Churchill and Harline, with Paul Smith) that Care has characterized as "nostalgic operetta" (Care, 2002: 26) rather than based on the styles of musical comedy then popular in stage productions and cartoons; the first one-third of this film features one music number following another in rapid succession and linked by continuous orchestral scoring using a theatre ensemble. A few years later, Oliver Wallace and Frank Churchill won an Academy Award for best musical score for their brassy music for *Dumbo* (Ben Sharpsteen, 1941).

Disney's post-war return to animation features took place with *Cinderella* (Clyde Geronimi, Wilfred Jackson and Hamilton Luske) in 1950 and, for the first time, brought in popular songwriters (New York's Tin Pan Alley artists Mack David, Jerry Livingston and Al Hoffmann) to work with the company's musical staff (see Newsom, 1980). These were the first songs to be administered by Disney's own music publishing division and the soundtrack songs album released by RCA sold more than 750,000 copies in the first year (Tietyen, 1990: 93), demonstrating the potential of this music merchandising approach. This example informed the establishment of the Disney record company (Disneyland Records) in 1956 and resulted in the employment of well-known entertainers such as Dinah Shore, the Andrews Sisters and Nelson Eddy (see Hollis and Ehrbar, 2006).[6]

In a further centralization of creative assets, the songwriting brothers Richard and Robert Sherman were employed under exclusive contract for eight years in the 1960s and located in Disney's Burbank Studios as a songwriting team. The use of contracted songwriters was a first for the Disney company, which had previously used commissioned songwriters such as Sammy Fain or staff composers, sometimes with lyrics written by different people in the studio (including, for example, staff nurse Hazel George under the pseudonym 'Gil George'). The songs were used in conjunction with understated underscores (created by George Bruns) in a style influenced by Buddy Baker, a UCLA teacher and later musical director, arranger and conductor for many Disney television, film and theme-park productions. The Sherman brothers created a complex musical production for the live-action, animation, song-and-dance numbers, and special-effects sequences in the successful *Mary Poppins*. Other live-action musical movie successes in the 1960s (*My Fair Lady* [George Cukor] and *The Sound of Music* [Robert Wise], both released in 1964) confirmed the lucrative appeal of the song-and-dance formula.[7] After Walt died in 1966, song-and-dance numbers continued to be incorporated into several animation features (for example, 'Bare Necessities' in *The Jungle Book* [Wolfgang Reitherman, 1967]), but it was a series of non-Disney films that provided fresh confirmation of the formula's appeal in novel contexts.

Saturday Night Fever (John Badham, 1977) represented a turning point in the general history of the US movie musical. The film soundtrack generated five US No.1 hits on *Billboard*'s singles charts, and clearly demonstrated that pop songs could be a primary force within the musical format. Songwriter and popular music producer Giorgio Moroder recalls:

> Saturday Night Fever *was an enormous hit and made everybody think "Wait. Let's try to do something similar", and that's when we started to have songs which were really driving the movie.*[8]

The success of subsequent movies such as *Flashdance* (Adrian Lyne, 1983), *Footloose* (Herbert Ross, 1984) and *Dirty Dancing* (Emile Ardolino, 1987) proved beyond doubt that movie musicals were highly effective vehicles for the creation of popular hits, especially when supported by intensive cross-media promotion. Songs and other popular music numbers were incorporated into television spots and trailers, and key melodic elements were woven throughout the film so that the music was integrally associated with the film narrative and themes. Significantly, though, many of these films relied more on (extra-diegetic) recorded song and performance of dance rather than singing. As music writer Richard Coles suggests, the downside of the obsession with hit songs was a loosening of the connection between song and movie narrative:

> ...sometimes you think the raison d'être of films like Footloose *or* Top Gun *or* Flashdance *is ... they're not interested in telling you a story, it's not about a narrative, it's this kind of stringing together of marketing focuses ... it's the single, it's the video, it's the doll and you sometimes think that the*

narrative idea of the film is secondary to that. (Richard Coles, WOB interview, part 7)

Alongside these synergistic music/media practices, in the 1980s Disney's film-making approach was affected by personnel changes. In 1985 Walt's nephew Roy E. Disney commenced as Head of Animation at the Disney Studios with Vice President Peter Schneider. A team of new personnel was appointed including, as Chair of Disney animation, Jeffrey Katzenberg from Paramount Studios, who had a track record in live-action film production. Katzenberg took over business while Roy moved into overseeing creative production. Together with the initiatives of Eisner, Wells and Miller, the corporation set out to invigorate Disney enterprises and establish a dynamic post-Walt and Roy profile, one that especially impacted on animation feature-film production.

Music for the mermaid

Disney had moved away from musical films since *Pete's Dragon* in 1977, despite this having been a strength in the past, and *The Little Mermaid* was not originally planned as a musical film (Miller, 2000: 47). Ultimately, however, it was created by putting songs together with orchestral accompaniment and underscore, in a working method influenced by Broadway. Loosely based on Hans Christian Andersen's short story, the film tells of a defiant teenage mermaid, Ariel, who falls in love with a human prince she rescues from a shipwreck. Accompanied by her father's minder, Sebastian the crab, and with the help of a vengeful sea-witch, Ursula, she acquires legs and follows the prince on shore to his castle, intending to attract his attentions. Tricked by the sea-witch, she is unable to persuade the prince to commit to her before the sea-witch claims her soul. King Triton sacrifices himself for his daughter, and his power and authority are claimed by Ursula, who aspires to rule the world. However, Prince Eric and an assortment of bird and sea creature friends destroy the sea-witch, and King Triton's and other lost souls previously claimed by the witch are revived. In a predictably Disney upbeat resolution, Ariel and her father are reconciled, and the prince and Ariel are married.[9]

The music for the film was created by Alan Menken and Howard Ashman. One of the team of producers on *The Little Mermaid*, lyricist Ashman came to film music from Broadway, where he had worked with Menken — a partnership that culminated in the successful production of *Little Shop of Horrors*[10] (that itself spawned an eponymous film musical [Frank Oz, 1986]). As observed in the quote opening this chapter, Menken was initially warned off working on an animated film but his score was integral to the success of *The Little Mermaid* (and gained him an Oscar in 1989). Menken went on to score numerous other Disney films and stage musicals.

In writing music for the new Disney animation feature, Menken and Ashman were keenly aware of the movie's place within a long tradition of high-quality animated features, and felt a responsibility to create a score that would bear comparison with earlier Disney classics.

I remember Howard said our assignment was to write a score for an animated musical that could sit on the shelf alongside Cinderella *and* Dumbo *and* Peter Pan *and* Pinocchio. (Menken, 2006 DVD audio commentary)

Menken and Ashman therefore aimed to closely integrate music and narrative (as had been done in the earlier Disney films) – rather than following the hit-song approach of successful 1980s film musicals such as *Flashdance* and *Dirty Dancing.*

We wanted to make songs that would tell the story, songs that would really move the story forward, really push the plot along and keep things driving ahead, so it's not like you stop and sing a song. *(Ashman, interview with Alan Menken and Howard Ashman, 2006 DVD audio commentary)*

Menken also approached the creation of the orchestral score (his first) with older models in mind, and as a result the music is notable for its 'busy' quality – offering an almost continual underscore, and at times providing stingers to emphasize visual elements in lively action sequences (such as the storm scene).

I made a choice to do this very much in the style of the earlier animated features in which, instead of sound effects, you're basically using music for a falling or music for an impact or for anything, almost like a ballet. (Menken, 2006 DVD audio commentary)

The link with the past (and the central role of music within the movie) is further evident in some of the ways in which music and animation evolved during the creation of the film. In many instances songs and instrumental score led the animation process:

In the old days a lot of the music was written first before they animated a thing. Just even the background music was written first and in some ways we've gone back to some parts of that old tradition in deciding the songs as the story itself was getting developed so there are lots of places where they've animated right to the music. (Ashman, interview with Alan Menken and Howard Ashman, DVD 2006 audio commentary)

Indeed, producer Ron Clements recalls that Menken wrote "almost a silent film score" (DVD 2006 audio commentary), sometimes without having seen the action. He played the themes on piano and the recorded cues were placed against the action. In the final film, music is used to provide many key scenes with strong support for the narrative momentum; for example, it is used prominently when characters are introduced, when they express their desires or approach to life in song, or to offer musical support for romance or comic relief. As Miller notes, the music draws on Broadway conventions for diegetically significant numbers:

From expository opening number ("Daughters of Triton") to heroine Ariel's "I want" ballad ("Part of Your World") to Busby Berkeleyesque production number ("Under the Sea") to villainess Ursula's plot-forwarding tour de force ("Poor Unfortunate Souls") to comic divertissement ("Les Poissons") to choral love song ("Kiss the Girl"), it carefully hit all the marks of a classic Broadway score. (Miller, 2000: 47)

Further emphasizing the overall focus on music within the film are 'musical-within-a-musical' elements, a trope commonly employed in both stage and screen musicals (see Feuer, 1993). For example, Ariel and her sisters are singers, a performance of an operetta introduces Triton, and sailors sing and dance to a sea shanty on board the prince's ship.

Popular-song approach

The composers made a conscious decision to include an eclectic mix of musical styles. Ashman recalls how trying to match other Disney classics such as *Peter Pan* and *Snow White* gave the composers "latitude to work in all kinds of musical styles – just to dream" (Menken, 2006 DVD audio commentary). Working in this manner in the early 1990s meant that Menken and Ashman built on a history of Broadway scores (ranging from early revues to work by Stephen Sondheim) and they had several decades of popular song (in a variety of genres) at their disposal.

At the same time, the composers were concerned that reverence for the past could result in old-fashioned music, and their solution was to use popular music in the form of calypso-influenced pop songs. Ashman also acknowledges that he and Menken employed something of a "trick" – creating a Jamaican character for the crab – to allow them to place the fairy-tale in Caribbean musical settings[11] in various sequences through-out the film.

> *It's very hard to write contemporary-sounding music in a fairy-tale context. You're dealing with long ago and far away and you really still want to have a feeling that modern kids and adults can enjoy and start to move to, 'cause that's how you get energy. And it was sort of a trick ... before the script was actually written we had a long conference about that and was there a way we could give the crab something in his personality that would make it possible to have a special kind of music that had some kind of rhythmic edge or contemporary feeling to it. And what we came up with was that there would be a 'Jamaican' flavour.* (Ashman, interview with Alan Menken and Howard Ashman, 2006 DVD audio commentary)

In addition to Caribbean elements, Menken and Ashman use a broad musical palette to create an appealing musical pastiche. Examples include: a sea shanty (opening boat scene); operetta (performance for Triton); French music hall ('Les Poissons'); medieval/Renaissance dance music (dance scene on boat); baroque counterpoint (tour of king-dom); Romantic-period orchestral music (when Ariel sees the prince); and early Disney-style high-set female choirs (various scenes). Menken acknowledges the deliberate pastiche quality of the music, recalling that "we did a pastiche [in *Little Shop of Horrors*] of 50s' rock and roll, and in *The Little Mermaid* we did really our own pastiche of Disney" (2006 DVD audio commentary). In this sense, the pastiche operates as both a composite of musical elements and a style imitative of existing idioms without overtly parodying the styles and techniques.[12]

Songs represent a highly significant component of the film's musical soundtrack. As well as moving the story forward, the catchy songs contribute in a significant way to the emotional content and narrative flow of the movie. Various approaches are apparent in 'Kiss The Girl' (a sweet and gentle, almost hypnotic, romance song), 'Les Poissons' (a wild and zany comedy song) and the extravagant camp performance by Ursula for 'Poor Unfortunate Souls'. Two especially memorable and narratively significant songs that illustrate contrasting techniques are 'Part Of Your World' and 'Under The Sea'.

'Part Of Your World' is a sophisticated song that draws on the traditions of the Broadway musical by providing an 'I wish' number, that is, a classic narrative driver that establishes the scenario and the central protagonist's desire for change and dictates the plot direction and focus. The song is neatly integrated into the narrative: it conveys Ariel's desire to join the human world – and thereby achieve independence and metaphorical upward mobility – and outlines the obstacles in her way. The song structure is 'theatrical', with an extended introductory verse, use of a pre-hook (or pre-chorus) section, a relatively undefined chorus, and a long bridge section that adds more lyric content.

All aspects of the music are driven by the lyrics, and the melody, although uplifting, is not especially memorable. The vocal delivery is theatrical and yearning, including extensive rubato, and alternates between singing and half-spoken delivery. Jodi Benson, who voiced Ariel, worked with Ashman on his Broadway show *Smile* (1986), and was coached by him to interpret the song and deliver it in a style consistent with music theatre.[13] The song's central role was highlighted by its use for a screen-test sequence. Table 13.1 matches the song lyrics with a description of the musical elements.

'Part Of Your World' is also important because, for much of the rest of the film, Ariel is mute (after the sea-witch has provided her with legs in exchange for her voice) and the musical score becomes her voice.[14] Prince Eric recalls his rescuer's sonic motif (centred on three ascending notes), and Sebastian speaks (and sings in 'Kiss The Girl') for her. Ariel's muteness replicates the musical contrast that occurred in earlier Disney productions, such as *Bambi* (David Hand, 1942), which has very little dialogue and in which the musical impetus that speaks for the animal characters is provided by the orchestra (see Care, 1985). Ariel's lack of voice is particularly important as a key personal attribute (she is the most accomplished singer of her sisters) and in relation to the semiotics of mermaid song (she is unable to use the 'siren song' to ensnare her prince).

The melodic motifs from 'Part Of Your World' also serve as a foundation of the musical score and are cleverly woven into the soundtrack by Menken. For example, the pentatonic theme that accompanies the verse melody of the song (Figure 13.1) appears

Table 13.1 An analysis of 'Part Of Your World' lyrics and music

Summary of lyrics	Musical description
Conveys how Ariel's collection of human artefacts offers a treasure trove and she's "got everything" a girl could want.	The song begins with an evocative, watery instrumental figure (used as a recurring motif throughout the song and orchestral soundtrack). The introduction/verse is lightly orchestrated and harmonically ambiguous. Rather than beginning on the tonic chord (which is not heard until the chorus), it alternates the IV and V chords. Together, the watery motif and unresolved chord progression (i.e., no resolution to the tonic) give the music a sense of 'floating' or suspension.
But despite the "gadgets and gizmos" she wants more.	The song moves to a pre-hook section that ends with a long high-set note on "more" at the end of the phrase "I want more". "More" is on the second scale degree and over the dominant chord – a typical, music-theatre device that signals the arrival of the chorus.
Ariel yearns to be "where the people are", where they dance, walk, stroll down streets, to be "part of that world".	The chorus continues to focus on the articulation of the lyric content, rather than a memorable melodic idea. It begins in understated fashion, in mid-range vocally and with minimal instrumental backing. From "up where they walk" the melody begins to rise, reaching a high note with a pause over the minor iv chord (a very theatrical technique). A subsequent break in the orchestral texture serves to highlight the lyric hook (which is almost whispered) against minimal backing.
Ariel would give anything to be there where "bright young women" are "ready to stand".	A bridge section allows for the inclusion of still further lyric content. Once again, the music moves to a long high note on the dominant chord (on the word "stand") to set up the second version of the chorus.
Ariel wishes to leave the sea and learn about the world above and to be part of it.	The chorus is repeated and the music moves to a reprise of the watery figure that began the song. This time the chord progression is at last allowed to resolve to the tonic chord, suggesting her resolution to make a change.

in the first scene of the movie, and reappears throughout the film as the primary 'watery' motif. The song's chorus is reprised when Ariel rescues the prince, and her voice is represented by a segment of the verse melody when she is captured by Ursula. The prince plays a version of the chorus melody on recorder as he wistfully ponders his lost love, and orchestral strings reprise the verse melody to signal Ariel's return during the disrupted wedding scene.

Figure 13.1 'Watery' accompaniment motif in 'Part Of Your World' (this and all subsequent transcriptions from the DVD music by Jon Fitzgerald)

The gentle melodicism of 'Part Of Your World' markedly contrasts to the exaggerated "camp drag show" (Sells, 1995: 182) by Ursula in which she both instructs Ariel in gender performativity and provides a powerful role model for how to achieve the independence (and conscious sexuality) the teenager so desires (see Colless, 2007). The gender-performing, camp-styled villain song has significant roots in Broadway, where the theatrical form allows for this highly exaggerated style perhaps more than in some other popular music contexts. Prior to Ursula's performance in *The Little Mermaid*, however, King Triton's court musician, Sebastian the crab, has employed a different persuasive tactic and performative style. 'Under The Sea' (which won Menken and Ashman an Academy award in 1989) is performed by Sebastian with a fish ensemble, as he tries to convince lovesick Ariel of the benefits of her home environment (to no avail as she continues to yearn and plan for a new life). The song is a lively and happy ensemble piece imbued with calypso musical flavours. Its lyrics are humorous and involve imaginative, carefully crafted rhyme schemes, including internal rhymes such as:

> *Under the sea, under the sea,*
> *Nobody beat us, fry us and eat us in fricassee…*
>
> *When the sardine begin the Beguine it's music to me*[15]

Caribbean (especially calypso) elements abound. Sebastian the crab is a Broadway-style character who speaks and sings with a thick Jamaican patois and this signals the (inauthentic) link to calypso-styled music. 'Under The Sea' is set in a major key and uses an up-tempo groove in 4/4 with a characteristic bass riff. Rhythmic elements and percussion instruments (including steel pans[16]) are prominent. A syncopated brass riff is used in the introduction and as a repeated song hook. The song uses a simple verse–chorus form (with bridge) with a very catchy, singalong chorus melody. Its harmony is simple, consisting mostly of primary chords.

A number of elements also demonstrate the influence of both Broadway and Hollywood musicals. These include the use of the secondary dominant II chord (in the last phrase of the chorus), modulation up a semitone for the last chorus, and the inclusion of a bridge section that lists all the creatures playing different sea instruments. Here, fast-paced orchestral 'hits' (much as in earlier Disney classics) are matched in a literal way with fish images and lyrics such as, "The newt play the flute, the carp play the harp, the plaice play the bass". A musical theatre-style choral backing provides reinforcement for the last chorus.

The Little Mermaid featured a form of 'hybrid' score in which score and song were carefully integrated, as Miller notes: "*Mermaid*'s musical riches did not end with its songs: Menken punctuated the story with a forceful musical underscoring recalling Max Steiner or Erich Wolfgang Korngold" (2000: 47). However, the significance of the songs was later reinforced by *The Little Mermaid* CD release in Disney's Karaoke series (2006), a CD that comprised updated versions of the songs by contemporary popular artists such as Jessica Simpson. The Platinum Editions reissue DVD, released in 2006, features singalong versions of the major songs.

Music, marketing and merchandise

Part of the reason for the financial success of *The Little Mermaid* was its focused marketing and merchandising, a strategy that had been exploited as early as *Cinderella*[17] but was particularly lucrative for *The Little Mermaid* and subsequent features. As Miller notes:

> The Little Mermaid *won two Oscars, earned $84 million in its initial domestic theatrical release, and laid the foundation for a marketing franchise that turned Disney from a profitable but moldering old-guard corporation into an unstoppable entertainment phenomenon. Impressive as that $84 million was in 1989, it was chump change compared to the millions to be made from* The Little Mermaid's *international rights, video sales and rentals, cable showings, fast-food tie-ins, and, especially, product licensing: Little Mermaid toys, clothes, watches, trinkets, books, even a Saturday morning TV series. Disney had stumbled on a gold mine, and it spent the rest of the decade extracting the riches.* (Miller, 2000: 48)

While Disney had successfully and inventively used music to support, enhance and feature in its animation feature films, *The Little Mermaid* enabled this to take a new direction insofar as the music was a key driving force in the film. This direction for the feature-animation format was critically endorsed, as it was the first of five Disney film animations in a row to win Oscars for score and song. In addition, the successful partnership of Menken and Ashman was brought into several of these, prior to Ashman's death in 1991. *The Little Mermaid* established a template that was followed to various extents by *Beauty and the Beast* in 1991 and *Aladdin* (Ron Clements and John Musker, 1992).[18] The former film exceeded the box-office success of *The Little Mermaid* and later was adapted for a Broadway stage production.

Disney's blockbuster musicals were an important boost for the animation film industry and a catalyst for the production of several animated musicals such as *An American Tail* (Phil Nibbelink and Simon Wells, 1991), *FernGully: The Last Rainforest* (Bill Kroyer, 1992), and others in the early 1990s. However, as Miller argues:

> *Lacking the budgets, merchandising savvy, and storytelling acumen of Disney's best, most flopped. Nor were their scores as distinguished as the*

> Ashman-Menken movies, settling for a few wannabe pop ballads and deriva-
> tive production numbers. (Miller, 2000: 50)[19]

In the early 1990s, the income that came from the success of *The Little Mermaid* and *Beauty and the Beast* enabled Disney's development of another major project. Five years after *The Little Mermaid*, another animation feature was released that drew on musical techniques such as pastiche, elements of 'world' musics, Broadway personnel and techniques, as well as some new musical approaches – *The Lion King*. But where *Beauty and the Beast* and *Aladdin* drew on several of the musical techniques successfully exploited in *The Little Mermaid*, *The Lion King* exploited a fresh approach to the synthesis of popular music and staged musicals, without the involvement of Menken and Ashman, and used fewer songs and a different approach to those numbers.

The Lion King's blend of musical elements

The Lion King was the thirty-second film in the Disney animated feature canon, and the highest-grossing 'traditionally animated' (in the sense of incorporating hand-drawn components[20]) feature film in the USA. The film focuses on a young African lion named Simba, who learns of his place in the 'Circle of Life' while struggling through various obstacles to become the rightful king.[21] Tricked by his evil uncle Scar to kill his father, Simba flees the Pridelands. Befriended by a meerkat (Timon) and warthog (Pumbaa), Simba lives a carefree life as he grows to adulthood in exile. His childhood playmate, Nala, finds him and a romantic connection develops but she cannot persuade him to return and save the Pridelands from Scar's corrupt and destructive dictatorship. Eventually the Shaman baboon Mafiki reminds him of his role as proper leader, and Simba reclaims the pridelands, a new cub is born and the circle of life is confirmed. *The Lion King* storyline has significant religious undertones[22] and the US-centric approach to cultural representation was evident in Disney storylines for subsequent animated features including *Pocahontas* (Mike Gabriel and Eric Goldberg, 1995), *Mulan* (Tony Bancroft and Barry Crook, 1998) and *Brother Bear* (Aaron Blaise and Robert Walker, 2005).[23]

The music for *The Lion King* garnered two Academy awards: Best Original Score and Best Original Song ('Can You Feel The Love Tonight') and the film won the same two categories in the Golden Globe Awards.[24] Yet, as with *The Little Mermaid*, the film was not originally intended as a musical; as the project evolved, *The Lion King* drew on diverse individual talents and musical genres and eventually the music became a prominent feature in the film.

> One of the things people don't know about The Lion King *is that it was not
> actually anticipated to be a musical. It was in a sense like a National
> Geographic special that would be animated. Tim Rice had come to work at
> the studio because he had sold his play and I sat down ... one day and said,
> "Could this thing be a musical?" and he said, "Well, anything can be a
> musical."* (Executive Producer for *The Lion King*, Thomas Schumacher,
> interview[25])

Rice, already highly regarded for his collaborations with the British stage music composer Andrew Lloyd Webber on *Evita* and *Jesus Christ Superstar* had been brought in to work on *Aladdin* when Howard Ashman died (three of Rice's songs were used in that film). He brought a wealth of experience as a lyricist for music theatre, and he was also the driving force behind UK pop songwriter Elton John's involvement in the project:

> *I think perhaps my biggest contribution to the entire project was suggesting Elton John, and I did say, "Well, you'll never get him because he'll be too busy, he'll be too expensive", and to my amazement very quickly Elton came on board.* (Tim Rice)

John noted the appeal of being involved in a new Disney project: "I think everybody in England that was a kid looked forward to seeing Disney movies." John's commitment to the film meant that the soundtrack would include strong pop-rock elements and his involvement also facilitated a valuable connection to the popular music market. Rice and John co-wrote five original songs for the film, and John performed 'Can You Feel The Love Tonight', which played during the end credits and was a marketable, radio-friendly number.

Elton John's involvement in *The Lion King* can be seen as a logical development within the evolution of the 1990s Disney musical. *The Little Mermaid* had demonstrated that a return to the ideals of the classic Disney animated film, in which the 'pop-hit' approach of the standard 1980s musical was eschewed in favour of an integrated approach to animation, dialogue, songs and music, could produce a 'hit' movie. However, it also demonstrated that popular songs used in a film of this type could become hits in their own right (as was the case with Oscar-winning 'Under The Sea'[26]), even if the composers and producers did not have this as a primary aim. It is not surprising then that producers should want to include songs that were potential pop hits, and they ensured this by using an established pop songwriter. From an aesthetic point of view, however, Elton John's musical sensibilities led the songs in more of a popular song than musical theatre direction – thereby somewhat weakening the connection with Disney classics that had been forged by Menken and Ashman in *The Little Mermaid* and *Beauty and the Beast*. Rice argues that "I wasn't really deliberately trying to break through with rock in Disney movies … it was just that I thought 'This is a great composer'" ('Making' interview). In terms of the effect on the songs, these take a more obvious verse–chorus form consistent with standard pop songs (unlike the way lyrics drive the form in *The Little Mermaid* songs).

The other major contributors to *The Lion King* soundtrack were German composer Hans Zimmer and South African musician Lebo Morake (commonly known as Lebo M). Zimmer is an established Hollywood film composer and orchestrator, and the driving force behind the Media Ventures (later Remote Control Productions) company. For *The Lion King* Zimmer created an orchestral film score supplemented by African musical arrangements and choral elements by Lebo M, who was recommended to Disney by Zimmer. Lebo M provides the first human voice in the film (singing the chant heard over the opening sequence) and he also formed and conducted the African choir used in various places within the soundtrack.[27]

Music and the African setting

The collaboration between Zimmer and Lebo M lay behind the distinctive blend of European and African elements that provided some of the memorable music in the movie. Zimmer describes Lebo M as his "tour guide" through African music but suggests that Lebo was not overly concerned with musical 'authenticity':

> ...the way [Lebo M's] role works is I write something and I say, "Lebo, does this sound African?", and he goes, "Yeah, sure" and he makes up some story ... that some tribe somewhere in Africa probably writes just like this, so if I play bits of Mozart he still goes "No, No, No, No, No, we can still make this work." (Zimmer, 'Making' interview)

Although Zimmer's humorous insight provides a salutary caution about assigning African authenticity to the music merely because an African musician was involved,[28] Lebo M's contribution was of critical importance. In (director) Rob Minkoff's opinion, Lebo M "had found the heart of the movie" when he wrote the chant that begins the film. Chris Montan (president of Walt Disney Music) argues that the opening chant provided an instant sense of Africanness:

> It immediately took you to Africa. I mean at that point it wasn't a bunch of Hollywood people trying to do what we thought Africa should be. It was somebody from that place able to express his feelings about that place. (Montan, 'Making' interview)

Lebo M's chant is indeed striking. His voice is high-set (moving around an F# note in the tenor range), in full voice rather than falsetto, and the sound is loud, strong and unrestrained. Lebo M's voice is supported by an African choir — at first with female voices on the tonic, and then with a full chorus singing a standard IV–V–I progression. This progression, sung in close harmony, is a hallmark of Zulu choral music, and was made familiar to many western listeners through Paul Simon's (1986) *Graceland* album and subsequent Ladysmith Black Mambazo recordings and tours that reflected a revival of Africanism in the context of 'world music'. The distinctive tone of Lebo M's 'character' voice finds a match in the warmth and humanness of the choral timbre.[29] This is consistent with African choir (and gospel) music that often features individual voices within group textures and highlights improvised lines, call-response and other distinguishing elements, rather than obscuring the individual in the blend. Zimmer has contended: "When you hear an African choir, it's innocence. There's no holding back ... you can hear every individual in the group" ('Making' interview), thereby connecting the sound with familiar cultural associations. As Kassabian notes: "music signifies ethnicity … within our particular musical heritage, not simply by borrowing directly from the culture it attempts to evoke" (2001: 58). The theatrical context for such music had also been introduced to the USA through the *Ipi Ntombi* stage production that was first performed in South Africa in 1974 and staged at the Harkness Theatre on Broadway in 1977.[30]

African choral singing plays a central role in establishing the 'Africanness' of the soundtrack throughout the movie, and the importance of African choral music is underlined as the opening scene progresses. After Lebo's chant, African voices continue in a hypnotic, rhythmic accompaniment to the opening song 'The Circle Of Life' (discussed below). This accompaniment involves a repeated I–vi–ii–V progression together with the catchy syncopated rhythm illustrated in Figure 13.2, and the African style is reinforced through the addition of drums and vocal and environmental sound effects. The opening music ultimately proved so strong that Rob Minkoff decided dialogue was unnecessary. This resulted in an unusual opening (four uninterrupted minutes of visuals and music before the titles appear) that immediately signals music's central place in the film and its key role in informing the narrative and emotional affect.

Figure 13.2   Rhythmic motif used in the choral accompaniment to 'The Circle Of Life'

Zimmer's orchestral music also plays a critical role in evoking the vast African landscape, and in supporting action and dialogue scenes. Initially, he avoided the use of a 'western' orchestra, but changed his mind after commencing the scoring.

> *I had done a film called* The Power of One [John G. Avildsen, 1992] *which was all based on huge Zulu choirs and percussion … I thought, well, let's do the same thing again, big Zulu choirs and just percussion, let's not book an orchestra … and then I started working and of course that concept went straight out of the window.* (Zimmer, 'Making' interview)

Zimmer blends a western orchestra with African percussion and western and African vocal music to create an underscore that complements a wide range of landscapes, actions and moods. For example, when Simba is chased by a stampeding herd of wildebeest, Zimmer combines orchestra, voices, drums and percussion to create a dramatic underscore, with the repetitive vocal chants and prominent rhythmic elements reminiscent of classical works such as Carl Orff's *Carmina Burana*. Rhythmic elements are prominent throughout the underscore (and within the songs), as might be expected given the importance of rhythm within African musical styles. Maultsby, for example, describes "rhythmic complexity" as the "most noticeable feature" in African American music (1990: 193). Fitzgerald observes the "significance of rhythm within various African American musical styles" (2007: 129) and lists other elements that typically appear in African-influenced music:

> Melodic elements include the flattened third and seventh scale degrees (associated with the blues in particular), pentatonic scales, improvisation, melodic embellishment, pitch variation, melisma, varied and expressive (sometimes 'raw') vocal tone, riffs and other repetitive elements. (Fitzgerald, 2007: 130)

Zimmer deliberately uses rhythm (and melody) as 'universal' elements, contending: "I think everybody understands tunes and rhythm. That's the thing that goes across the whole world" ('Making' interview).

Not all of the underscore is imbued with 'African' elements. A version of the evocative and flexible main melody (detailed below) is often employed to provide the feeling of a vast landscape, while at other times traditional orchestral colours are used to help establish the mood. For example, when Simba wakes his father Mufasa (who would prefer to stay asleep), Zimmer creates a suitably playful, childlike underscore using orchestral winds and strings, while the tragedy of Mufasa's death is accompanied by music that resembles a classical-period requiem mass.

Another notable feature of the orchestral underscore is Zimmer's effective creation and manipulation of thematic material (a characteristic of his approach to film composition[31]). The main minor-key theme (see Figure 13.3) is a flexible motif that appears in many guises and is particularly associated with Mufasa (and Simba's recollections of him and his teachings). For example, it is used when Simba and Mufasa first talk about the idea of death, and reappears in the quasi-requiem style when Mufasa is killed in the stampede. During this event, the minor theme appears in a dramatic, rhythmic fashion. The main theme is also used when Simba remembers his father during his period of exile and, when Simba returns to his family, the minor theme takes on a majestic quality as rain falls on the Pridelands, symbolizing a return to life and productivity.

Figure 13.3   Recurring minor-key motif associated with Mufasa

Similarly, the major pentatonic theme illustrated in Figure 13.4 is a simple, flexible melodic idea capable of evoking a variety of moods, and it is particularly associated with Simba's relationships with his friends. For example, it is heard when Pumbaa (the warthog) and Simba look at the stars, and when Simba and (girlfriend) Nala nuzzle each other before the song 'Can You Feel The Love Tonight'. It reappears as a grand, theatrical, orchestral motif after Simba returns to the Pridelands.

Figure 13.4   Recurring major pentatonic theme for Simba's friendships

These themes, then, are flexible enough to complement a range of emotions — sadness, grandeur, hope, nostalgia — and Zimmer has stressed the importance of the 'versatile' motif:

> *When you write a theme, one of the things you want to do is to see how much life it really has, how many possibilities there are … that's the thing when you really figure out if a tune is any good or not. Does it have more than just one shallow little character?* (Zimmer, 'Making' interview)

The other principal recurring motifs are primarily rhythmic in nature. Grooves that alternate between 6/8 and 3/4 are used on many occasions (for example, when Simba first plays with Nala and when Simba decides to return to the Pridelands). Repetitive drum patterns and rhythmic vocal chanting also appear as recurring motifs throughout the film.

A further example of Zimmer's compositional approach is provided during the scene where Simba looks at his own reflection, understands that his father lives within him, and decides to return home. At this highly significant moment, all of the major motifs are reprised. The minor theme is heard in quasi-requiem form, the major pentatonic theme is grand and orchestral, and the rhythmic themes enter in dramatic fashion.

Added to this emotionally affective scoring are the songs used in *The Lion King*. Of the five original songs co-written by Rice and John, 'Circle Of Life' and 'Can You Feel The Love Tonight' are typical Elton John-style 'big ballad' numbers; 'I Just Can't Wait To Be King' is a relatively simple, funky pop song that functions in the film as Simba's 'I want' song; 'Be Prepared' is the most dramatic and theatrical of the songs; and 'Hakuna Matata' has the most obvious African connections. 'Circle Of Life', 'Be Prepared' and 'Hakuna Matata' are discussed below as three contrasting illustrations of how the songs operate within the narrative and the context of the musical score overall.

'Circle Of Life' provides a lyrical summary of the essence of the film — the life-journey from birth through childhood, adolescence, adulthood and the passing of responsibility from one generation to another. A lengthy opening sequence introduces the animals and the landscape, culminating in a scene in which, on a rock above the assembled animals, the shaman baboon Rafiki holds the newborn Simba aloft, the clouds part and a beam of sunlight glows on the future leader of the Pridelands, while the animals bow below. Rice notes that: "'Circle Of Life' had to be, both lyrically and musically, a strong, powerful song that would also set some of the agenda for the film" ('Making' interview). Musically, the song evolves out of Lebo M's chant, as African choral voices morph into a regular rhythmic pattern that forms part of the backing for the song. 'Circle Of Life' is a musical hybrid that blends a pop-style verse–verse–chorus form, a theatrical pre-hook and instrumental section, gospel backing vocals, and African chanting and drums.

The low-set verse is followed by a rising pre-hook melody that culminates in the catchy, high-set chorus (containing the main lyric/melodic hook). The bVII chord is used in the pre-hook to delay the arrival of the dominant (V) chord – thereby adding to the 'theatrical' build-up of tension before the chorus enters on the tonic chord with the highest note of the melody (on the word "circle"). The catchy melody clearly draws on Elton John's considerable experience as a pop ballad writer. African drums feature prominently as the chorus begins and then continue strongly. An instrumental version of the song follows as underscore for the scene with the arrival of baby Simba, before choral voices join in for a repeat of the chorus and a dramatic, Broadway-style, high-set ending.

A more theatrical performative song is 'Be Prepared', sung by the villain of the movie. Scar, Mufasa's estranged brother, performs the song as he plots the king's downfall and accompanies highly stylized animation scenes featuring striking design elements, dramatic lighting and colour contrasts. The minor-key song begins with a groove featuring prominent African percussion, with vocals adding to the rhythm. Numerous theatrical elements are used to enhance the drama. Vocal delivery alternates between sung and spoken or half-spoken sections, and dialogue sections are blended into the song. A lengthy build-up eventually leads to the dramatic high-set chorus, where the "be prepared" lyric hook is supported by high backing vocals. The visuals display masses of hyenas with choreographed movements – including 'goosestep' marching. Overall, the lavishness of the scene and accompanying music bears comparison with the grandest of the 'golden age' 1940s Hollywood movie musicals.

Reflecting Simba's release from his responsibilities and guilt, 'Hakuna Matata' is the musical 'comedy' offering in the film, and takes the form of a happy, up-tempo, major-key 'buddy' song built over a foot-tapping, swung sixteenth groove. 'African' elements include the quasi-African lyric hook, emphasis on groove and percussion, bright electric bass sound, improvised elements, and instrumental and vocal interpolations. Once again, gospel-style backing vocals support the lead vocals, and the song has a simple, singalong chorus. Theatrical elements include the extended musical form, opening spoken section, changing tempos, dialogue sections, operatic (tenor) delivery by Pumbaa, the warthog, and the alternation of vocal and instrumental sections. At times, raw rock vocal delivery and rock piano riffs are used to increase dynamic intensity in a manner reminiscent of rock musicals such as *The Rocky Horror Show* (first staged in the UK in 1973).

Although the songs featured in *The Lion King* were very successful, both commercially and in terms of awards, they have been subjected to some criticism – for example, Stephen Holden, writing in the *New York Times*, described the songs as "mediocre" and "not a good sign for the artistic future of the animated musical" (cited in Miller, 2000: 53). Several elements lend some support to this assessment. 'Circle Of Life' and 'Can You Feel The Love Tonight', the most successful of the songs, hold few surprises for the listener familiar with Elton John's pop hits and represent relatively safe, predictable pop offerings in terms of melodic and harmonic content. In addition, the strong melodies in these two songs tend to overpower, rather than serve, the lyrics – an approach a specialist music-theatre composer would avoid. The most notable example occurs in 'Can You Feel The Love Tonight', which ignores one of the basic theatrical lyric-setting conventions, namely, that important words should receive emphasis in the melody. In the main lyric hook ("Can you feel the love tonight") the high points of the melody occur on the words "can" and "the" rather than "feel" and "love".

'Circle Of Life' also lacks subtlety in 'giving away' the essence of the narrative before the story is allowed to unfold, and the song receives what can be considered undue attention by being played in 'stand-alone' fashion to open the film. This places it at odds with the otherwise well-integrated nature of the soundtrack (and differentiates it from the successful formula employed in *The Little Mermaid*). In addition, despite the award of an Oscar for his music, and the considerable public acclaim generated through this, Zimmer does not consider *The Lion King* score to demonstrate his best skills. Since it was written in just three and a half weeks, and was based on pre-production drawings rather than animated scenes, Zimmer argues that he "got the orchestration wrong in a few places".[32] Nevertheless, *The Lion King* not only proved to be extremely lucrative for Disney as a feature film (generating US$1 billion total and $313 million in gross domestic revenue) but provided a vehicle that would be a smash hit as a Broadway musical, thereby paving the way for several musical-theatre techniques exploited in Disney animation films to be 'returned' to Broadway.

Completing the circle: Disney on Broadway

Disney's move into Broadway musical production in the late 1990s was in some ways a logical step, given that several leading members of Disney's animation staff had Broadway experience, and the theme park entertainment division had been staging live mini-musicals for years (see Carson, 2004). Added to this, the corporation was offered an extremely attractive incentive to locate a show on Broadway, with New York mayor Rudolf Giuliani linking Disney's family-friendly associations to a clean-up of a notably run-down area of the theatre district around 42nd Street and Seventh Avenue (Maslon and Kantor, 2004: 418). After *Beauty and the Beast* followed on the heels of *The Little*

Mermaid in winning Academy awards for Best Song (for the 'Beauty And The Beast' number) and Best Original Score, the Disney company was convinced that the music and the musical spectacular could be further exploited. A theatre script was devised that included additional songs by Alan Menken and Tim Rice, and *Beauty and the Beast* was brought to the stage in Houston in 1993, and later in Broadway's Palace Theater in 1994. Despite negative press and industry resentment, the show generated considerable box-office sales and in 2001 it became the longest-running American musical since *A Chorus Line*, which was first staged in 1975 (*ibid.*: 421).

Disney restored the New Amsterdam Theater (on 42nd Street) and launched *The Lion King* there in 1997. The show has continued to play on Broadway and in various other cities for many years and is currently celebrating a decade of near-continuous performances. While some have claimed the stage musical success to be due to the story and characters being 'right' for Broadway "because that's where they'd come from in the first place" (Clive Owen, *WOB* narrator, Part 7), its success was also due to clever marketing and merchandising on the part of Disney. This form of "business art" (John Luhr, cited in Maslon and Kantor, 2001: 423) was derided by critics but enabled a revitalization of both animation film and musical theatre. A major part of the success of *The Lion King* stage musical was the music, as director Judy Tamor (costume designer, mask/puppet co-designer, and additional lyricist for the stage version of *The Lion King*) noted:

> I was completely excited by the combination of music. The Elton John songs joined with Lebo's South African influence with the chorus seems to me a fantastic combination and very unusual for a Broadway score. It's much more innovative, it's much more fresh, it's new. ('Making' interview)

A staged musical of *The Little Mermaid* was launched in 2007. While the show did not prove to be as successful (see Saltzman, 2008), it could not have been attempted without the two other Disney animation film-based Broadway shows. These shows demonstrated how Broadway and musical theatre itself were reinspired by animated features.[33] The success of the musicals also cemented the importance of music for Disney productions and for animated features.

The Broadway-experienced team of Menken and another American musical-theatre lyricist and composer Stephen Schwartz worked on the subsequent Disney animations *Pocahontas* and *The Hunchback of Notre Dame* (Gary Trousdale and Kirk Wise, 1996). While several songs were considered memorable in these films, they did not have the same musical impact, integrated character-bursting-into-song numbers and instrumental score of the earlier productions, and, despite attracting profits, were not as overwhelmingly successful as *The Little Mermaid, Beauty and the Beast* or *The Lion King*. The music of these films was important for the cross-media success of the audio-visual works but it was the musical approach – one that was significantly influenced by Broadway – that offered a fresh momentum for Disney's animation features, as well as providing suitable material for staged musical productions. In this sense, then, extending a familiar association of Disney with music, it was musical products that facilitated Disney's animated feature-film renaissance in the late 1980s. Added to this, it was Disney's ability to reinvent itself – aided by music and new musical styles – that enabled a viable future for the corporation's animation division as well as subsequent diversifications.

The successful integration of animation and stage production elements in Disney's *The Little Mermaid* and *The Lion King* demonstrates that animation is not a domain of niche productions. Furthermore, the interaction of animation with another cultural phenomenon (staged musicals) highlights the adaptability and diversity offered by animation. In the final decade of the twentieth century, *The Little Mermaid* and *The Lion King* stand out as landmark animated features. They did this through a convergence of elements that were particular to the time and production factors. These elements were not consistently applied in such combinations to subsequent Disney animation features, due to the changes that were occurring in animation techniques and approaches towards the end of the millennium. Nevertheless, *The Little Mermaid* and *The Lion King* highlighted the input of music to such audio-visual products and the significant impact music can provide for animation cinema.

Acknowledgements

Thanks for much assistance on this project provided by Philip Hayward, and for insights into Broadway history provided by (Richard) Dan Blim.

Notes

1. Audio commentary, for the 2006 DVD re-release of *The Little Mermaid* in Walt Disney's Platinum Editions line of classic Disney animated features. Audio Commentary version, with Ron Clements (co-writer and co-director), John Musker (co-writer and co-director) and Alan Menken (composer).
2. Disneyland in Los Angeles had opened in 1955 and by 1965 the amusement park had attracted 50 million visitors. See Smoodin (1994) for more on the 'Magic Kingdom'.
3. The Experimental Prototype Community of Tomorrow (EPCOT) addition to the Florida park had opened in 1982, and the first international theme park, Tokyo Disneyland Park, opened in 1983.
4. A successful box-office production was *Three Men and a Baby* (Leonard Nimoy, 1987).
5. Walt Disney Classics were usually released each year in time for December sales. See Watts (1997) for a discussion of the notion of 'classic' Disney.
6. This exploited a model that had been employed in *The Lady and the Tramp* (Clyde Geronimi, Wilfred Jackson and Hamilton Luske, 1955), which featured songs by Peggy Lee.

7. The Broadway connection is notable here, in that Julie Andrews was a Broadway performer and starred in the 1956 *My Fair Lady* stage show (with music by Frederick Loewe and lyrics by Alan Jay Lerner) that was a smash hit.

8. Interview with Giorgio Moroder, extracted from episode 8 of the BBC TV series *Walk on By: The Story of Popular Song* (Andrew Graham-Brown, Peter Jamieson, Jeremy Marre, Jeff Morgan and Ian James Pye) produced in 2001. All *WOB* references are extracted from this source.

9. This is a recognizable Disney-style rewrite of the original story ending, a feel-good culmination that also allows for a sequel. *The Little Mermaid II: Return to the Sea* (Jim Kammerud and Brian Smith, 2000) features Ariel's strong-willed daughter. See Schickel (1986) for a discussion of Disney's revisions of stories to ensure broadly palatable narratives.

10. This tongue-in-cheek rock musical originally played off-Broadway in 1982, and then appeared on Broadway and internationally. It was itself based on a low-budget black-comedy movie by Roger Corman released in 1960.

11. The association is, of course, inappropriate to Calypso's origins as a southern Caribbean music.

12. Philip Hayward notes that:

    The term 'pastiche' is often used by composers and critics to refer to a work that imitates aspects of a pre-constituted musical style without the element of satire implicit in the practice of parody. There is, however, a degree of subjectivity in how such terms are assigned and how textual imitation is interpreted. What may have been intended as pastiche may be interpreted as parody and vice versa. (personal communication to the authors, 17 January 2008)

13. *Treasures Untold: The Making of Disney's 'The Little Mermaid'*, documentary produced for the 2006 DVD release of *The Little Mermaid* in the Walt Disney Platinum Editions line of classic Disney animated features.

14. See an extended discussion of Ariel's voice in relation to feminist readings in Sells (1995), Colless (2007), and others.

15. The beguine is a lively ballroom dance and 'Begin The Beguine' is a jazz song written by Cole Porter and introduced by June Knight in the Broadway musical *Jubilee* (1935), as well as being referenced in several films.

16. The steel pan (also known as the steel drum), originally from Trinidad and Tobago, is a distinctive-sounding pitched percussion instrument devised from a 55-gallon storage drum.

17. Notably for a children's album, the RCA album of *Cinderella* songs was a number-one seller on *Billboard*'s pop album chart, and both Perry Como and the Andrews Sisters achieved notable sales of recordings of songs from the movie (Tietyen, 1990: 93). According to Tietyen, "To promote *Sleeping Beauty*, [Disney] licensed 55 companies to manufacture more than 100 "Sleeping Beauty" items, including a Princess Aurora doll, a Prince's hat complete with plume-shaped pen, games, puppets, jewellery, and even baby's diapers. There were 2.1 million

Sleeping Beauty comic books and more than 5 million hardbound books. Fourteen different *Sleeping Beauty* records were produced" *(ibid.:* 106).

18. Another animated feature released in this period was *The Rescuers Down Under* (Hendel Butoy and Mike Gabriel, 1990).

19. See Smith (1998) for more on Disney's synergistic strategy in the 1990s. This is not to say that animation features incorporating music from other studios had not been successful – see *The Land Before Time* (Universal/MGA, 1988) that includes catchy songs.

20. After some of the animation for *The Little Mermaid* was drawn in China, *Beauty and the Beast* was the second feature to be produced using the CAPS system developed by Disney. CAPS enabled the artists' hand-drawn animation to be scanned into the computer, then coloured and combined with background painting. *The Lion King* animation was largely completed by SEK studio in Korea.

21. While not the focus of this chapter, the storyline for *The Lion King* has been discussed in relation to its strong connection to earlier work and the characterization of a young lion, Kimba, by the well-known Japanese manga and animation artist Osamu Tezuka (Patten, 2007).

22. Disney ideologies are discussed in numerous sources (see, for example, Dorfman and Mattelart, 1991; Murphy, 1995; Byrne and McQuillan, 1999; Schulz, 2002). See also Paul Wells (2002) for Disney's impact on animation history and association (and contrast) to other aspects of US culture.

23. See Chapter 7 by Janice Esther Tulk, analysing the music in *Brother Bear*, in this volume.

24. It also won Best Motion Picture – Musical or Comedy, and another Golden Globe for film editing. In the Annie Awards, it won Best Animated Film, Best Individual Achievement for Story Contribution in the Field of Animation, and Jeremy Irons also won Best Achievement for Voice Acting (in his character for Scar).

25. *The Making of 'The Lion King'*, documentary directed by Dan Boothe (1994), first broadcast on the Disney Channel, and included on the Walt Disney Platinum Edition of *The Lion King*, 2003. The subsequent quotations from Tim Rice and Elton John are taken from interviews in this same documentary.

26. The film-industry awards for music and songs assisted sales of *The Little Mermaid* CD soundtrack, which reached triple platinum figures, an extraordinary achievement for a soundtrack album, especially one for an animation film. The music continues to be lucrative for Disney. The Original Broadway Cast Recording entered the *Billboard* 200 chart, ranking at number 26, the highest debut for a cast recording in twelve years (BWW News Desk, http://www.broadwayworld.com/printcolumn.cfm?id=25625, accessed 6 August 2008). See deCordova (1994) for more on marketing.

27. Lebo M made a major contribution to the sequel to the film's soundtrack, *Rhythm of the Pride Lands*, and the film's direct-to-video sequel *The Lion King II: Simba's Pride* (Darrell Rooney and Rob LaDuca, 1998).

28. Tagg (1989) argues that it can be difficult to assign 'black' and 'white' musical elements.

29. Disney's *Dumbo* included music by an African American choir (specifically, the Hall Johnson Choir from a black church in Los Angeles) that could be seen as a precedent for the chorus style used in *The Lion King* (see further discussion of these stylistic elements in Burnim and Maultsby [2006]).

30. The use of the song 'The Lion Sleeps Tonight' in a scene with Timon and Pumbaa led to disputes between Disney and the family of South African Solomon Linda, who composed the song (originally titled 'Mbube') in 1939. In July 2004, the family filed suit, seeking US$1.6 million in royalties from Disney. In February 2006, Linda's heirs reached a legal settlement with Abilene Music, who held the worldwide rights and had licensed the song to Disney for an undisclosed amount of money.

31. See the discussion of Zimmer's thematic approach in relation to *Wallace & Gromit: The Curse of the Were Rabbit* in Chapter 11 by Rebecca Coyle and Peter Morris.

32. E. Black, 'Hans Zimmer Interview by Edwin Black', *Film Score Monthly*, online at: http://www.filmscoremonthly.com/features/zimmer.asp (accessed 7 February 2008).

33. It is significant that many Broadway musicals have been successful first as films; for instance, recent Broadway shows generated from films include *Legally Blonde* and *Billy Elliot*. Although specific narratives have spawned several cultural and media products, not all have a close link in terms of music – see examples such as the play, films, musicals, etc. deriving from the 'Chicago' story.

References

Allan, R. (1999), *Walt Disney and Europe: European Influences on the Animated Feature Films of Walt Disney*, Bloomington: Indiana University Press.

Burnim, M., and Maultsby, P. (eds), *African American Music: An Introduction*, New York: Routledge, 2006.

Byrne, E., and McQuillan, M. (1999), *Deconstructing Disney*, London: Pluto.

Care, R. (1985), 'Threads of Melody: The Evolution of a Major Film Score – Walt Disney's *Bambi*', in I. Newsom (ed.), *Wonderful Inventions: Motion Pictures, Broadcasting, and Recorded Sound at the Library of Congress*, Washington: Library of Congress, pp. 76–98.

Care, R. (2002), 'Make Walt's Music: Music for Disney Animation, 1928–1967', in G. Goldmark and Y. Taylor (eds), *The Cartoon Music Book*, Chicago: A Capella Books, pp. 21–36.

Carson, C. (2004), '"Whole New Worlds": Music and the Disney Theme Park Experience', *Ethnomusicology Forum*, 13(2), 228–35.

Colless, E. (2007), 'Between the Legs of the Mermaid', in A. Cholodenko (ed.), *The Illusion of Life II: More Essays on Animation*, Sydney: Power Publications, pp. 229–42.

Culhane, J. (1983), *Walt Disney's Fantasia*, New York: H. N. Abrams.

Culhane, J. (1999), *Fantasia 2000: Visions of Hope*, New York: Disney Editions.

deCordova, R. (1994), 'The Mickey in Macy's Window: Childhood, Consumerism and Disney Animation', in E. Smoodin (ed.), *Disney Discourse: Producing the Magic Kingdom*, New York: Routledge, pp. 203–13.

Dorfman, A., and Mattelart, A. (1991), *How to Read Donald Duck: Imperialist Ideology in the Disney Comic* (trans. David Kunzle), New York: International General.

Giroux, H. (2001), *The Mouse That Roared: Disney and the End of Innocence*, New York: Rowman and Littlefield.

Feuer, J. (1993), *The Hollywood Musical*, 2nd edn, Indianapolis: Indiana University Press.

Fitzgerald, J. (2007), 'Black Pop Songwriting 1963–1966: An Analysis of U.S. Top Forty Hits by Cooke, Mayfield, Stevenson, Robinson, and Holland-Dozier-Holland', *Black Music Research Journal*, 27(2), 97–140.

Hollis, T., and Ehrbar, G. (2006), *Mouse Tracks: The Story of Walt Disney Records*, Jackson: University Press of Mississippi.

Johnston, O., and Thomas, F. (1995), *The Illusion of Life: Disney Animation*, New York: Disney Editions.

Kassabian, A. (2001), *Hearing Film: Tracking Identifications in Contemporary Hollywood Film Music*, London: Routledge.

Maslon, L., and Kantor, M. (2004), *Broadway: The American Musical*, Boston: Bulfinch Press.

Maultsby, P. (1990), 'Africanism in African-American Music', in J. Holloway (ed.), *Africanisms in American Culture*, Bloomington: Indiana University Press, pp. 185–210.

Miller, M. (2000), 'Of Tunes and Toons: The Movie Musical in the 1990s', in W. Dixon (ed.), *Film Genre 2000: New Critical Essays*, New York: State University of New York Press, pp. 45–62.

Murphy, P. (1995), '"The Whole Wide World Was Scrubbed Clean": The Androcentric Animation of Denatured Disney', in E. Bell, L. Haas and L. Sells (eds), *From Mouse to Mermaid*, Bloomington: Indiana University Press, pp. 125–47.

Newsom, J. (1980) '"A Sound Idea": Music for Animated Films', *Quarterly Journal of the Library of Congress*, 37(3–4), 279–309.

Patten, F. (2007), 'Simba versus Kimba: The Pride of the Lions', in A. Cholodenko (ed.), *The Illusion of Life II: More Essays on Animation*, Sydney: Power Publications, pp. 275–313.

Saltzman, S. (2008), 'A CurtainUp Review: *The Little Mermaid*', *CurtainUp: The Internet Theater Magazine of Reviews, Features, Annotated Listings*, online at: http:www.curtainup.com/littlemermaid.html (accessed 1 August 2008).

Schickel, R. (1986), *The Disney Version*, London: Michael Joseph.

Schulz, M. (2002), 'Analytical Essay: Disney's Full Length Animated Films', in *Kid Culture*, online at: http://www.uleth.ca/edu/kid_culture/disney/essay.html.

Sells, L. (1995), '"Where Do the Mermaids Stand?" Voice and Body in *The Little Mermaid*', in E. Bell, L. Haas and L. Sells (eds), *From Mouse to Mermaid*, Bloomington: Indiana University Press, pp. 175–92.

Smith, J. (1998), *The Sounds of Commerce: Marketing Popular Film Music*, New York: Columbia University Press.

Smoodin, E. (ed.) (1994), *Disney Discourse: Producing the Magic Kingdom*, New York: Routledge.

Tagg, P. (1989), 'Open Letter: Black Music, Afro-American Music and European Music', *Popular Music*, 8(3), 285–98.

Taylor, D. (1940), *Walt Disney's* Fantasia, New York: Simon and Schuster.

Tietyen, D. (1990), *The Musical World of Walt Disney*, Milwaukee: Hal Leonard Publishing.

Watts, S. (1997), *The Magic Kingdom: Walt Disney and the American Way of Life*, Boston and New York: Houghton Mifflin.

Wells, P. (2002), *Animation and America*, Edinburgh: Edinburgh University Press.

Index